LIBRARY AND LITERACY MOVEMENT FOR NATIONAL DEVELOPMENT

LIBRARY AND LITERACY MOVEMENT FOR NATIONAL DEVELOPMENT

Dr. Sahib Singh

CONCEPT PUBLISHING COMPANY, NEW DELHI-110059

ISBN 81-8069-065-2

First Published 2003

Published and Printed by
Ashok Kumar Mittal
Concept Publishing Company
A/15-16, Commercial Block, Mohan Garden
New Delhi-110059 (INDIA)

Phones : 25351460, 25351794
Fax : 091-11-25357103
Email : publishing@conceptpub.com

कृष्ण चन्द्र पन्त
K.C. PANT

सत्यमेव जयते

उपाध्यक्ष
योजना आयोग
भारत
DEPUTY CHAIRMAN
PLANNING COMMISSION
INDIA

Foreword

The roots of many social problems like poverty, crime, superstition, regionalism, communalism, unemployment and corruption can be traced to illiteracy. With the largest illiterate population in the world, every third person in India is illiterate, with all its attendant ills. Therefore, eradication of illiteracy from the map of India is a basic requirement for making her a prosperous and developed nation.

To achieve the goal of making India a literate nation, substantial efforts are being made by Central and State Governments, NGOs, individuals and national as well as international agencies, and we have made significant progress in this direction. But most of the ongoing literacy programmes do not provide long time support to neo-literates. Unless their newly acquired skills are made meaningful by effective support through ready availability of reading and learning materials, they may again slip back into the category of illiterates. Here libraries can play a vital role by providing the basic requirements for maintaining and upgrading literacy skills.

The vital role of libraries is examined in this book entitled *Library and Literacy Movement for National Development*, authored by Dr. Sahib Singh, who not only has long experience as a practising librarian, but is also privy to government plans and policies, being a Cabinet Minister in the Central Government. In this book, he not only highlights past, present and future scenarios of literacy in the country, but also correlates growth of population and illiteracy. Defining the desiderata of a good public library, its functions and objectives, Dr. Sahib Singh takes a close look at various literacy and adult education programmes, and what is necessary to make them effective. One of the most innovative aspects of this study is its emphasis on the creation of a rural network of libraries and literacy centres for eradication of illiteracy and poverty in India.

(K.C. Pant)

Delhi
May 29, 2003

Preface

Illiteracy breeds ignorance, which in turn leads to poverty. It is closely related to crime and superstitions. It sows the seeds of regionalism, communalism, unemployment and corruption. Illiterate people are always susceptible to exploitation. On the other hand, literacy makes people easy to lead, but difficult to drive; easy to govern, but difficult to enslave. It is a tool to be used in every day life and can be constantly sharpened and perfected so that it can become a person's life long companion. It equips an individual to safeguard his interests by having a thorough knowledge of his duties and democratic rights. It is a key to solve most of the problems and can produce better responsible citizen and effective functioning of democracy in India. Thus the literacy is a prerequisite for building up the monument of development and a progressive society. A literate person can develop national consciousness because he has the power to make informed choices and effective participation in the affairs of the country.

Today, the world's largest democracy is the home to the largest illiterate population in the world. Now every third illiterate person in the world is an Indian. Therefore, eradication of illiteracy from the map of India is the basic requirement of making it a prosperous and developed nation. Since a nation is made great by its people and people in turn become important citizen of that great nation. Therefore, each individual in our country need to be made literate, otherwise they may not be aware of their constitutional rights and also they may not be able to participate in the developmental process.

In this era of communication and information, one's inability to read and write makes him handicapped that not only affects his individual growth but also arrests the development of nation. During the past several decades, India has made significant progress in eradication of illiteracy. About two-third of the country's population has been made literate. The total average literacy rate of the country has increased from 5.35 per cent in 1901 to 65.40 per cent in 2001 with an average growth rate of 0.6 per cent per year. This achievement is still far below the level of satisfaction.

To achieve the goal of making India a functionally literate nation, we have to work a lot in this direction. Central and State Governments, NGOs, individuals, national and international agencies have launched many programmes and projects pertaining to eradication of illiteracy. The NLM, DAE, ILP, UNESCO, NSLM, ILP, SIDA, European Union, World Bank and other agencies have rendered financial support to enhance literacy programmes in India. These further need concerted and coordinated participation by all sections of the society. Unless all of us come together and work for this noble cause, the dream of a fully literate India will continue to be elusive.

The goal can be achieved by accelerating the growth of literacy rate and simultaneousely by arresting the population growth. Unless it is taken as a people's movement to eradicate illiteracy within a time bound period, it may not be possible to achieve the desired goal. Now each one of us should feel proud by participating in this venture.

Most of the ongoing literacy programmes do not provide long time support to neo-literates. Unless they are provided effective support through reading and learning materials, they may again fall in the category of illiterates. Here libraries can play vital role by providing reading and learning materials to them. Literacy programmes should also be oriented towards income generation and improvement of quality of life of individuals to raise their living standards. This all is possible if literacy programmes are implemented through libraries which necessitates linkage of literacy movement with library movement in the country.

Network of libraries should be expanded to the whole country and one library should be established in each of 640,000 villages of the country with proper infrastructure, resources and consistent financial support so that these can sustain and contribute to literacy programmes. These libraries can be used as information windows to disseminate information about government plans and policies for national development. A portion of funds of each developmental programme may be diverted to the libraries to strengthen their information resources and services. These libraries need to be managed by the PRIs. A Delhi based NGO, Gramin Swabhiman has created a model library network, which operates Libraries and Literacy Centres (LLCs) in each village of Delhi with a mission to make rural Delhi functionally literate by 2005.

The book intends to through light on the role of libraries in eradication of illiteracy and alleviation of poverty in India. It has been organised in six chapters. Chapter 1 deals with general information about illiteracy, population explosion, unemployment and poverty. It highlights past, present and future scenario of literacy and illiteracy along with the major factors responsible for illiteracy. It also correlates growth of population and illiteracy in India. Chapter 2 defines a public library, its functions and objectives and also barriers in their effective use. Some of the major public libraries, their roles in preservation of our rich cultural heritage, library legislations enacted by various States/UTs and library associations in India have also been discussed in this chapter. Chapter 3 defines oracy and literacy, need for literacy, growth of population and literacy in various ethnic communities in India. Chapter 4 presents an account of various literacy and adult education programmes organised by the Government, national and international agencies, individuals and NGOs. Chapter 5 deals with library and literacy movement in Delhi and sustainable development and eradication of illiteracy from rural Delhi through a network of library and literacy centres. Chapter 6 concludes by drawing attention to overall considerations for library and literacy movement for the prosperity of the country. Glossary of terms used in the text to explain various concepts, along with bibliography, appendices and index have been given at end of the book.

Dr. Sahib Singh

Acknowledgements

It is indeed a matter of great pleasure and satisfaction to record encouragement and assistance received from a variety of sources during the whole process from preparation of manuscript to the printing and publication of the book. At the very first instance, I would like to express my deep sense of gratitude to my supervisors in the doctoral work for their valuable guidance and inspiration with intellectual stimuli in my research work, which formed the basis of this book. The present book is an outcome of the intellectual and personal assistance provided by a number of volunteers associated with Gramin Swabhiman, Gomati Sewa Sansthan and Netaji Subhash Literacy Mission.

I would like to record my warm appreciation for all the heads of Library and Literacy Centres (LLCs) functioning in the rural areas of Delhi and also to those who are contributing in making Delhi, a functionally literate state. I would like to acknowledge the efforts of authors and writers of books and articles whose intellectual inputs have helped me in consolidating my ideas and enhancing the quality of the end product. I would like to appreciate the spirit and cooperation shared by my family members who supported me in preparation of manuscript and its finalisation for printing. I would also like to thank my personal staff for constantly encouraging and supporting me to give the final shape of my ideas. I must give due credit to the officers and staff of library and secretariat of the Ministry of Labour at Shram Shakti Bhavan for providing me secretarial assistance.

Last but not least, I would like to thank the officials of the National Literacy Mission, National Adult Education Association, Directorate of Adult Education and Ministry of Human Resource Development, fellow librarians and legislators who gave me a great deal of encouragement and support in bringing out this work in the present form, otherwise, it would not be possible for me to complete this task without their consistent support. I am also thankful to the printer and publisher for helping me in dissemination of knowledge to the society in a tangible form.

Dr. Sahib Singh

Contents

List of Tables

List of Figures

Abbreviations

AAAL	Alberta Association of Adult Literacy
AC	Appex Committee
AEP	Adult Education Programme
AIDS	Acquired Immuno Defeciency Syndrome
ALA	American Library Association
ARWSP	Accelerated Rural Water Supply Programme
BARC	Bhabha Atomic Research Centre
BC	Backward Classes
BIMARU	Bihar, Madhya Pradesh, Rajasthan and Uttar Pradesh
BSY	Balika Samridhi Yojana
CABE	Central Advisory Board of Education
CAS	Current Awareness Service
CBT	Children Book Trust
CDP	Community Development Programme
CD-ROM	Compact Disc - Read Only Memory
CEP	Continuing Education Programme
CGHS	Central Government Health Scheme
CRL	Central Reference Library
CRSP	Central Rural Sanitation Programme
CSL	Central Secretariate Library
DAE	Directorate of Adult Education
DDP	Desert Development Programme
DLA	Delhi Library Association
DLB	Delhi Library Board
DMA	Delhi Medical Association
DPAP	Drought Prone Area Programme
DPEP	District Primary Education Programme
DPL	Delhi Public Library
DSS	Document Supply Service
DTP	Desk Top Publishing
EAS	Employment Assurance Scheme

EC	Executive Committee
EFA	Education For All
EIP	Eradication of Illiteracy Programme
EP	Equivalency Programme
FFLP	Farmer's Functional Literacy Project
FID	International Federation of Documentation
FLAW	Functional Literacy for Adult Women
GDP	Gross Domestic Product
GNP	Gross National Product
HDI	Human Development Index
HLA	Haryana Library Association
HPI	Human Poverty Index
IAY	Indira Awas Yojana
ICDS	Integrated Child Development Scheme
IDA	International Development Agency
IFLA	International Federation of Library Associations and Institutions
IGNOU	Indira Gandhi National Open University
IGP	Income Generating Programme
IIC	India International Centre
IIPP	Individual Interest Promotion Programme
ILA	Indian Library Association
ILP	India Literacy Project
IMA	Indian Medical Association
IMY	Indira Mahila Yojana
INB	Indian National Bibliography
IPCL	Improved Pace and Content of Learning
IRC	Information Resource Centre
ITPO	India Trade Promotion Organisation
IWDP	Integrated Wasteland Development Programme
JGSY	Jawahar Gramin Samridhi Yojana
JRSY	Jawahar Rojgar Samridhi Yojana
JSN	Jan Shiksha Nilayam
JSS	Jan Shikshan Sansthan
KANFED	Kerala Association for Non Formal Education and Development
KGS	Kerala Granthasala Sangham
KVIC	Khadi and Village Industry Commission
KVK	Krishi Vigyan Kendra
LAN	Local Area Network
LC	Local Committee
LISA	Library and Information Science Abstract

LLC	Library and Literacy Centre
MLA	Member of Legislative Assembly
MLC	Member of Legislative Council
MP	Member of Parliament
MS	Mahila Samakhya
NACO	National AIDS Control Organisation
NACP	National AIDS Control Programme
NAEP	National Adult Education Programme
NAPLIS	National Policy on Library and Information System
NASP	National Social Assistance Programme
NBT	National Book Trust
NCT	National Capital Territory
NDC	National Development Council
NEFA	North East Frontier Agency
NEP	National Education Policy
NER	Net Enrolment Rate
NFBS	National Family Benefit Scheme
NFE	Non Formal Education
NGO	Non Governmental Organisation
NICNET	National Informatics Centre Network
NLM	National Literacy Mission
NLRC	National Literacy Resource Centre
NMBS	National Maternity Benefit Scheme
NOAPS	National Old Age Pension Scheme
NREP	National Rural Employment Programme
NRI	Non Resident Indian
NSAP	National Social Assistance Programme
NSLM	Netaji Subhash Literacy Mission
NSSO	National Sample Survey Organisation
OB	Operation Blackboard
OPAC	On-line Public Access Catalog
PHC	Primary Health Centre
PLC	Post Literacy Campaign
PLP	Post Literacy Programme
PLS	Public Library System
PMGSY	Pradhan Mantri Gram Sadak Yojana
PMGY	Pradhan Mantri Gramodaya Yojana
POPI	Poverty of Opportunity Index
PP	Prehar Pathshals
PRI	Panchayati Raj Institution
QLIP	Quality of Life Improvement
RC	Resettlement Colony

RCC	Referral Contact Centre
RFLP	Rural Functional Literacy Project
RLA	Rajasthan Library Association
RLEGP	Rural Landless Employment Guarantee Programme
RMK	Rastriya Mahila Kosh
RRRLF	Raja Rammohun Roy Library Foundation
RSKB	Rajasthan Shiksha Karmi Board
RSSP	Rural Social Sanitation Programme
SAEP	State Adult Education Programme
SAI	Sports Authority of India
SAY	Samagra Awas Yojana
SC	Scheduled Caste
SCL	State Central Library
SDI	Selective Dissemination of Information
SGSY	Swarnajayanti Gram Swarojgar Yojana
SIDA	Swedish International Development Authority
SK	Swabhiman Kendra
SKP	Shiksha Karmi Project
SRC	State Resource Centre
SSA	Sarva Shiksha Abhiyan
SSP	Sahaj Shiksha Programme
ST	Scheduled Tribes
SV	Shramik Vidyapeeth
SWRC	Social Work and Research Centre
TFR	Total Fertility Rate
TLC	Total Literacy Campaign
TMSSML	Tanjaur Maharaja Serfoji Saraswati Mahal Library
TSC	Total Sanitation Campaign
TSP	Target Specific Programme
UEE	Universalisation of Primary Education
UGC	University Grant Commission
UNDP	United Nations Development Programme
UNESCO	United Nations Educational Scientific and Cultural Organisation
UNICEF	United Nations International Children Emergency Funds
VA	Volunteer Agency
VEC	Village Education Committee
WB	World Bank
ZSS	Zilla Saksharata Samiti

Chapter 1

Introduction

If you just help in creating an atmosphere, the rest will be done by the atmosphere itself, even the wingless leaves rise high like birds when a powerful storm comes.
—*Vinoba Bhave*

1.1 INTRODUCTION

India is a great country with different regions having different strengths and weaknesses. It is known for its oldest civilisation and culture. It is the second largest populous country in the world covering an area of 3,287,263 sq km with total population of 1027 millions. It consists of 28 States, 7 UTs, 593 Districts, 35 cities with population of more than one million, 5564 Tehsils/Talukas, 5161 towns and 640,000 villages. After achieving independence in 1947, India has made tremendous progress in agriculture, science, healthcare, literacy and education. After over five decades of independence, we still have various categories of people; some with the best of education, training, exposure and experiences. Others with average educational opportunities and comparatively less work experience. There is another class of people who are engaged in many activities for their day-to-day survival, which takes up all their attention.

It has been observed that the less fortunate people also have ability to learn and develop skills. Indians are having great learning capability and competitive spirit. There is a need to channelise their spirit constructively and productively. We should aim for proper channelisation and utilisation of our huge human resource base, which is one of the greatest core competencies of the nation. Due to lack of educational opportunities, a large segment of human resources are unable to properly utilize the available opportunities for employment and to improve their standard of living. Non-availability of preventive healthcare further weakens their physical bodies and working capabilities. About two-third of India's population do not get the minimum level of education and healthcare necessary for functioning human capabilities.

Besides so many constraints, attitudinal abilities and professional capabilities. Indians are second to none in the international scene. One segment of our population is contributing remarkably in India and abroad in many areas like space sciences, medical sciences, military technology, software engineering, management, etc. The other segment is passing through hardship in accessing quality education, adequate medical facilities, clean water, nutritious food, proper shelter and other basic necessities. These people are easily slipped into illiteracy and susceptible for many kinds of diseases, inequalities in opportunities, ignorance and finally to poverty.

1.2 ILLITERACY, POPULATION EXPLOSION, UNEMPLOYMENT AND POVERTY

At the beginning of the past century, India's population was 238 millions. It increased to 1027 millions at the end of 20th century with a total progressive growth of 331 per cent. In an estimate, our population will cross the population of China before 2045. With the overall increase in population, our illiterate population forms a black mark on the progressive map of India. There is a growing feeling that the growth of population has not only stagnated the economic progress of the country but also eaten away a large share to be utilized for various developmental programmes. These programmes include community development, eradication of illiteracy, poverty alleviation, generation of employment, infrastructure development like roads, transport and housing, generation of electricity, sanitation, healthcare and nutrition, drinking water, etc. Thus we have to think and work in both the directions: one for population control and the other to increase literacy, education, healthcare systems and basic infrastructure facilities.

We felt proud to become a billionaire on 11 May 2000 in terms of population. It was not the day of proud but the alarming day when our population crossed one billion mark. On that very day our Prime Minister Shri Atal Bihari Vajpayee said:

> "Today India's population has crossed one billion mark. This is a serious matter that is both cause for concern and introspection – concern over the impact that a runaway population growth is bound to have on the nation's

ecological, natural and other resources; introspection over where went wrong and how we can stabilize the population."

There is a definite relationship between the size of population and the level of its development. The population of a country has to be within the bearable limits of its economy and resources. It has to be stabilized at a particular level, otherwise a large segment of the society will remain deprived of even basic necessities of life. In an estimate, every year about 15.5 million children are born in India, making it virtually impossible for the government to ensure their healthcare, nutrition, education, etc, which are their fundamental needs. They are born just for their existence and not for happiness. Generation of employment and creation of necessary infrastructure facilities cannot keep pace with population growth. Once population is stabilized, resources can be diverted for eradication of illiteracy, alleviation of poverty, better healthcare and economic development. Thus the stabilization of population is an essential need for sustainable development with equitable distribution and poverty alleviation. The growth of population has serious implications on food and water security, clean air, healthcare, rural and urban services and also sustainability of ecosystem. All these come from illiteracy, which leads to poverty and due to poverty haphazard urbanization, destructive exploitation and overuse of natural resources, environmental stress and ecological degradation are inevitable. Therefore, the cycle of illiteracy, population growth, unemployment and poverty has to be broken down and cycle of library, literacy and prosperity has to be created. These two cycles are shown in Figure 1.1 and Figure 1.2 respectively.

Important indicators of development i.e. Population Growth Rate, Life Expectancy at Birth, GDP and Under-five Mortality Rate of some of the developing and developed countries are shown in Table 1.1.

It shows that the China, which is the most populous country in the world, was emerged with a strong GDP of 6.5 per cent during 2000-2001 by restricting its population growth to one percent per year. India also has to lower its population growth from presently 1.8 per cent to less than one per cent during the current decade (2001-2011) and further to zero in the next decade (2011-2021). This may positively affect the other factors for development. In terms of Under-five Mortality Rate, India comes only after Pakistan and Nepal. All efforts should be made to lower the mortality rate in single digit and also to increase our GDP in double digits.

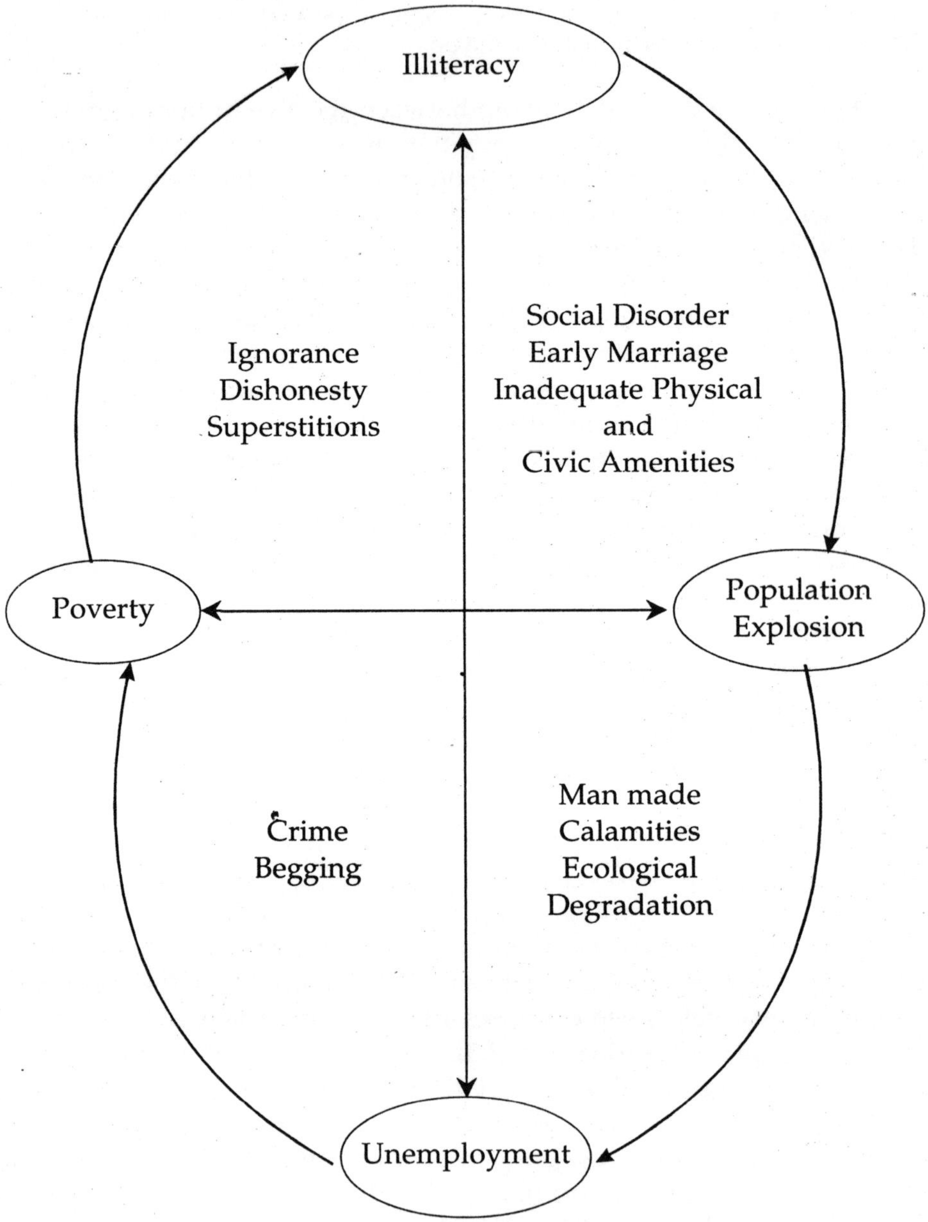

Fig. 1.1: Illiteracy, Population Explosion, Unemployment and Poverty Cycle

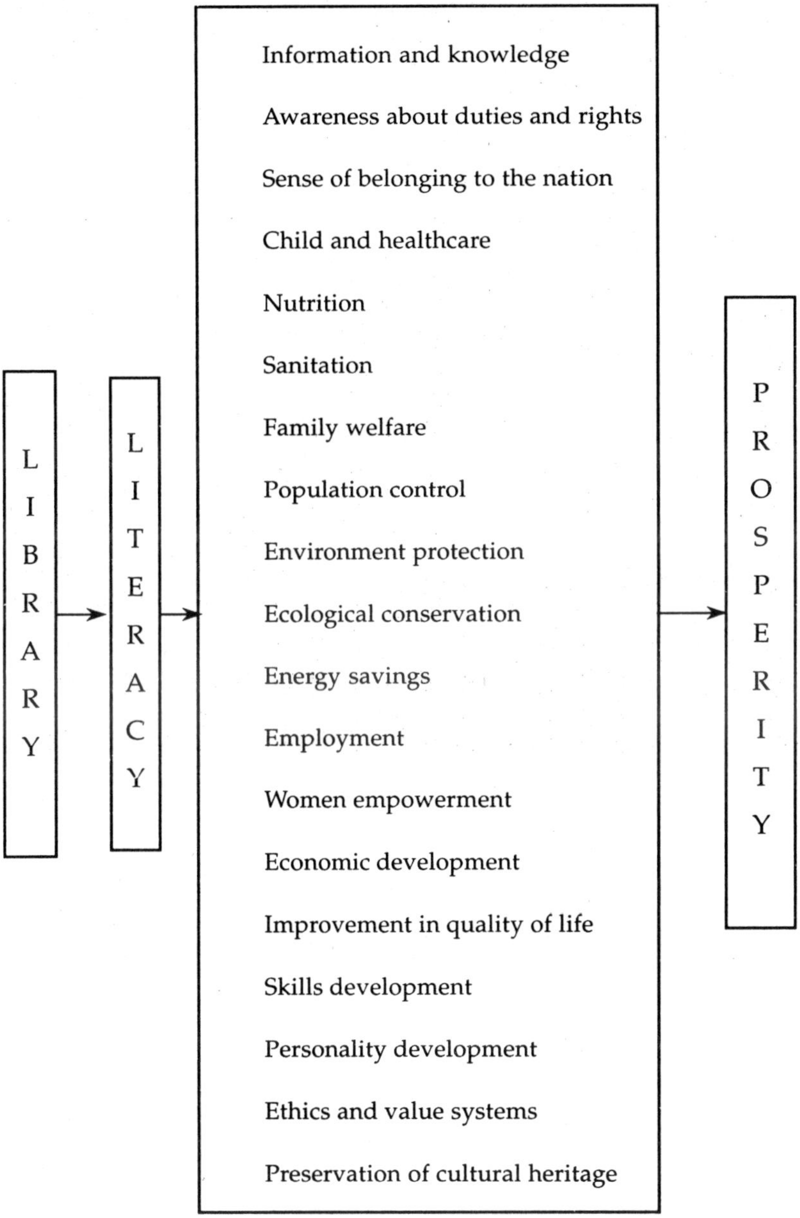

Fig. 1.2: Library, Literacy and Prosperity

Table 1.1: Key Indicators of Development

Country	*Average Annual Population Growth (in %) (1991-2000)*	*GDP Per Capita Growth (in %) (2000-2001)*	*Life Expectancy at Birth (in Year) (2000)*	*Under-five Mortality Rate (per 1000) (2000)*
India	1.8	2.7	63	88
Bangladesh	1.8	3.3	61	83
Pakistan	2.5	0.9	63	110
Sri Lanka	1.3	1.0	73	18
Nepal	2.4	3.4	59	105
China	1.0	6.5	70	39
USA	1.2	0.3	77	9
UK	0.4	1.9	77	7
Japan	0.3	-0.6	81	5
Russia	-0.2	5.5	65	19
France	0.4	1.6	79	6
World	1.4	0.2	66	78

Source: World Development Report 2003

During the past couple of decades, India has made good progress in reduction of population living below the poverty line and also the number of the poor in rural and urban areas. The data related to poverty position in India has been reflected in Table 1.2.

Table 1.2: Poverty Position in India

Year	*Area*	*Total Population Below Poverty Line (in Lakh)*	*Population Below Poverty Line (in %)*	*Decrease in Poverty (in %)*
1983				
	Rural	2519.57	45.65	—
	Urban	709.40	40.79	—
	Total	3228.97	44.48	—
1993-94				
	Rural	2440.31	37.27	8.38
	Urban	763.37	32.36	8.43
	Total	3203.68	35.97	8.51
1999-2000				
	Rural	1932.43	27.09	10.18
	Urban	670.07	23.62	8.74
	Total	2602.50	26.10	9.87

Source: Planning Commission, Government of India

At the national level, the incidence of poverty on the Head Count Ratio declined from 44.48 per cent in 1983 to 26.10 per cent in 1999-2000. There was a decline of 8.51 per cent in 10 years period between 1983 to 1993-94 and it further declined to 9.87 per cent between 1993-94 to 1999-2000. In absolute terms, the number of poor declined from about 323 million in 1983 to 260 million in 1999-2000. While the population of poor in the rural area has declined from 45.65 per cent in 1983 to 27.09 per cent in 1999-2000, then decline in urban area has been from 40.79 per cent to 23.62 per cent during the same period. Distribution of population living below the poverty line in States and UTs during a survey conducted in 1999-2000 is presented in Table 1.3.

Table 1.3: Rural, Urban and Total Poverty Ratio of Major States and UTs During 1999-2000

State/UT	*Rural Poverty Ratio (in %)*	*Urban Poverty Ratio (in %)*	*Total Poverty Ratio (in %)*
INDIA	27.09	23.62	26.10
Andhra Pradesh	11.05	26.63	15.77
Arunachal Pradesh	40.04	7.47	33.47
Assam	40.04	7.47	36.09
Bihar	44.30	32.91	42.60
Goa	1.35	7.52	4.40
Gujarat	13.17	15.59	14.07
Haryana	8.27	9.99	8.74
Himachal Pradesh	7.94	4.63	7.63
Jammu and Kashmir	3.97	1.98	3.48
Karnataka	17.38	25.25	20.04
Kerala	9.38	20.27	12.72
Madhya Pradesh	37.06	38.44	37.43
Maharashtra	23.72	26.81	25.02
Manipur	40.04	7.47	28.54
Meghalaya	40.04	7.47	33.87
Mizoram	40.04	7.47	19.47
Nagaland	40.04	7.47	32.67
Orissa	48.01	42.83	47.15
Punjab	6.35	5.75	6.16
Rajasthan	13.74	19.85	15.28
Sikkim	40.04	7.47	36.55
Tamil Nadu	20.55	22.11	21.12
Tripura	40.04	7.47	34.44
Uttar Pradesh	31.22	30.89	31.15
West Bengal	30.85	14.86	27.02
Andaman and Nicobar Islands	20.55	22.11	20.99
Chandigarh	5.75	5.75	5.75
Dadra and Nagar Haveli	17.57	13.52	17.44
Daman and Diu	1.35	7.52	4.44
Delhi	0.40	9.42	8.23
Lakshadweep	9.38	20.27	15.60
Pondicherry	20.55	22.11	21.67

Source: Planning Commission, Government of India

Poverty ratio of rural Delhi was less than one per cent and recorded as the lowest in the country. There was no gap found in rural and urban poverty ratio in Chandigarh. Orissa, Bihar, Madhya Pradesh, Sikkim, Tripura, Meghalaya, Assam, Nagaland and West Bengal were the States in which poverty ratios were recorded higher than 30 per cent. In 1983, about 50 per cent of the population of Tamil Nadu, West Bengal, Orissa and Bihar as living below the poverty line. By 1999-2000, Tamil Nadu and West Bengal reduced their poverty ratio by half but Orissa and Bihar continued to be with poverty ratio of 47 per cent and 43 per cent respectively. Even rural Orissa and rural Bihar continued to be the poorest in 1983 as well as today. Though the progress is in positive direction, even we have to accelerate this speed and alleviate poverty to make a prosperous India.

1.3 LITERACY: PAST, PRESENT AND FUTURE

It is not true that our great leaders had not made efforts to make our country a literate nation. The efforts to eradicate illiteracy in India has had a long history. The first Indian nationalist leader, who stressed the need for the eradication of illiteracy, was Shri Gopal Krishna Gokhale. After his death, Mahatma Gandhi became the main crusader in India for the eradication of illiteracy. Sir M. Visveswarya, the Dewan of Mysore State, opened 7,000 literacy classes in 1912 to literate adults. He established a network of circulating libraries through out the Mysore State. Dr. D.N. Maitra started a variety of community development programmes in 1915 by setting up of literacy classes, youth clubs, community libraries and various other cultural programmes. Lala Lajpat Rai and Bal Gangadhar Tilak, prominent nationalist leaders, organised night schools and summer schools in 1921 to literate people in northern and western parts of India. During the same time Rabindra Nath Tagore started literacy activities in 1922 from his newly established Rural Reconstruction Institute by bringing out literature for neo-literates. The Provincial Governments of Bengal, Bihar, Madras and Bombay Presidencies, headed by Indian National Congress, launched mass literacy campaign in 1937. The Governments expanded primary education and spread literacy among adults. These campaigns could not be sustained because the Indian National Congress Government resigned just a couple of years after its formation. Further, the Central Advisory Board of Education (CABE) proposed in 1944 that in 40 years *i.e.* by the end of 1984, the country should provide universal education for children and liquidate adult illiteracy.

The First National Seminar, after independence, was organised in 1950 by the Indian Adult Education Association (IAEA) at Jabalpore. The theme was the liquidation of illiteracy and to discuss the techniques of eradication of illiteracy in India. Government of India established National Book Trust (NBT) in 1957 for production of literacy materials like books. The Trust was involved in organising book exhibitions for the mass awareness of people. After that a number of literacy programmes and projects were launched but the work of eradication of illiteracy was accelerated after the launch of National Literacy Mission (NLM) in 1988 with the basic objective to impart functional literacy to 80 million illiterates by 1995. Since then, Central and State Governments, international agencies, NGOs and individuals have taken up this task as people's movement.

During the past century, India made enormous efforts to improve literacy rates from 5.35 per cent in 1901 to 65.4 per cent in 2001 at the average growth rate 0.60 per cent per year. As soon as this literacy rate will come closer to the saturation, the speed of growth of literacy will become slower. Government and the NGOs claim that the absolute literacy can be achieved by the year 2020. But we still think that this is a far-reaching goal because it depends upon many factors. In all our policies we have to put stabilisation of population and eradication of literacy on top priority. Arresting population growth and the speeding up the literacy growth together can put India on the actual path of progress.

1.4 LITERACY AND HEALTHCARE

A healthier, functionally literate, well educated and higher skilled population is the surest route of higher productivity and better standards of living in any country. Countries occupying developed status today have followed the same route and India still has to follow. Due to wide spread of illiteracy and ignorance of benefits of small family norms, India's fertility and total mortality rates are very high as compared to the countries of the western world. In rural areas it is much higher than the urban areas. It has been seen that the States and UTs having higher literacy rates (like Kerala) recorded minimum Rural Infant Mortality Rates (RIMR) and Total Fertility Rates (TFR) as shown in Table 1.4 and Table 1.5 respectively.

There was a constant decrease in RIMR in the successive years. States with higher literacy rates have less RIMR. Kerala with 90.9 per cent literacy rate and 15 RIMR has taken the lead followed by Maharashtra, Himachal Pradesh, Tamil Nadu, Punjab and Gujarat. Conditions of Uttar Pradesh and Bihar were not satisfactory.

There is a co-relationship between the female literacy rates and TFR. Again, Kerala with the highest female literacy rate and minimum TFR has taken the lead which is below the set goal of TFR. BIMARU States have higher rural, urban as well as total TFR as compared to relatively higher literate states. This indicates that making people literate can control the growth of population.

Table 1.4: Rural Infant Mortality Rates During 1995-98

		Rural Infant Mortality Rates				*Total Literacy Rate*
Rank	*India/States*	*1995*	*1996*	*1997*	*1998*	*2001*
	INDIA	80	77	77	77	65.4
1.	Madhya Pradesh	104	102	99	103	64.1
2.	Orissa	107	99	100	101	63.6
3.	Uttar Pradesh	89	88	89	89	57.4
4.	Rajasthan	90	90	89	87	61.0
5.	Assam	78	79	79	82	64.3
6.	Andhra Pradesh	74	73	70	75	61.1
7.	Haryana	70	70	70	72	68.6
8.	Gujarat	68	68	69	71	70.0
9.	Karnataka	69	63	63	70	67.0
10.	Bihar	74	73	73	68	47.5
11.	Himachal Pradesh	63	63	64	66	77.1
12.	Maharashtra	66	58	56	58	77.3
13.	Punjab	58	54	54	58	70.0
14.	Tamil Nadu	61	60	58	58	73.5
15.	West Bengal	61	58	58	56	69.2
16.	Kerala	16	13	11	15	90.9

Source: Registrar General India, SRS Bulletin

To analyse the impact of literacy on the growth of population— the Birth Rate, Death Rate, Natural Growth Rate and Total Literacy Rate of the country during the past half-century have been tabulated chronologically in Table 1.6.

During 1950-51, Birth Rate was 39.9 per thousand which was reduced to 26.1 per thousand in 1998-99 showing a decrease of 13.8 per thousand (34.6%) in the past 50 years. Similarly, during the same period, Death Rate was also decreased from 27.4 per thousand to 8.7 per thousand (68.2%). But the Natural Growth Rate was increased from 12.5 per thousand to 17.5 per thousand (4.9%). Keeping Natural Growth Rate for the year 1950-51 as exception, this growth varied between 17 per thousand to 22 per thousand during the other periods. Literacy Rate during the past half century went on increasing from 18.33 per cent at the beginning to 64 per cent at the end with a net increase of 45.67 per cent .

Table 1.5: Total Fertility Rate During 1998-99

States	*Total Fertility Rate (15-49 Years)*			*Female Literacy Rate in 2001*
	Urban	*Rural*	*Total*	
1. Uttar Pradesh	2.88	4.31	3.99	43.0
2. Rajasthan	2.98	4.06	3.78	44.3
3. Bihar	2.75	3.58	3.48	33.6
4. Madhya Pradesh	2.61	3.56	3.31	50.3
5. Haryana	2.25	3.13	2.88	56.3
6. Gujarat	2.33	3.01	2.71	58.6
7. Maharashtra	2.24	2.74	2.52	67.5
8. Orissa	2.19	2.50	2.46	51.0
9. Assam	1.50	2.39	2.31	56.0
10. West Bengal	1.69	2.49	2.29	60.2
11. Andhra Pradesh	2.07	2.32	2.25	51.2
12. Punjab	1.79	2.42	2.21	63.6
13. Tamil Nadu	2.12	2.22	2.18	64.6
14. Himachal Pradesh	1.74	2.18	2.14	68.1
15. Karnataka	1.89	2.25	2.13	57.5
16. Kerala	1.51	2.07	1.96	87.9

Source: Compiled from preliminary reports of NFHS-2, 2000 (International Institute for Population Sciences, Bombay, 2000)

Table 1.6: Variation in Birth Rate, Death Rate, Natural Growth Rate and Total Literacy Rate in India During 1950-1999

	Year	*Birth Rate (per 1000)*	*Death Rate (per 1000)*	*Natural Growth Rate (per 1000)*	*Total Literacy Rate (in %)*
1.	1950-51	39.9	27.4	12.5	18.33
2.	1960-61	41.7	22.8	18.9	28.31
3.	1970-71	36.9	14.9	22.0	34.45
4.	1980-81	33.9	12.5	21.4	43.56
5.	1990-91	29.5	9.8	19.7	52.21
6.	1991-92	29.2	10.1	19.1	—
7.	1993-94	28.2	9.3	18.3	—
8.	1995-96	27.5	9.0	18.5	—
9.	1997-98	26.5	9.0	17.5	62.00
10.	1998-99	26.1	8.7	17.4	64.00

Source: National Human Development Report 2001

To compare the above indicators among major states of India and to correlate them with the literacy, the data is presented in Table 1.7

Table 1.7: Birth Rate, Death Rate, Natural Growth Rate and Total Literacy Rate of Major States of India in 1998 and 1999

Year	*Birth Rate (per 1000)*		*Death Rate (per 1000)*		*Natural Growth Rate (per 1000)*		*Total Literacy Rate (in %)*
	1998	*1999*	*1998*	*1999*	*1998*	*1999*	
INDIA	26.4	26.1	9.0	8.7	17.4	17.4	65.4
1. Uttar Pradesh	32.4	32.8	10.5	10.5	21.9	22.3	57.4
2. Rajasthan	31.5	31.1	8.8	8.4	22.7	22.7	61.0
3. Bihar	31.1	31.5	9.4	8.9	21.7	22.6	47.5
4. Madhya Pradesh	30.6	31.1	11.2	10.4	19.4	20.7	64.1
5. Assam	27.7	27.0	10.1	9.7	17.6	17.3	64.3
6. Haryana	27.6	26.8	8.1	7.7	19.5	19.1	68.6
7. Orissa	25.7	24.1	11.1	10.7	14.6	13.4	63.6
8. Gujarat	25.3	25.4	7.8	7.9	17.5	17.5	70.0
9. Himachal Pradesh	22.5	—	7.7	—	14.8	—	77.1
10. Punjab	22.4	21.5	7.7	7.4	14.7	14.1	70.0
11. Maharashtra	22.3	21.1	7.6	7.5	14.7	13.6	77.3
12. Andhra Pradesh	22.3	21.7	8.8	8.2	13.5	13.5	61.1
13. Karnataka	22.0	22.3	7.9	7.7	14.1	14.6	67.0
14. West Bengal	21.3	20.7	7.5	7.1	13.8	13.6	69.2
15. Tamil Nadu	18.9	19.3	8.4	8.0	10.5	11.3	73.5
16. Kerala	18.2	18.0	6.4	6.4	11.8	11.6	90.9

Source : Registrar General, India SRS Bulletin

The Birth Rate, Death Rate and Natural Growth Rate of northern states like Uttar Pradesh, Bihar, Madhya Pradesh, Haryana and Rajasthan are higher than the southern states like Kerala, Karnataka, Tamil Nadu and Andhra Pradesh. It shows that more the literacy less the population growth rate. Here literacy is also considered to be one of the important factors to increase Life Expectancy at Birth. For the last fifty years, it has become doubled. It was 30 years at the time of independence and now it is over 63 years. There is a significant difference in Life Expectancy at Birth across the states. In Kerala, a person at birth is expected to live over 73 years (70 years for male and 76 years for female), followed by Punjab 67.4 years (66.4 years for male and 68.4 years for female). In other states like Assam, Bihar, Madhya Pradesh, Orissa, Uttar Pradesh, Rajasthan, it ranges between 55-60 years. The difference in life expectancy between male and female is less in relatively higher literate states like Kerala (0.8 years), Punjab (1.7%)

and it goes up to 8-9 years in other states like Madhya Pradesh, Bihar and Orissa.

In another study, (Table 1.8) it has been found that the TFR of literate women is lower than the illiterate women in both rural and urban areas. This further decreases in case women attained matriculate or higher education. This justifies that the making women literate is a long time investment in success of the family planning programmes, leading to reduction in RIMR, birth rate, death rate, natural growth rate and TFR. In this regard, Kerala has set an example for other States and UTs to follow.

Table 1.8: Literacy Level and Health Awareness

Level of Literacy	*Illiterate*	*Less than Middle School*	*Up to Middle School*	*Up to High School*
Infant Mortality Rate (per thousand)	86.5	58.6	48.1	32.8
Under Five Mortality Rate (per thousand)	122.8	75.8	58.1	37.1
Child Vaccination	27.8%	52.3%	62.7%	72.7%
Awareness about Family Planning	42.9%	76.4%	85.9%	94.0%
Awareness about AIDS	18.0%	54.0%	74.0%	92.0%

Source: National Human Development Report 2001

As the level of literacy increases, the Infant Mortality Rate decreases. There is a significant decline in Under-five Mortality Rate as the level of literacy goes up. People with higher literacy level are much aware of the child vaccination, family planning and dreaded diseases like HIV/AIDS. As the literacy increases, the awareness about the small family norms also increases.

1.5 LITERACY AND ECONOMY

It is a well-established fact that higher the literacy rate better the economical development and higher the per capita income as well as improved quality of life. Thus, the literacy is prerequisite for economic development of any country. It is a lack of investment in human capital, not a lack of investment in physical capital, that prevents developing countries, like India, from catching up with the developed ones. Literacy attainment and public spending on literacy are correlated positively to the economic growth of any country.

It has been evidenced in many developed countries and also in the Indian state like Kerala, where human capital is given more priority than the physical capital. Therefore, result is before us in the form of increased literacy and awareness. Thus for India to be on the development path, the public spending should increasingly focus on enhancing literacy through primary education and promoting skill-based vocations and ushering in an environment of *dignity of labour.* The corporate sectors should also be motivated through some incentives to support literacy programmes, education and healthcare facilities.

Now the time has come that all round development of a country is to be judged not by its military power, natural resources, oil reserves, agricultural and industrial products, economic strength, capital cities, huge and ornamental buildings, etc. It will be judged by the well being of the people living in it, level of the people's health, nutrition, literacy and education, the opportunities to earn a fair reward for its labours, ability to participate in problem-solving and decision-making process which affects the lives of the existing people and the future generations.

1.6 HUMAN RESOURCE DEVELOPMENT

Human resource development is the most important input for promoting economic growth and development of any country. Poverty also persists under the conditions where the human resource is under-valued and land and other material resources are over-valued. Development of any nation depends mostly upon the human resource than any other resource. Since it is the core competency of this great country, therefore, its development is directly related to our progress and prosperity. According to Human Development Report 1999 of UNDP, India was ranked 132 among the list of 174 nations in terms of Human Development Index (HDI). Its rank was increased to 124 in 2000. Our aim should be to put India within the category of top ten developed nations by 2020. During the past five and half decades we have made considerable progress in the areas concerning well beings of the people. But in this area we have to do some more efforts. HDIs of some of the developed and developing countries are given in Table 1.9 whereas, HDIs of selected states of India are given in Table 1.10.

Out of 173 countries in the world, Norway stood first in the rank of HDI. It is a matter of satisfaction that India has been categorised in medium HDI, whereas Pakistan is in the low HDI category. During the past two and half decades, India has made 42 per cent progress and in the same duration Pakistan and China have recorded 45 per cent and 39 per cent growth respectively.

Table 1.9: Trends in Human Development Index of Selected Countries of the World

Country	*Rank*	*Human Development Index*					
		1975	*1980*	*1985*	*1990*	*1995*	*2000*
Norway	1	0.859	0.877	0.888	0.901	0.925	0.942
United States	6	0.863	0.884	0.898	0.914	0.925	0.939
Japan	9	0.854	0.878	0.893	0.909	0.923	0.933
United Kingdom	13	0.841	0.848	0.858	0.878	0.916	0.928
Sri Lanka	89	0.616	0.650	0.676	0.697	0.719	0.741
China	96	0.523	0.544	0.591	0.625	0.681	0.726
India	124	0.407	0.434	0.473	0.511	0.545	0.577
Pakistan	138	0.345	0.372	0.404	0.442	0.473	0.499

Note: Countries are ranked as per HDI 2000
High HDI : 0.800 and above
Medium HDI : 0.500 to 0.799
Low HDI : Less than 0.500

Source: Human Resource Development Report 2001

Table 1.10: Trends in Human Development Index of Selected States of India

State	*Year 1981*	*Rank*	*Year 1991*	*Rank*	*Year 2001*	*Rank*
Andhra Pradesh	0.298	(7)	0.377	(8)	0.416	(9)
Assam	0.272	(8)	0.348	(9)	0.386	(13)
Bihar	0.237	(13)	0.308	(14)	0.367	(14)
Gujarat	0.360	(4)	0.431	(6)	0.479	(6)
Madhya Pradesh	0.245	(12)	0.328	(12)	0.394	(11)
Uttar Pradesh	0.255	(11)	0.314	(13)	0.388	(12)
Orissa	0.267	(9)	0.345	(12)	0.404	(10)
Haryana	0.360	(4)	0.443	(5)	0.509	(5)
Kerala	0.500	(1)	0.591	(1)	0.638	(1)
Punjab	0.411	(2)	0.475	(2)	0.537	(2)
Tamil Nadu	0.343	(6)	0.466	(3)	0.531	(3)
Maharashtra	0.363	(3)	0.452	(4)	0.523	(4)
Rajasthan	0.256	(10)	0.347	(10)	0.424	(8)
Karnataka	0.346	(5)	0.404	(7)	0.472	(7)

Source : National Human Development Report 2001

At the state level, Kerala, Punjab, Haryana, Gujarat, Karnataka, Maharashtra, Tamil Nadu and West Bengal were among the states with better HDI. States like Bihar, Uttar Pradesh, Madhya Pradesh, Orissa,

Rajasthan were not improved in their HDI. Tamil Nadu was at the 6th rank in 1981 and improved to 3rd position in 1991 and remained at the same status in 2001.

1.7 FORMAL AND NON-FORMAL EDUCATION

India's educational system is a mixture of a number of different traditions. During the British period, formal education was not affordable to masses. In 1947, when India gained independence, about 80 per cent population was illiterate. Mahatma Gandhi and other leaders developed programme for basic education with an idea to eradicate the prevalent illiteracy. As a result, about 40 per cent of the children between the age group of 6 years and 11 years and 29 per cent of the age group between 12 years and 14 years were enrolled in formal schools. During 1950-1960, various educational schemes were launched to eradicate illiteracy. This was the period when Delhi Public Library was established with the objectives to support non-formal and continuing education system. Prior to this, role of libraries was not much recognized as a force to literacy, to educate and to stimulate public interest in reading.

Before independence, the conditions of libraries were not so satisfactory. After 1947, the situation changed and it was realised that libraries could play a prominent role in socio-economic, cultural, scientific and technological development of the society. United Nations Organisation[1] (UNO) also stated in its Article 27 that *"it is the birth right of every individual to have free access to the results of human ingenuity exercised in art or science"*. Having free access to the recorded thought results not only in personal gain but also national welfare. Therefore, libraries are termed as builders of the nation's soul.

There is close relationship between the library and society. Library satisfies certain requirements of the society. It functions as an educational centre to support and promote all types of formal, non-formal, adult and life-long education by keeping adequate stock of books and other reading and learning materials and also making them available to all sections of the society. Thus, it plays a significant role in literacy movement.

Healthy recreation is also an essential requirement of the society. Library provides newspapers, magazines, books, audio-visual materials, films, cassettes, CD-ROMs, gramophone records, etc. and also organises various forms of performing arts, musical events for recreation of the masses.

It provides facilities for aesthetic appreciation that widens mental horizon and develops creative capacities of the individuals. Also contributes the cultural enrichment of the community by organising extension activities like lectures, seminars, symposia, book exhibitions and other cultural gatherings. It also serves as an information centre to provide information about the socio-economic need of the society *i.e.* employment opportunity and facilities provided by the government or other social welfare agencies, etc. People come to the library and collect information as per their requirements.

Even today, it is a well-known fact that the development of libraries has not taken place in relation to need of society in India. Mainly their existence were realised in urban areas, particularly in metropolitan cities. Thus libraries have been serving only a small segment of the society. As social institutions, they have failed to bring benefit of the dissemination of information, education and culture to majority of population. There is a lot of scope for libraries to satisfy the thirst of knowledge of the society and also to rectify the broken channel of flow of information from library to a common man. A huge gap has also been identified between information requirements of the society and collection development in libraries. A large number of documents acquired by them are not being properly used by the public. Libraries need to take active role in fulfilling the formal and non-formal educational requirements of people. These libraries should provide supportive educational materials to the students and teachers at various levels. These should also fulfill cultural and recreational need, which the society demands. This is the reason why the existence of libraries in India was not felt in the past. Some of the other reasons were - low literacy rates, lethargy among people to acquire education, lack of awareness among the people, non-availability of required materials in existing libraries, establishment of more libraries in the urban areas than rural areas and so on. In these circumstances, opening of libraries in the areas where majority of illiterate people are living, is like lighting of streets in a city of blinds.

Merely increasing the numbers of libraries may not fulfill the national goal to achieve total literacy. A mass population should be persuaded to take trouble of learning to read and write. Until they are convinced that knowledge will open up new avenues of advancement, the objectives of libraries and literacy movement may not be fulfilled, which are directly related to the poverty alleviation. Modern libraries can have a variety of information materials to attract masses and perform the persuasion functions. They also have an appeal to untutored minds. Through variety of means they can inspire illiterates towards eradication of illiteracy in the country.

Necessity for having libraries for the masses was felt by the Government and NGOs. To liquidate mass illiteracy, there was a growing demand that libraries should collaborate and complement the national campaign against eradication of illiteracy by providing suitable reading and learning materials and proper services to the new literates. In the present context, libraries should not complement, rather these should take lead in the literacy programmes. Support of libraries are required to fill up the gaps between basic education and adult education up to a large extent. At present, there is a large gap in coordination between functioning of libraries and literacy programmes organized. All efforts should be made to identify the areas where libraries and literacy programmes are lacking in coordination and how these gaps could be fulfilled to meet the common goals of these two. The outcomes may be quite useful in strengthening the coordination among various libraries and literacy movement and programmes in the country.

1.8 NATIONAL HERITAGE AND LIBRARIES

Who are we? What is our national identity as Indian? What is our shared perception of history, life styles, values and beliefs? These are some of the serious questions having a bearing on the life and well beings of the nation and its people. In the changing world there is a fear of loss of our traditional values, ethics and culture. We have to propagate, preserve and conserve our cultural heritage. Though enriched by diversity during this long course of evolution, our culture has retained its distinctive character. Now we have to attempt to build bridges between the past and the present. Our tangible and intangible cultural heritage include monuments, folk, arts, literature, manuscripts, handicrafts, performing arts including music, drama and dance, visual arts in the form of paintings, sculpture and graphics, etc. These are our national heritage and preserved by the museums, art galleries, archives and libraries. These are the repositories of the nation's valuable treasures and play important roles in moulding people's tastes and making them aware of the history and creative talent available in India. Some of the important libraries involved in preserving our cultural heritage have been discussed in the following chapter.

1.9 ILLITERACY IN INDIA

Illiteracy is not a fatality. It is just the product of time. Nobody is born literate. An illiterate is just a victim of situations because he did not have opportunity of going to school or having gone to school. He has been dropped out of the systems not of his own violation but due to economic or social compulsions. He grew up to adulthood and remained illiterate. He is cut off from the rest of the world without access to the print media, and to the world of communication and information. Illiteracy, therefore, is not his own making but it is the outcome of the forces and situations beyond his control.

Illiteracy is a growing phenomenon and unless nipped in the bud, it is likely to grow further and pose a menace to development to the human evolution and growth. It is a serious impediment to the individual's growth. It is also a hindrance in the way of a country's socio-economic progress.

Democracy can flourish only when the people are enlightened with the power of literacy. Thus, ignorance needs to be uprooted and illiteracy should be done away with. The poor and the illiterates can rise to their liberation through literacy, dialogue and action. Illiteracy breeds ignorance, which, in turn, leads to apathy. In any democratic system, citizens are required to participate in political process and to take interest on matters of public importance. The illiterate masses are most susceptible to exploitation and superstitions and also closely linked with poverty and crime. On the other hand, literacy empowers the individual. Mahatma Gandhi said that:

> "Illiteracy is a sin, a blackmark on India and must be eradicated"

According to Noble laureate Prof Amartya Sen, India suffered two major social failures – one concerning gender inequity and the other concerning illiteracy. He said that:

> "Illiteracy is unfreedom – not just lack of freedom to read but also the curtailment of all other freedoms that are conditional on communication, both oral and written"

As we have entered into the new millennium, we are in great danger of the knowledge revolution bypassing one third of our adult population. India today has the dubious distinction of having the largest number of illiterates in the world. To know the status of increasing or decreasing number of illiterates and literates in the country during the past one decade, the data is presented in Table 1.11 and Table 1.12 respectively.

On one side, the number of literates have increased and on the other side the total number of illiterates have decreased in 2001 as compared to 1991. Surprisingly, the percentage of female literate population has increased by about 74 per cent as compared to male literates by 47 per cent. This is a positive sign of women empowerment. For the first time since independence, there was a declined trend in absolute number of illiterates during a decade. Efforts should be made to make this trend permanently irreversible till the goal of literacy is achieved.

Table 1.11: Decrease in Male, Female and Total Illiterate Population in India During 1991-2001

Year	*Illiterate Population*		
	Persons	*Male*	*Females*
1991	328,167,288	128,099,211	200,068,077
2001	296,208,952	106,654,066	189,554,886
Absolute decrease (over 1991)	-31,958,336	21,445,145	-10,513,191
Percentage decrease (over 1991)	-9.73	-16.74	-5.25

Source: Census of India 1991 and 2001

Table 1.12: Increase in Male, Female and Total Literate Population in India During 1991-2001

Year	*Literate Population*		
	Persons	*Male*	*Females*
1991	358,402,626	228,983,134	129,419,492
2001	562,010,742	336,969,695	225,041,048
Absolute increase (over 1991)	203,608,117	107,986,561	95,621,556
Percentage increase (over 1991)	56.81%	47.16%	73.88%

Source: Census of India 1991 and 2001

Table 1.13 gives number of illiterate population of states and UTs in India in 2001. The states of Uttar Pradesh, Bihar, Andhra Pradesh, West Bengal, Maharashtra, Rajasthan and Madhya Pradesh constitute about 3/4th illiterate population of the country. The four BIMARU states along with newly created States of Chattisgarh, Uttaranchal and Jharkhand account for 49.5 per cent of illiterate female population, 49.6 per cent of illiterate male population and 49.5 per cent of total population of the country.

Table 1.14 gives percentage distribution of illiterate male, female and total population of states and UTs in India in 2001 and the same has been reflected in Figure 1.3.

To know the decadal growth trend of total population and the number of illiterates in India after independence, the data has been presented in Table 1.15 and Figure 1.4.

Table 1.13: Distribution of Male, Female and Total Illiterate Population in India in 2001

	Iliterate Population (age 7+ years)		
State/UT	*Persons*	*Male*	*Females*
India	296,208,952	106,654,066	189,554,886
Uttar Pradesh	57,810,542	21,306,282	36,504,260
Bihar	34,968,650	13,799,477	21,169,173
Andhra Pradesh	25,689,502	9,724,534	15,964,968
West Bengal	21,266,590	8,031,792	13,234,798
Maharashtra	18,998,379	5,968,562	13,029,817
Rajasthan	17,935,918	5,627,181	12,308,737
Madhya Pradesh	17,860,686	6,020,438	11,840,248
Karnataka	15,132,802	5,537,162	9,595,640
Tamil Nadu	14,668,772	4,905,357	9,763,415
Gujarat	12,469,293	4,202,730	8,266,563
Orissa	11,472,584	3,838,038	7,634,546
Jharkhand	10,143,063	3,661,286	6,481,777
Assam	7,960,619	3,248,618	4,712,001
Punjab	6,379,994	2,743,910	3,636,084
Chattisgarh	6,033,286	1,925,087	4,108,199
Haryana	5,598,873	1,978,457	3,620,416
Kerala	2,559,343	789,032	1,770,311
Delhi	2,155,932	826,149	1,329,783
Uttaranchal	1,984,993	579,642	1,405,351
Himachal Pradesh	1,194,777	368,182	826,595
Tripura	727,997	263,070	464,927
Meghalaya	678,184	316,995	361,189
Manipur	646,287	231,946	414,341
Nagaland	561,941	254,027	307,914
Arunachal Pradesh	403,266	169,570	233,696
Goa	212,484	68,064	144,420
Pondicherry	159,372	47,656	111,716
Chandigarh	144,413	64,423	79,990
Sikkim	140,495	58,035	82,460
Mizoram	86,259	36,115	50,144
Dadar and Nagar Haveli	72,448	27,184	45,264
Andaman & Nicobar Islands	58,646	23,716	34,930
Daman & Diu	26,108	9,525	16,583
Lakshadweep	6,454	1,824	4,630

Source: Census Report 2001

Table 1.14: Percentage Distribution of Male, Female and Total Illiterate Population in India in 2001

	Iliterate Population (in %)		
State/UT	*Persons*	*Male*	*Females*
Uttar Pradesh	19.52	19.98	19.26
Bihar	11.81	12.94	11.17
Andhra Pradesh	8.67	9.12	8.42
West Bengal	7.18	7.53	6.98
Maharashtra	6.41	5.60	6.87
Rajasthan	6.06	5.28	6.49
Madhya Pradesh	6.03	5.64	6.25
Karnataka	5.11	5.19	5.06
Tamil Nadu	4.95	4.60	5.15
Gujarat	4.21	3.94	4.36
Orissa	3.87	3.60	4.03
Jharkhand	3.42	3.43	3.42
Assam	2.69	3.05	2.49
Punjab	2.15	2.57	1.92
Chattisgarh	2.04	1.80	2.17
Haryana	1.89	1.86	1.91
Kerala	0.86	0.74	0.93
Delhi	0.73	0.77	0.70
Uttaranchal	0.67	0.54	0.74
Himachal Pradesh	0.40	0.35	0.44
Tripura	0.25	0.25	0.25
Meghalaya	0.23	0.30	0.19
Manipur	0.22	0.22	0.22
Nagaland	0.19	0.24	0.16
Arunachal Pradesh	0.14	0.16	0.12
Goa	0.07	0.06	0.08
Pondicherry	0.05	0.04	0.06
Chandigarh	0.05	0.06	0.04
Sikkim	0.05	0.05	0.04
Mizoram	0.03	0.03	0.03
Dadra & Nagar Haveli	0.02	0.03	0.02
Andaman & Nicobar Island	0.02	0.02	0.02
Daman & Diu	0.01	0.01	0.01
INDIA	100.00	100.00	100.00

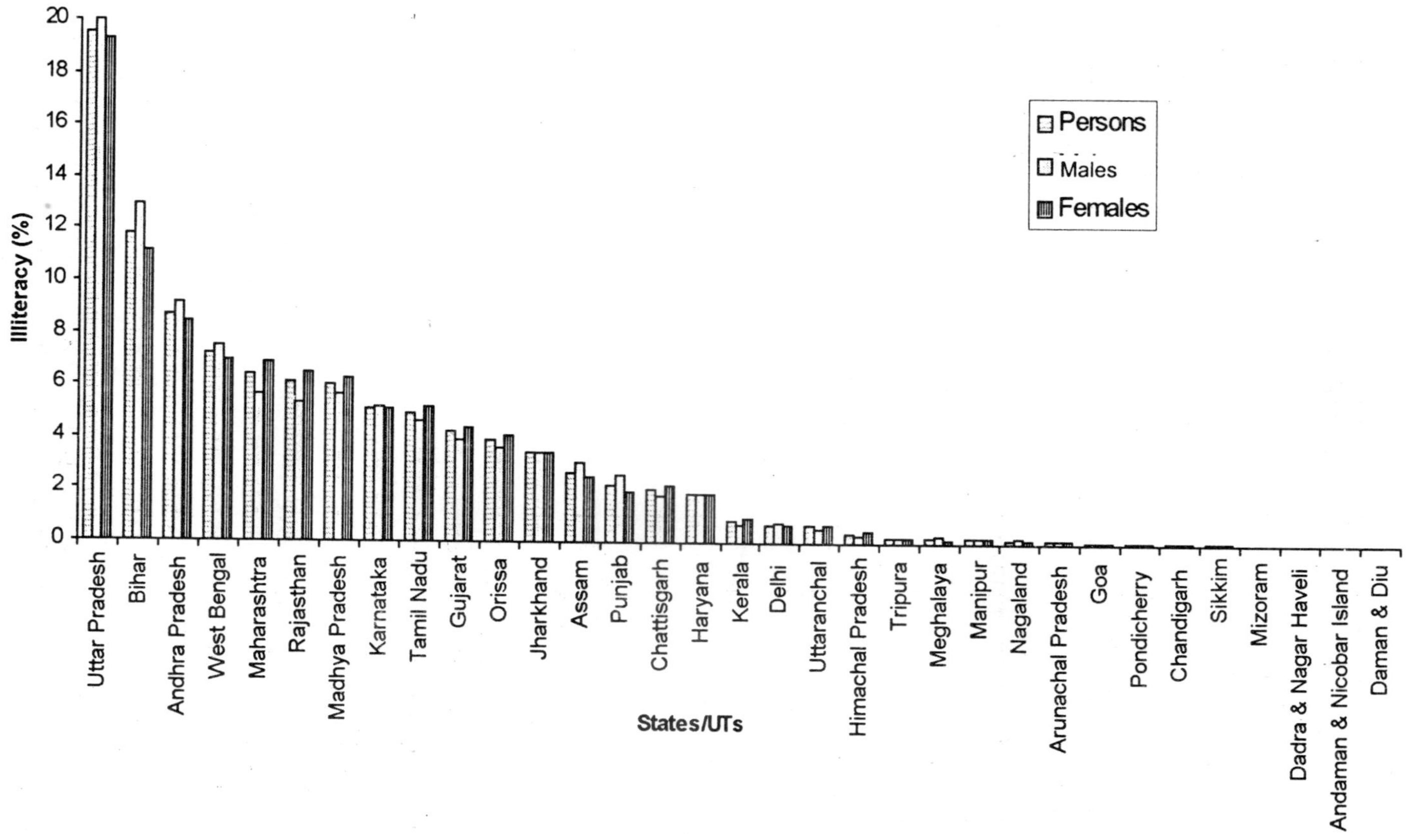

Fig. 1.3: Percentage Distribution of Male, Female and Total Population in India in 2001

Table 1.15: Growth of Total Population and Number of Illiterates in India During 1951-2001

Year	*Total Illiterates (in million)*	*Age Group*	*Number of Population (in million)*
1951	361.09	5+	300.09
1961	439.23	5+	267.32
1971	548.16	5+	307.17
1981	683.32	7+	305.31
1991	846.30	7+	328.88
2001	1027.02	7+	296.21

Source: Census of India

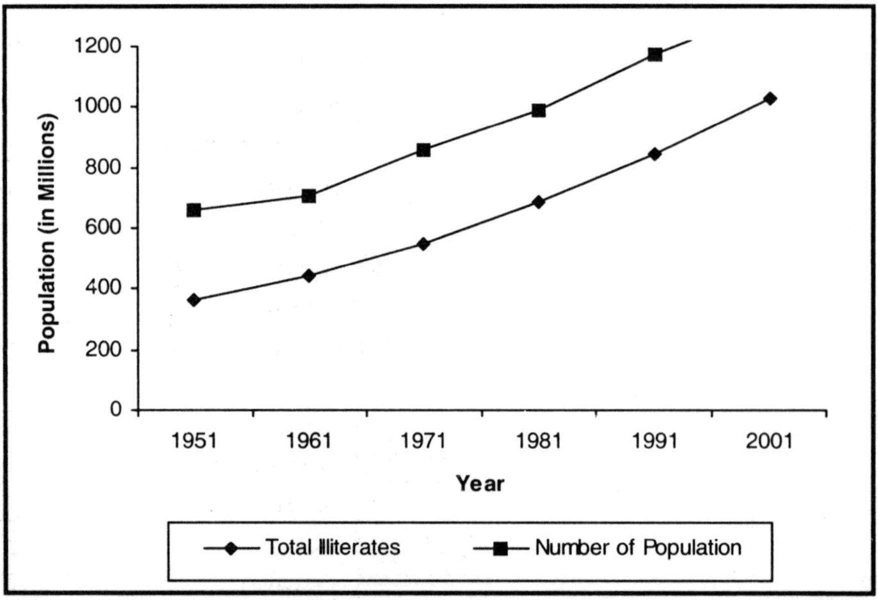

Fig. 1.4: Growth of Total Population and Number of Illiterates in India During 1951-2001

The number of illiterates have decreased during the period 1951-1961, 1971-1981 and 1991-2001 by 32.77 million, 1.86 million and 32.67 million respectively. The number of illiterates was increased during the period 1961-1971 and 1981-1991 by 39.85 million and 23.57 million respectively. There was a tremendous increase in the population of the country, the number of illiterates has gone down. This actually shows a marked decline of 3.88 million illiterates, despite population growth since 1951. This was a significant achievement made by our country in the area of literacy.

1.10 WORLD WIDE ILLITERACY

At the beginning of this century, illiteracy was very common world over, perhaps because education was not widely available to everybody as it is available today. With the growth of population, the number of both literates and illiterates have also increased. The world's population was 1.6 billion in 1900, which has increased more than three and half times and became 5.75 billion in 1995. Thus, there is an increase of 4.15 billion people during the period of 95 years. During the same period, the number of illiterates have also increased more than three times, from about 300 million in 1900 to about 1 billion in 1995. Thus the numerical growth of non-literates is in the same proportion as the population growth. Following are some of the facts about growth of population and illiteracy:

- The world's population has sharply increased after the Second World War.
- Illiteracy is not yet in the process of being wiped out. The number of non-literate persons has increased slowly but steadily during the last century i.e. size of illiterate population is still growing.
- It is conceivable that the growth of illiteracy may be halted but the elimination of illiteracy is not likely in the foreseeable future.
- To eradicate illiteracy from the world's map may not be possible without halting the growth of population.
- While UNESCO and many governments had launched campaigns to wipe out illiteracy by the year 2000, but the number of illiterates still continued to grow.

It is a well-known fact that the largest number of illiterates are living in India. It may be of interest to know the position of India in the world in this regard. The numerical distribution of world's non-literate population and India's position in 1991 is given in Table 1.16 and presented graphically in Figure 1.5.

On the map of illiteracy, India has the maximum number of illiterates in the world, followed by China, Africa, South Asian and Arabian States. Taking India and China together, more than half of the total world's illiterates live in these two countries.

The following are some of the well-known facts about the illiteracy:

1. There are about one billion illiterate adults (persons of 15 years of age and above) in the world today.

Table 1.16: World-wide Illiteracy in 1991

Country/Region	*Percentage Population of Illiterates*
India	30.99
China	20.10
Sub-Sahara Africa	15.34
South Asia	12.95
Arab States	06.73
East Asia/Oceania	05.63
Latin America/Caribbean	04.74
Others	03.52
Total	100

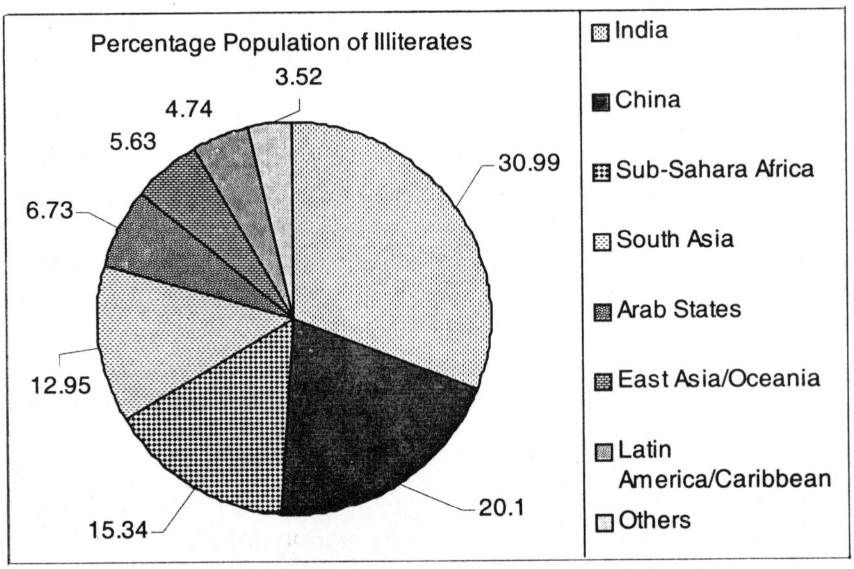

Fig. 1.5: World-wide Distribution of Illiteracy in 1991

2. Ninety-eight per cent of all illiterates are in developing countries. Two-third of all illiterates are women.
3. More than one-half of all illiterates are in India and China i.e. every second illiterate person in the world may be either Indian or Chinese.
4. One-third of all illiterates are in India i.e. every third illiterate person in the world is an Indian.
5. India, China and South Africa constitute two-third illiterate population of the total number of illiterate population of the world.

6. It is estimated that 30-50 million people are added each year to the numbers of illiterates.
7. Twenty-seven per cent of all the adults are illiterate.
8. World-wide, the percentage of adult literacy is declining, but the absolute number of illiterates is increasing.
9. In the poorer countries, population growth is believed to be one of the prime factors of growth in the number of illiterates.

1.11 FACTORS RESPONSIBLE FOR ILLITERACY

There are so many reasons and factors, which influence the Indian scene for the total eradication of illiteracy. Persistence of illiteracy is because of a number of historical reasons. India is a land of many religions, castes, ethnic groups, etc. Caste system, foreign languages, foreign rulers and their personal interests deprived the Indians of basic facilities, like education. SCs, STs and people with poor economic conditions continued in the same conditions for about 2000 years or more. An access to libraries and education was confined to only the privileged class consisting of families and children of upper castes, rulers, big landlords, rich persons, etc. Members of only these classes received benefit of access of libraries, literacy and educational programmes.

Another major factor influencing literacy is the linguistic diversity. There are dozens of major languages in the country, which are used as communication medium, either verbal or written. Many languages are not having good printed materials for learners. It has been observed that the countries having less numbers of spoken and written languages, are relatively more literate than those having more number of languages.

These are well-known facts that even more than fifty years after Independence from almost two centuries of British rule, to check the large scale poverty remains the most difficult task. India still has the world's largest number of poor people in a single country. About 400 million people are below the poverty line and 75 per cent of them are in rural areas. The main causes of poverty are described as illiteracy and population growth rate by far exceeding the economic growth rate during the past five and half decades.

It has also been realised that the poverty and illiteracy, more or less, overlap each other. Poverty in a broader sense refers to denial of opportunities in education, health, material well-being, access to markets, job security, political and social freedom and several other factors. It is measured in terms of Human Poverty Index (HPI) and Poverty of

Opportunity Index (POPI). It is a composition of three major human deprivations, namely,

Health Deprivation, which is measured by a weighted average of three variables:

- The percentage of people not expected to survive to age of 40 years;
- The percentage of people without access of safe drinking water;
- The percentage of malnourished children under the age of 7 years.

Education Deprivation, which is a composition of two variables:

- The percentage of illiterate adults;
- The percentage of primary school-age children who are out of school.

Income Deprivation, which is the percentage of people living below the poverty line.

All these three deprivations are the real causes of human poverty. In 2000, the HPI of India was 55 as compared to China's 24, Sri Lanka's 31, and Pakistan's 68 among all 88 developing countries of the world.

The poverty of resources may not be considered as the only real cause for low literacy rate of any country. Many countries, which are poorer than India, have managed a much higher rate of literacy. For instance, Tajikistan has real per capita income of US $1,117 and a literacy rate of 98 per cent, while Vietnam enjoys a literacy rate of 94 per cent at a per capita income of only US $1,208. Kenya also has a literacy rate of 78 per cent with a real per capita income of US $1,404. In 1994, India's real per capita income was US $1,348 but its literacy rate was only 52 per cent. A brief view of the situation is given in Table 1.17.

Table 1.17: Per Capita Income and Literacy Rates of Developing Countries in 1991

Country	*Real GDP Per Capita Income*	*Literacy Rate*
India	US $1348	52%
Kenya	US $1404	78%
Vietnam	US $1208	94%
Tajikistan	US $1117	98%

Following are some of the various other factors responsible for poor female literacy rate in India.

- Gender-based inequality.
- Social discrimination and economic exploitation.
- Occupation of girl child in domestic chores.
- Low retention rate and high drop-out rate.

To eradicate illiteracy in women of all categories, the literacy campaigns have contributed in many ways, such as:

- Heightened social awareness.
- Increased school enrollment.
- Increase in self-confidence and personality development.
- Gender equity and women's empowerment.
- Status in family.
- Educational equality.
- Women as entrepreneurs.
- Household savings and access to credit.
- Health and hygiene.

1.12 FUTURE TARGETS

Over the years, we have made significant progress in various fields in the social sectors. A considerable improvement of demographic indicators, healthcare services, education and adult literacy has been made particularly after independence. Still there is a lot of scope for accelerating development process in these areas. In spite of several budgetary constraints being faced, the Government has enhanced allocations for the social sectors. The following attainment of monitorable targets has been set up by the Government, which are to be achieved during the next couple of Five Year Plans.

- Reduction of Poverty Ratio by 5 per cent points by 2007 and by 15 per cent points by 2012.
- All children in school by 2003 and all children to complete 5 years of schooling by 2007.
- Reduction of gender gaps in literacy by at least by 50 per cent by 2007.
- Reduction in the decadal rate of population growth between 2001 and 2011 to 16.2 per cent.
- Increase in literacy rate to 75 per cent within the current Plan.
- Reduction of Infant Mortality Rate (IMR) to 45 per one thousand live births by 2007 and to 28 by 2012.

- Reduction of Maternal Mortality Ratio (MMR) to 2 per one thousand live births by 2007 and to 1 by 2012.
- Potable drinking water to all villages within the current.
- Cleaning of major polluted rivers by 2007 and other notified stretches by 2012.

1.13 NATIONAL VISION

Country's glorious past should be taken as a source of inspiration to instil and motivate and should not constitute a burden on our back. A *"National Vision"* needs to be created through the ever-widening mass media. Necessary environment should be created so that people should realise sense of belonging to the country, patriotism, mantra of work is workship and other such features should be built in the coming generations so that we could achieve the status of developed nation at least within a couple of decades from now. Hence a long term strategy for literacy, education and building work culture is very essential for transforming our society to the developed one.

President of India Dr. A.P.J. Abdul Kalam[2] said:

> "Any organization, society or even a nation without a vision is like a ship crusing on the high seas without any aim or direction. It is clarity of national vision which constantly drives the people towards the goal".

Before independence, our national vision was to make India free from British Rule. This vision was set by the people of India itself and led by our great leaders at that time. Therefore, it went deep into the minds and hearts of the millions of Indians. As a result, they plunged into the freedom movement irrespective of their castes, creed or religions. The goal was achieved in the form of independence in 1947. Since then, we framed out various goals and sub-goals like self-reliance in food grains, primary health, eradication of illiteracy, alleviation of poverty, education and employment for all, social justice, women empowerment and so on. Some of these are met partially or wholly, some are yet to be achieved. During the past half century, we have not been able to set any national vision.

Presently, every one of us is feeling that we must stand in the frontline of developed nation and gain a status of developed nation from developing nation at least during our life time. After all, how many years we shall remain in the underdeveloped or developing status. It means, we should transform our existing resources to make it as one of the largest economies of the world. Every one of us has to live above the poverty line and high standard of health and education. Our national security should be fully assured. Thus the strength and potential of each and every Indian should be realised and transformed to improve our national economy.

One of the important goals in achieving the status of developed nation is eradication of illiteracy from the map of India. Government of India, State Governments, international agencies, NGOs and many individuals are working in this direction for the past so many years. They are making enormous efforts but this can be speed up with proper co-ordination and co-operation among them and synchronisation in their activities. Efforts made by various agencies in this direction have been described in the following chapters. The main focus was given to eradicate illiteracy through library movement, adult education, literacy programmes and non-formal education systems and finally to alleviate poverty. Because India has billion minds which form our national human resource base, some are well ignited, some have to be ignited and others to be made for ignition so that they can participate effectively in national development. Imparting literacy and education are the best ways of igniting minds of millions illiterate Indians.

To enhance literacy rate and make it sustainable, necessity of libraries have been given main focus in the text. Delhi, being the national capital, has been as a model state to implement library and literacy programmes in depth.

REFERENCES

1. POWER (Jonathan), *Ed.* A vision of hope: The fiftieth anniversary of the United Nations. Regency Corporation. London. 1995. p. 293.
2. ABDUL KALAM (APJ) and RAJAN (YS). *India 2020: A Vision for the New Millennium*. Viking. 1998. p. 21.

Chapter 2

Library Movement in India

Ignited young minds, we feel, are powerful resources. This resource is mighter than any resource on the earth, in the sky and under sea. We must all work together to transform our "developing India" into a "developed India", and the revolution required for this effort must start in our minds. —*Dr. A.P.J. Abdul Kalam*

2.1 INTRODUCTION

Library is a social institution. It collects, selects, processes, organizes, maintains, preserves, retrieves and disseminates information. Public library makes information available to the public. It forms the prime communication channel and information intermediary in any society. There are a number of definitions given by the institutions/professional associations/individuals on the basis of the objectives and functions of public libraries. UNESCO[1] defines public libraries as:

> "Those which serve the population of a community or region free of charge or for a nominal fee. They may serve the general public or special categories of the public such as children, members of armed forces, hospital patients, prisoners, workers and employees."

Dr. S.R. Ranganathan[2], father of library science in India, defines:

> "Public library is one which is open to any member of the public and is usually free of any charge paid as so much for so much service. It is usually supported by local rate and grants from government."

Harrod's Librarians' Glossary of Terms used in Librarianship, Documentation, Book Crafts and Reference Books[3] defines:

> "A library provided wholly or partly from public funds and the use of which is not restricted to any class of persons in the community but is freely available to all."

ALA Glossary of Library and Information Science[4] defines public library as:

> "Any library which provides general library services without charge to all residents of a given community, district or region. Supported by public or private funds, the public library makes its basic collections and basic services available to the population of its legal service area without charges to individual users, but may impose charges on users outside its legal service area. Products and services beyond the library's basic services may or may not be provided to the public at large and may or may not be provided without individual charges. Earlier, a library accessible to all residents of a given community, but not generally free, as distinguished from a private library."

Shri K. P. Sinha[5] in his report, prepared in 1957, describes:

> "A public library is financed for the most part out of public funds. It charges no fees from readers. It is open for full use by the public without distinction of caste, creed or sex. It is intended as an auxiliary educational institution providing a means of self-education, which is endless. Public library houses learning materials giving reliable information freely and without partiality or prejudice on a wide variety of subjects which satisfies the interest of the readers".

William Frederick Poole[6], the librarian of the Chicago Public Library, states that:

> "The public library is established by the State Laws, is supposed by local taxation and voluntary gifts, is managed as a public trust, and every citizen of the city and town which maintains it has an equal share in its privileges of reference and circulation."

The above definitions of public library may be consolidated as:

- The public library should be supported by public funds.
- The public library should be established and managed by State legislation.

- Its services should be available to all residents coming under its legal service area and it may charge from users outside its legal service area.
- It should provide learning and reading materials and render its library services to its users without distinction of caste, creed, sex or religion.
- It should collect and preserve reading and learning materials for use by the users.
- It should not be a Store House but an Information Centre and provide reliable and authenticated information to right user at right time in a right manner.

UNESCO issued Public Library Manifesto[7] in 1949 and revised[8] it in 1972. It says that:

- The public library is a practical demonstration of democracy's faith in universal education as a continuing and life-long process, in the appreciation of the achievement of humanity in knowledge and culture.
- It is the principal means whereby the record of man's thoughts and ideas and the expression of his creative imagination are made freely available to all.
- It is concerned with the refreshment of man's spirit with the provision of books for relaxation and pleasure and with provision of up-to-date technical, scientific and sociological information.
- Melvil Dewey called public library as people's university, meaning thereby a place where people of all age groups can come and acquire knowledge or supplement their knowledge either themselves or under the guidance of able librarians in an unbiased personal way.
- The above objectives can be fulfilled when the public library should have the following features:

  — As organisation and management should be wholly based on public funds, and no direct charge should be made to individual for its products and services.
  — Regardless of nationality, race, colour, religion, language, status, age, sex, caste or educational qualification, its doors should be open to all members of the community residing in a defined geographical area.
  — It should be established under the clear mandate of law.

Further, the UNESCO Manifesto[8] has clearly stated the role of public library:

> "The public library must offer to adults and children the opportunity to keep in touch with their tunes, to educate themselves continuously and keep abreast of progress in the science and arts. Its contents should be a living demonstration of the evolution of knowledge and culture, constantly reviewed, kept up-to-date and attractively presented. In this way, it will help people from their own opinions, and develop their critical capacities and powers of appreciations. The public library is concerned with the communication and ideas, whatever the form in which these may be expressed."

2.2 OBJECTIVES OF PUBLIC LIBRARY

The following are the objectives of the public library.

- To infuse awareness among people on the sources of information and encourage them to make use of information which are available in the library;
- To take care of economic, educational, social, cultural and informational needs of the local people;
- To convert uneducated illiterate and neo-literate into potential users; and
- To provide information on all aspects such as agriculture, finance, public hygiene, family planning, legal matters, etc.

To achieve all these objectives, the public library should co-operate and co-ordinate with other social organisations and institutions in the community and create a comprehensive collection of reading and learning materials in the form of text or graphics or any other form relevant to the community.

2.3 FUNCTIONS OF PUBLIC LIBRARY

The public library should provide timely, accurate and reliable information services to the community. It should provide the informational services on:

- Local history, commerce and industries, agricultural and industrial products.
- Funding agencies for housing and personal loans, commerce and trade, education, agriculture, technology and industries.

- Career development information and scope for employment opportunities for unemployed youth, prematured and voluntary retired people.
- Guiding and counselling on all matters such as agriculture, public health and hygiene, family welfare and population control, legal matters, etc.
- Audio-visual reading and learning materials should be provided to the illiterates, neo-literates, adults and children, retired and in-service people, etc.
- As a part of its functions, public library should organize exhibitions in festivals and local fairs from time to time to propagate its services.

These can be elaborated further as:

- Library equipped with audio-visual aids can carry on successful motivation through charts, pictures, films and television shows and through various social education activities.
- Library can prepare annotated bibliographies for all grades of pupils and organise book exhibitions and thus help the teacher in selection of right type of reading material.
- Library can select, stock and serve easy-to-read materials for the actual work of literacy and the follow up reading materials to those who have picked up functional literacy.
- Library can function as a co-ordinating agency for various departments of the State and Central Governments and deliver authentic information about the guidelines, programmes and policies of the Government to the people.
- By supplying the teachers and organisers of the literacy campaign with books on latest techniques and reports on research methods and policies, they can prevent the teacher from going stale on knowledge and techniques.
- Library and book publicity techniques, including organising book fairs more frequently, should be adopted at national, state and local levels.

In more comprehensive terms of functions of a public library, it should satisfy the following requirements of the society.

2.3.1 Information Requirement

A public library should not be confined to only provide traditional library services i.e. lending and borrowing, reference service, etc. It should also provide information service to the society for its socio-economic development. It should serve as an Information Resource Centre (IRC) to provide specialised as well as general information to its users. It should act as a Referral Contact Centre (RCC) for users where they may exchange information directly or through library services for improvement of their quality of life and living standards. It should also provide Current Awareness Service (CAS) to people about various programmes and schemes launched by the State and Central Governments and other Non-Governmental Organisations (NGOs) on rural development, poverty alleviation, eradication of illiteracy, health and family welfare programmes, employment schemes, welfare schemes for Scheduled Castes, Scheduled Tribes, ex-servicemen and other classes of the society. The public library should collect, process and store information relevant to the societal needs for further retrieval and dissemination to its users.

2.3.2 Educational Requirement

The public library should function as an educational centre to support and promote all types of formal, non-formal, adult, life-long and continuing education by collecting and acquiring of various types of reading and learning materials in print and non-print forms and making them available to all users of the library.

2.3.3 Cultural Requirement

The public library should work towards cultural enrichment of the society by organising extension activities like lectures, seminars, symposia, workshops, conferences, book exhibitions, social and cultural gathering, etc. It should also provide opportunities to the members of library to participate in these extension activities to exhibit their talent, intellect and creativities. It plays a vital role in collecting and preserving cultural heritage of the locality and making it readily available to the people of the locality to enrich their cultural awareness, which helps in development of cultural heritage of the society.

2.3.4 Recreational Requirement

The public library needs to provide healthy recreation to its users. This can be done by providing books of fiction, light reading magazines, newspapers, audio-visual materials, television, radio, Internet browsing facilities, etc. Library can also organise various types of paintings, vocal/ instrumental music, sports, magic shows and other recreational programmes from time-to-time to divert human mind towards positive use of leisure time. It may help people to get rid of the stress and strain of modern complex and mechanical life by offering them books, audio-visual and other healthy recreational materials.

2.3.5 Public Libraries Help Children

It is well-established fact that babies are born with under-developed brains that are wired in the first few months and years of life for cognitive and emotional development. Book reading can nurture this development in important ways, and libraries have to offer:

1. Children learn by being exposed to spoken language and using visual materials stored in various formats in the library.
2. Libraries have children materials and offer programmes such as lapsits, story hours and read-to-me programmes.
3. Libraries have to select children's materials with the help of parents and caregivers.
4. Libraries can help babies and young children to:

    - Develop language skills;
    - Develop positive habits;
    - Learn to socialise;
    - Stimulate their imaginations;
    - Develop the ideas of sequences by experiencing the beginning, middle and end of the stories;
    - Understanding the functions of the words and pictures in the books; and
    - Develop the cognitive skills through sensory stimulation, which helps foster the intellectual development — hearing words and music, viewing pictures and text, teaching objects and scanning pages of the books.

2.3.6 Public Libraries Help Parents

The libraries can help parents to:

- Share activities, which enhanced their child's emotional

development;

- Realise them that they are the first and the most important teacher of their child;
- Read aloud to their child;
- Provide opportunity to learn how to select appropriate books and materials helpful for the development of their child's interest;
- Practice their own reading skills while reading for pleasure;
- Gain access to information on parenting;
- Gain access to children's reading and learning materials that they might not otherwise have in their homes;
- Learn about other agencies, organisations in the community that provide services for parents and children.

Thus the public library acts as a community centre for social, recreational, cultural and information activities, where people from all classes, castes, communities, religions, professions, congregate and enjoy services rendered by it. Now application of information technology and communication technology has changed the role of public libraries. With the help of these technologies, libraries can store giga billion pyramid of information, process in fast mode and then communicate to the user by using fast communication modes i.e. e-mail, fax, etc. Various methods are available for abstracting, indexing, press cutting and clipping service and other documentation work. In the developing countries like India, there is a great demand for modernisation of public libraries to meet set goals because 'Nation that reads is a Nation that leads'. and 'Knowledge is Power'. A nation, which has knowledgeable/educated society, is a powerful nation!

2.4 BARRIERS IN USAGE OF LIBRARIES

2.4.1 Illiteracy

Illiteracy is one of the major barriers to make use of libraries. At present, majority of libraries are having reading and learning materials in printed forms and some of them are having in audio-visual forms also. To make their use effectively, one should be literate. Libraries located in metropolitan cities are using computer, communication technology and multimedia to break the barrier of illiteracy. But the case of rural libraries is not the same as urban libraries in the context of reading and learning materials. Many course materials and other reading materials are available in electronic, optical, audio-visual forms. These may help new literates to acquire more knowledge. Therefore, libraries have to acquire all kinds of reading and learning materials in variety of formats for their effective use by the new literates.

2.4.2 Poverty

Poverty is considered as the main cause of illiteracy. Alleviation of poverty and eradication of illiteracy are the integral parts of any developmental endeavour. About 35 per cent of country's population is living below the poverty line. The World Bank estimates declination of poverty to another 10 per cent by the year 2005. At present the Government spends about 12 per cent on anti-poverty programmes and food subsidy, which is diverted from other resources. These anti-poverty programmmes may not be completely successful unless the population is made educated and literate, because they may not utilise their knowledge and resources properly.

A major proportion of enrolled students leave their education due to poverty. Earlier, only one third of all children who enrolled in grade one reach grade eight. Just one out of one hundred girls enrolled in grade one reaches grade eight. This situation has now improved in many states. Still this dropout case in India is very high as compared to western countries. This results in increase in illiteracy. Unfortunately, in our country, there is no provision in any library to support learners, dropout students, those are financially weak, to continue their study. On the other hand, educational institutions have various schemes for encouragement of new learners. The Society for Information Science in its 12th Annual Convention recommended:

> "To improve the quality of the life of rural masses and to take full advantage of the technologies developed for meeting the challenges of the 21st century in respect of fuel, food and fibre, a well organised rural technical network providing for a package of services for the benefit of the masses living in the villages and backward areas should be developed to improve the quality of their life".

2.4.3 Unemployment

Unemployment is another major factor, which affects the usage of libraries. Unemployed youths have their priority to search the job opportunities rather to sit in the library and gain knowledge. Of course, students preparing for their competitive examinations are using public libraries very effectively. Dr. Vijay Pal Memorial Library, Keshav Puram, Delhi, is a live example, which has enrollment of students preparing for competitive examinations and using library at least twelve hours a day. Students, not only from NCT of Delhi but also from other nearby states i.e. Haryana, Rajasthan, Uttar Pradesh, etc come to use library for their competitive examinations.

2.4.4 Lack of Infrastructure and Resources

Majority of libraries, especially in rural areas, are not having good and functional buildings, furniture, equipment storage racks and other resources. Most of these libraries are not having electricity connections to use electricity-run equipments i.e. computers, television, etc. Libraries need to be provided proper infrastucture with functional buildings and adequate library materials to attract user community.

2.4.5 Lack of Reading and Learning Materials

The role of a librarian is not only to devise means to get the more number of books to the more number of readers but also to ensure that more people read more and more of worthy literature. In this country, there is practically no agency and author producing and publishing suitable follow up literature for the mass of new literate. Therefore, this should be taken as one of the responsibilities of the librarians and social and adult education agencies working in the field to devise means of discovering and in some cases training the right type of authors, finding publishers and overcoming the practical difficulties in publishing such literature attractively and yet at cheaper rates. National Book Trust (NBT) and Children Book Trust (CBT) are producing, reprinting and translating books of general interest. Gita Press, Gorakhpur has set an example by producing educative and religious reading materials in various Indian languages at a highly subsidised rate. Publications of Gita Press are helping millions of rural and urban population to gain knowledge. Such activities need to be augmented.

The Government of India, Ministry of Human Resource Development can take up necessary steps and adopt definite measures and policies for encouraging the production of good quality literature as cheaply as possible. Another method is to award prizes in all the Indian languages for outstanding works written specially for new literate adults. In order to encourage writers and publishers, books intended for competition for these prizes should be allowed to submit even in the manuscript form. The Government should buy multiple copies of every book, which secures prize, and distribute them to all public libraries as per their requirements.

2.4.6 Non-availability of Information/Communication Technology

In this information technology age user-friendly technology in user acceptable formats and in local languages should be spread to the extensive part of rural and urban areas to ensure eradication of illiteracy. This can accelerate the process of poverty alleviation and achieve quality rural development leading to prosperity. Knowledge has to be imparted to people by creating innovative programmes and projects through libraries. A librarian, being a professional expert in the management of personnel and material, can play a dynamic role in eradication of illiteracy in the world of on-line inter-connectivity and multimedia.

At present an exclusive and separate satellite channel is needed in the future generation of INSAT satellite systems to meet the education/ entertainment/training needs, especially that of illiterates and neo-literates. Indira Gandhi National Open University (IGNOU) and some other universities/institutions/organisations can take up the responsibility of launching library services and librarians as resource persons. Because the libraries have the largest communication and information network and are well equipped to produce very good multimedia instructional material for the literacy programme.

2.5 DEVELOPMENT OF PUBLIC LIBRARIES IN INDIA

The first significant date in the development of libraries for the public in India is 1808 when the Bombay Government initiated a proposal to register libraries, which were to be given copies of books published from the funds for the encouragement of literature. Three Presidency towns of Bombay, Calcutta and Madras had founded their public libraries by the mid of nineteenth century. These libraries were opened with the initiative and active support of the Europeans living in these cities. These libraries were not meant for the public in full sense because the usage of these libraries were confined to only upper section of the society. The public libraries grew beyond the metropolitan cities and spread over to the provincial capitals and many districts. Due to thin literacy in the country, people were not prepared to take advantage of these libraries. Government of India enacted the Press and Registration of Books Act (XXV) in 1867 under which the printer of a book had to deliver a copy of a book free to the State Government concerned. In 1900 Calcutta Library opened its door to the public. This was later known as Imperial Library and now as National Library.

The ruler of Baroda, Sir Sayaji Rao Gaekwad III, built up an elaborate library system composed of central library, village libraries and travelling libraries. Marindra Dev Rai Mahashaya of Bengal founded the Bengal Library Association in 1927 and tried hard to give Bengal a Library Act. Andhra Provincial Library Association, established in 1914, gave an impetus to the growth of libraries in Andhra Pradesh. Khan Bahadur Asadullah made enormous efforts in founding of Indian Library Association and his dream came true in 1933. By the mid of the twentieth century, many provinces had set up their Library Associations. These associations started disseminating information in the form of printed newsletters, bulletins, journals, etc.

Before Independence, in 1937 when Congress came to power in many provinces, many libraries were established on popular demand of the public. State Education Department had set up 80 rural libraries in Travancore in 1955. Assam, Bihar, Bombay, Orissa, Punjab, Cochin and some other provinces and States set up village libraries and mobile libraries. By the end of 1942, there were 13,000 village libraries in India. The growth of these libraries was the product of Indian Adult Education Movement, which swayed the country at that time. Opening of these public libraries was a part of the recommendation of the Central Advisory Board of Education in 1940.

The Library Development Committee published a report in 1940 and recommended to set up public libraries in Bombay province. It recommended setting up of one central library, three regional libraries, fifteen district libraries, 167 taluka libraries, 100 town libraries, 979 village libraries having population of 2000 or more, 2696 village libraries having population between 1000 to 2000 and 17,753 village libraries having population less than 1000. These recommendations were implemented partially. In 1948 the Library Act of Madras came into existence. In March 1956, nine states, namely, Assam, West Bengal, Madhya Pradesh, Punjab, Pepsu, Rajasthan, Saurastra, Bhopal and Vindhya Pradesh had prepared plans for setting up of their central libraries. By the end of 1956, Bombay, Bhopal, West Bengal, Assam, Madhya Pradesh, Rajasthan, Vindhya Pradesh, Saurastra, Bihar had started process of setting of district libraries.

In 1952 Government of India initiated Community Development Programmes (CDP) in which social education was assigned an important role. Gradually, the pattern of social education programme took a clear shape and public libraries occupied an integral place in this programme.

Government of India enacted the Delivery of Books (Public Libraries) Act in 1954, which was amended in 1956 to include newspapers also. According to this Act, a publisher was required to deliver a copy of his publications to the National Library, Calcutta; Connemara Library, Madras;

Central Library, Bombay and Delhi Public Library, Delhi. The implementation of the Act had resulted the establishment of four National Book Depositories in the country.

By the end of financial year 1953-54, the number of public libraries had gone to over 32,000 with the total stock of 7.10 million volumes of books with annual use of 3.77 million books. This shows that only one book was available for a population of fifty people in the country. Whereas, in UK and USA, this ratio was 1.24 volume and 1.15 volume per person, respectively. In a report of the Committee appointed by the Planning Commission for formulation of Eighth Five Year Plan, it was mentioned that per capita expenditure (as on 31 March 1987) on public libraries in India was Rs 0.46, at the same time, it was Rs 0.80 in Delhi. As on 1 July 1988, the total number of public libraries in India was 55,972. Of these, 219 were in Delhi. Per capita expenditure on public libraries in USA and UK was Rs 4.55 and Rs 3.50 respectively. The statistics reveal that India would go with fast speed to match the performance with the developed countries.

According to IFLA Standards[9] there should be one library for every 3000 people. With this standard, India needs 342,338 libraries for 1,027,015,247 people. In an estimation, there exist 60,000 number of libraries in the country in all categories. There is a gap of 282,338 number of libraries that are required to meet the international standards. Every year, there is an increase of about 600 libraries in the country. With this growth rate, India will take 470 years to meet the set target, provided the population remains stable during this duration. At present India's population is growing at a rate of 1.8 per cent per year. In Russia[10] there are 325,000 libraries with a stock of 6 billion books in 70 languages and serving a population of 22 crore. It means one library for a population of 667 people, which is above the IFLA Standards.

On 12 November 1958, Shri K.P. Sinha, Chairman, Advisory Committee, Government of India, submitted his recommendations to the Minister of Education on public libraries as given below:

1. State Government should encourage the setting up of Book Bureau in the capitals of each State in the first instance, to be extended later to district and other towns. All libraries run or assisted by the Government shall buy books from the Bureau.
2. Library associations are essential to the development of library movement and State Governments and Government of India should encourage development of strong library associations.
3. Government should give financial assistance to library associations for the following purposes:

- Rent for premises of headquarters office,
- Remuneration of the whole-time or part-time secretary or office clerk, and
- Projects of general usefulness to library movement, which Government may like to sponsor.

4. The library associations should strive to prepare the taxpayers' mind for accepting library legislation and persuade State Governments to enact legislation and set up State Libraries.
5. Libraries should encourage the formation of Mitra Mandals, wherever possible.
6. Every state or region should have a centre, where books weeded out from the public libraries are sent. Public libraries in the country should cooperate with other libraries as well as subscription libraries, school libraries, college libraries, departmental and research libraries, university libraries, etc.
7. In places, where it may not be possible to run independent public libraries, school libraries may serve the public after the school hours.
8. In places, where public libraries are not strong, an inter-lending arrangement with the college libraries should be made.
9. Leading establishment of efficient reference sections in public libraries, government departmental and research libraries should assist them in compiling annotated book lists on their special subjects and in answering reference inquiries from the public, etc.
10. The university library should cooperate with the public library system by:

- Issuing booklists on subjects of interest to certain groups in the public,
- Admitting as regular members the more serious minded readers among the public, and
- Perform reference functions of the State Central Library, where these libraries are not yet established.

11. Government of India should sponsor the preparation of four union catalogues as follows :

- A union catalogue of all publications in the various university libraries in the country. This can be undertaken by the University Grants Commission (UGC).

- A union catalogue of all publications in the departmental and research libraries under the Government of India. The Union Ministry of Education should take up this work.
- A union catalogue of all copyright holdings in the State Central Libraries. The National Library will probably be best fitted to take up this work.
- A union catalogue of all scientific and learned periodicals in the university and research libraries in the country. This should be entrusted to the Scientific Research Wing of the Ministry of Scientific Research and Cultural Affairs.

2.6 IMPORTANT PUBLIC LIBRARIES IN INDIA

India has had a rich wealth of Hindu, Buddhist, Jain, Christian, Muslim, Sikh and other religious and ethnic culture. This religious, cultural and ethnic wealth was not acquired in a day or a month. It took centuries to come to this stage. Manuscripts written by scholars had to be stored in safe places like archives and libraries. Over the passes of time, these had become rare collections and any society or library/archive had to feel proud of having these rare collections.

Collections of many rare books and manuscripts were stored in the Royal Houses at Srinagar, Varanasi, Patna, Rampur, Tanjaur, Mysore and Hyderabad in the shape of libraries. Libraries were established by the Asiatic Society of Bengal in 1784, the Asiatic Society of Bombay in 1808, the Madras Literary Society in 1812, the Calcutta Public Library in 1835 and the People's Library in 1846. These were followed by the establishment of libraries in Lucknow, Allahabad, Indore, Bhopal, Madras, Trivendrum and other places to serve the people. These laid down the foundation of the public libraries in India. Here it may not be possible to discuss all the public libraries of India. However, some of the important public libraries, established during the past, are being discussed below:

2.6.1 Khuda Baksh Oriental Public Library, Patna

An illustrious son of Bihar, an advocate by profession and a bibliophile by taste, Khuda Baksh Khan, established a "Public Library" in 1891 out of his family collection of manuscripts. Later on, he added a good number of manuscripts through his own resources, and, by a deed of trust, donated his entire collection to the public library the same year. The library is now well known world over as the Khuda Baksh Oriental Public Library. It has emerged as one of the richest collections of manuscripts in the sub-continent with over 21,000 manuscripts, 2,00,000 printed books and over 230 collections of original paintings of the Mughal, Rajput, Iranian and Turkish schools. The library also possesses a sizeable number of original letters of eminent persons written during their lifetime. It is now managed by a Board headed by the Governor of Bihar. An Act of Parliament in 1969 declared it to be an Institution of National Importance and the Government of India took over its control in the same year.

It acquires manuscripts and books through purchase, gift and exchange, which is a continuing feature of the library. The library has a scheme of acquiring copies of rare manuscripts available in other collections. Microfilms of several manuscripts were acquired from Aligarh, Rampur, Bhagalpur, Maner, Phulwarisharif, Asafiya (Hyderabad), the Asiatic Society (Kolkata) and British collection of the India Office and Cambridge. The library has modernized its facilities with the establishment of a Computer Centre with LAN, e-mail and the Internet. The library collection is being digitized and put on the Internet for use.

The *Khuda Bakhsh Library Journal*, which has been published over the last two decades, contains research articles. The library has set up a programme of translating some of the outstanding award-winning books within its area of specialization, in Hindi and other regional languages into Urdu and from Urdu into Hindi.

The library has also instituted an award to be given to scholars for outstanding research contributions in the library's special fields of Arabic/ Persian/Urdu/Islamic Studies/Tibb/South Asian Studies/Comparative Religion/ Sufism/Composite Culture of India. It is a center for Indo-Islamic Studies as it is a repository of classical and modern source material in Arabic, Persian, Sanskrit, Tamil, Telugu, Hindi, Urdu, Turkish and English.

2.6.2 Rampur Raza Library

It is a unique treasure house of Indo-Islamic learning and art. The library is of international importance. It was founded by Nawab Faizullah Khan who established the headquarters of his chiefdom in Rampur in 1774; his descendants continued to enrich the collection and it was under the last Nawab Sir Raza Ali Khan (1930-66) that the library attained its present eminence. After the attainment of independence and merger of the State into the Union of India, the library was brought under the management of a Trust and Nawab Raza Ali Khan was appointed as its President, and the District Magistrate of Rampur as the Secretary of the Trust. The arrangement continued till 1975 when the Central Government took over the library under an Act of Parliament, namely, the Rampur Raza Library Act 1975 and declared it as an Institution of National Importance.

The library has a valuable collection of about 16,000 manuscripts; 60,000 printed books in Arabic, Persian, Sanskrit, Hindi, Urdu, Tamil, Telugu, Pushto and Turkish, besides 5,000 miniature paintings representing the Mongol, Iran, Mughal, Rajput, Rajasthani, Pahari, Avadh, Deccani and Company styles, and thousands of specimens of Islamic calligraphy.

The Raza Library's most valuable and rare miniature paintings and manuscripts, selected for an exhibition (on Mughal Noblemen Bairam Khan), was displayed at the National Archives of India, New Delhi.

2.6.3 National Library, Kolkata

It came into being in 1948 with the passing of the Imperial Library (Change of Name) Act, 1948. However, the Library's lineage can be traced to the Calcutta Public Library of 1836, which was later converted into the Imperial Library in early nineteenth century.

The National Library is an institution of national importance and finds a special mention in Article 62 of the Seventh Schedule of the Union List in the Constitution of India. The library acts as a reference centre for research scholars; and coordinates and determines standards in the field of library services in the country. Some of the basic functions of the National Library are:

- Acquisition and conservation of all significant printed materials excluding ephemera;
- Collection of printed materials concerning the country, no matter where this is published, and as a corollary the acquisition of a photographic record of such materials that is not available within the country;
- Acquisition and conservation of manuscripts of national importance;
- Planned acquisition of foreign materials required by the country;
- Rendering of bibliographical and documentation services of current and retrospective material, both general and specialized. This implies the responsibility to produce current and retrospective bibliographies on various aspects of the country;
- Acts as a referral centre to disseminate accurate and authentic information of all sources of bibliographical information and participation in international bibliographical activities;
- Provision of photocopying and reprographic services; and
- Acts as a centre for international book exchange and international loan.

At the time of its establishment as the Imperial Library in 1903, it took over nearly 40,000 books belonging to the Calcutta Public Library, established in 1836. In addition, it received the collection of the Home Department Library and the Fort William College Library as well as gifts from other sources. Preservation and conservation of the precious and rare books and other documents stored in the Library is one of the major activities.

Under the on-going schemes for digitizing selected books and old documents through the CD-ROM technology, more than one million pages of the text have been scanned through and put into CD discs so far.

2.6.4 Central Reference Library (CRL), Kolkata

It was established as a subordinate office under the Department of Culture in 1955 in the National Library Campus (Kolkata). It functions as the National Bibliographic and Documentation Centre. At present, it is entrusted with the responsibility of implementing the following schemes:

- Production and sale of the Indian National Bibliography (INB) in Roman Script both monthly and with annual cumulations. The INB is a record of current Indian publications in 14 languages including English based on the receipt in the National Library, Kolkata under the provisions of the Delivery of Books Act, 1954;
- Compilation and publication of language fascicules of the Indian National Bibliography (INB); and
- Production and sale of index Indiana, which is an index to select articles appearing in current Indian periodicals in six languages.

2.6.5 Central Secretariat Library (CSL), New Delhi

This library in the Department of Culture, Ministry of Tourism and Culture, previously known as Imperial Secretariat Library in Kolkata, is one of the oldest libraries in terms of the size of its collection (over one million volumes). It is estimated to be second largest Central Government library after the National Library, Kolkata. It is located at G-Wing, Shastri Bhavan and its language wing is located at Bahawalpur House and a branch library at R.K. Puram, New Delhi.

The library is well known for its rich and valuable collections of rare books on Indian history and culture, Indian official publications, such as the Annual Administrative Reports, Budget and Plan Documents, Civil Lists, Census Reports, Legal Documents, Directories, Handbooks, Gazettes,

Gazetteers, Committee and Commission Reports, Parliamentary Legal Documents including microfiches and microfilms, General Reference Books, such as Encyclopedias, Dictionaries, etc., Foreign Official documents including Microfiche/microfilm collection of US Government Publications, UN documents and other out of print and rare materials. It is now developing a worthwhile collection in the field of electronic media.

CSL has a cooperative acquisition policy for the purchase of document resources for libraries under the Department of Culture in Delhi i.e. the National Archives of India, Archaeological Survey of India, National Museum and the National Gallery of Modern Arts. Under the cooperative acquisition policy, the reference collection including multi-volume titles are purchased by CSL as part of resource sharing with the participating libraries. The library is acquiring a unique collection of microfilms of Indian Official Documents published in India during the British period, which are available in the India Office Library, British Library, London. The CSL receives over thousand journals and newspapers on subscription and gratis basis. The library is mainly responsible for providing information for research and reference to registered members, policy planners, academicians, research scholars and to the general readers. Its resources are being utilized by more than two and half lakh readers. The CSL being the nodal agency for the Microfilming of Indian Publications Project, there is provision for a microfilm repository room in its premises for preserving the master negatives for archival purposes and for giving service to the readers on demand. The Library of Congress has deposited 3096 microfilm rolls of books in Indian languages published in the early twentieth century.

2.6.6 Connemara Public Library, Chennai

In recognition of the importance of library services, it was decided to establish a Public Library in Tamil Nadu by an enlightened administrator Lord Connemara, the then Governor of Madras, during the period 1886-1890. The foundation stone for the library was laid on 22 March 1890 and the library was formally opened on 5 December 1896. The library so founded was named after him in recognition of his efforts.

The Connemara Public Library building was designed and constructed by H. Irving, the then Consulting Architect to the Government of Madras. It is a semi-circle and oblong building in saracenic style with a magnificent hall with a splendid reading room and beautiful teak wood bookshelves. The roof is a truncated semi-circle. The truncated top has a wooden ceiling but the two curved sides are made of pieces of coloured glass artistically cemented to one another. Ornamental acanthus leaves and flowers adorn the marble slabs.

In commemoration of the Centenary of the Library, an additional multi-story building was constructed with a floor space of 21,823 sq. ft. at the cost of Rs. 1.79 crore and was opened on 24 June 1999.

The Connemara Public Library was renamed as the State-Central Library with effect from 1 April 1950, under the provision of Tamil Nadu Public Libraries Act of 1948 and from 10 September, 1955, it became one of the four Depositories for Indian Publications under the provision of the Delivery of Books and Newspapers (Public Libraries) Act of 1954. In 1955, this library became the UNESCO Information Centre to serve as a depository for selected publications of the UN and its allied agencies. It also serves as a Depository for the Asian Development Bank publications since 1992. As one of the four Depository Centres, it receives four copies of publications published in the State under the provisions of the State Central Library. A number of books are added every year by purchasing from funds made available by State Government. The stock of volumes in the library collection stands over five and half lakhs and it receives more than 3,500 periodicals and newspapers annually.

The Connemara Public Library provides the following services to the public:

- Civil Services Study Circle Service;
- Braille and Talking Book Section Service;
- Education Video Service;
- Home Delivery Service; and
- Bibliographic Service.

The expenditure for maintaining the library is met by the Government of Tamil Nadu. However, the Government of India meets 50 per cent of the recurring expenditure and 2/3 of non-recurring expenditure in respect of maintaining the Delivery of Books Act Section of the Library.

2.6.7 Thanjavur Maharaja Serfoji's Sarasvati Mahal Library, Thanjavur

It is one among the few medieval libraries existing in the world. It is an unparalleled repository of culture and an inexhaustible treasure house of knowledge built up by successive dynasties of Nayaks and the Marathas of Thanjavur. The library stocks very rare and valuable collection of manuscripts, books, maps and paintings on all aspects of art, culture and literature. The *Encyclopedia Britannica* in its Survey of the

Libraries of the World mentions this as "the most remarkable library in India". The library receives funds from the Government of Tamil Nadu for its maintenance and is funded by the Government of India for developmental activities.

The library has the richest collection of manuscripts in Sanskrit, Tamil, Marathi and Telugu, which reflect the history and culture of manuscripts, private libraries of Pandits and their patrons living in Thanjavur and its neighbourhood also came into the possession of the library. Even now this library receives manuscripts, books, etc. as donations.

Under the library's publication programme of original manuscripts, so far 422 books have been published in the field of literature, grammer, medicine, astrology, etc. A collection of rare manuscripts and books, illustrated manuscripts, paintings, rare atlases, portraits of kings, etc is a part of the library.

The library is preparing a list of institutions, mutts and individuals in possession of manuscripts in Tamil language in support of the National Mission for preservation of manuscripts project of Government of India.

A monthly literary programme is conducted; and eminent literary scholars deliver lectures every month. This is aimed to interact with the public and to develop library consciousness among them.

2.6.8 State Central Library (SCL), Mumbai

The library was functioning from the Asiatic Society, Mumbai. The Government of Maharashtra took over the assets of the library in 1994. In 1955, the library was notified as one of the National Depository Libraries in India under the provisions of the Delivery of Books Act, 1954. According to the Act, the main function of this library is to collect and preserve the books, periodicals and newspapers published in the country for posterity. The total collection received under the Press and Registration of Books Act is over 3 lakh. The total number of books and periodicals received under the Delivery of Books Act is over 5 lakhs. About 20,000 books and periodicals received annually under these two Acts are added to the collection of the State Central Library.

The Government of India, under an agreement with the Government of Maharashtra, provides 50 per cent grant under Plan and $2/3^{rd}$ under Non-plan for maintenance of the Delivery of Books Act Section in the Library. The Government of Maharashtra has allotted 4-acre land at the Kalina Campus in Mumbai University for a separate building for the State Central Library.

2.6.9 Delhi Public Library (DPL), Delhi

This library came into existence on October 27, 1951 as a pilot project under the then Ministry of Education in collaboration with UNESCO to introduce the concept of free public library and information services to the people of Delhi and also to eradicate illiteracy from the map of Delhi. The DPL has now grown into a premier public library system in the National Capital Territory (NCT) of Delhi and has become the busiest public library in the South Asia.

The DPL is administered by a Governing Body, called the Delhi Library Board (DLB), which is a society registered under the Societies Registration Act, 1860. The Board consists of Official, Non-official and Co-opted members headed by a Chairman, nominated by the Minister of Human Resource Development. The Director, DPL, is the ex-Officio Member-Secretary of the Board and also of all other Committees constituted by the Board. The main objects of the Board are to provide for the people of Delhi State without distinction of class, creed, occupation or race, a public library for popular education, which may serve as a model for all public library development in India.

There has been an over all increase in the activities of the library. The library has 192 Service Points in the NCT of Delhi. However, even this number is too small to serve the population of Delhi effectively. The library has been receiving requests from various organisations from both urban and rural areas to open libraries or to provide library services through mobile van in their localities. Some of these have offered free land for the purpose. But DPL is unable to construct buildings at its own acquired land due to paucity of funds.

The library is trying its best to attain its objectives by augmenting its services throughout the 1,483 sq. km area of the National Capital Territory of Delhi so that the enthusiastic readers from any place in Delhi may not be required to walk for more than 15 minutes to reach a service unit of DPL.

The DPL has a network of a Central Library with a well equipped separate Reference Section at Head Quarter; 4 Zonal Libraries; 4 Branch Libraries; 25 Sub-branch Libraries; 24 Libraries with book lending and reading room facilities at resettlement colonies; and 9 Exclusive Reading Rooms to inculcate reading habits among the weaker sections of society; a Braille Library with a network of 20 Mobile Service Points for the visually handicapped both for students and for adults; 3 Sports Libraries of the status of a Sub-Branch at National Stadium, Talkatora Stadium and Indira Gandhi Stadium; one Prison Library at Central Jail, Tihar for the prisoners;

16 Deposit Stations which are run by various societies/associations. Besides, the DPL has a network of 72 Mobile Service Stations to serve the remote urban and rural areas (Appendix A). Thus the Library provides its services to different segments of society including rural and urban folks, adults, children, students, visually handicapped, sportsmen and prisoners, etc., irrespective of any distinction of sex, religion, creed and caste. Various departments/sections of the DPL and their functions are summarised below:

Adults Lending Department: This department of Central Library lends books for home reading to the enrolled members.

Reference Section: The Reference Section at the Central Library is accessed by registered as well as non-registered members for consultation of reference sources in different languages and formats. The Reference Section also replies to a large number of queries on phone, in person and in writing. This Section also provides photocopying services to the readers on demand.

Children Department: The children department is exclusively open to readers below 15 years of age. It is well equipped with a variety of toys, picture books and other materials to attract infants, children and juvenile literates. This department also organises a number of competitions — music, painting, dance, story telling, extempore speech, etc. for the children from time to time.

Social Education and Cultural Activities Department: This department is responsible for organising cultural activities among adults and also caters to and promotes cultural interests of its members and the general public through group activities and audio-visual programmes. These include plays, group meetings, lectures, exhibitions, film shows etc. It also offers its infrastructure facilities to other educational organisations for socio-cultural activities either free or at a nominal charge.

Audio-visual Department: This department is fully equipped with audio-visual equipments and materials including slide projectors, tape recorders and players, audio and video tapes, etc. Members can use these facilities either in the library or at their home on loan basis.

Music Library Department: Users generally visit library not only for educational or information purposes but for entertainment purpose also. This department provides gramophone records/audio/video cassettes lending services for its registered members free of charge. These records/cassettes comprise of classical, instrumental and light music, bhajans, ghazals, film songs etc. Facilities for listening some songs through linguaphones is also extended by this department.

Painting Lending Library Department: Mounted paintings of master painters are kept here for the use by the members of the library. These are also lent out to the institutions free of charge.

Extension Services Department: This department provides library services to the people living at a distance from where they cannot come to the library. Mobile library facility is provided to them by this department. This department plays very important role in literacy programme in rural and remote areas. Mobile Library Vans provide library services to registered members in 72 areas in the NCT of Delhi and issues books to adults and children for home reading. Apart from the above mobile library services, this also operates Braille Mobile Library Services for the visually handicapped.

For efficient functioning of the library the entire system has been divided into zones, branches, sub-branches, etc.

Community Libraries: The library operates seven full-time and three part-time Community Libraries at different places in the NCT of Delhi.

Libraries at Resettlement Colonies: There are 31 libraries (22 RC Lending Libraries with reading rooms and 9 exclusively RC Reading Rooms) in resettlement colonies inhabited by the weaker sections of the society.

Deposit Stations: The DPL is operating 16 Deposit Stations in collaboration with various organisations at different places in the NCT of Delhi. These deposit stations have a large membership of adults and children. Besides the above, the Braille Department also operates 7 Deposit Stations of Braille books.

Mobile Libraries: Five Mobile Library Vans provide library services to its registered members in 72 areas in the NCT of Delhi.

Braille Department: The Braille Department, under the specialised service of the DPL, is devoted to cater to the reading needs of the visually handicapped to cultivate reading habits among them. This department not only provides Braille books but also transcribes books in Braille. A provision of regular Braille Mobile Service to 17 different institutions/ hostels has been made for the visually handicapped in the NCT of Delhi. This department maintains its seven Deposit Stations of Braille books at different institutions for the blinds. Efforts have been made to purchase record books and cassettes and made them available to its readers. Braille books are sent to readers by registered post free of charge to all parts of the country on request.

Prisoners Library: The DPL also provides its services to the prisoners in the Central Jail, Tihar in the NCT of Delhi.

Sports Libraries: The DPL is operating three Sports Libraries in collaboration with the Sports Authority of India at the National Stadium,

Talkatora Swimming Pool Complex and Indira Gandhi Indoor Stadium. These libraries have collections exclusively on sports and have been named as the Nehru Sports Library, Feroz Gandhi Sports Library and Indira Gandhi Sports Library respectively.

Reading Rooms: The library is continuously engaged in developing reading habits in its members as well as in the general public. It has provision of Reading Rooms at different service units to provide free of charge recent information by making available daily newspapers and current magazines.

Legal Deposit Division: On 16th December, 1981 the DPL was declared by the Government of India as the 4th recipient library under the Delivery of Books and Newspapers Act 1954 (as amended in 1956). As per the provisions of the Act, the DPL is to receive one copy of each publication from publishers in India free of cost in all languages. Besides books, approximately 800 popular periodicals and all leading dailies are being received regularly under the Act in all languages. The Division also compiles a monthly list of new arrivals along with bibliographic citations as a part of current awareness service of the books received in English, Hindi and other languages. This CAS is important for other libraries and considered a very useful bibliographic tool for selection of Indian books. The valuable collection received under the Act has been kept separately as a distinct collection for the use of readers as reference material in Zonal Library, Sarojini Nagar. The use of this collection is gaining popularity among the readers because such books are not easily available elsewhere.

Not much reading material was available for neo-literates when DPL was established. This task was later on undertaken by the DPL. It published many titles in Hindi and Urdu, and distributed to the neo-literates. Its activities are not confined only to its traditional library activities such as acquiring and issuing of books and journals to the borrowers, but ever since its establishment, it has also been continuously engaged in diversifying its activities for overall personality development of its clientele by organising social and cultural meets, with emphasis on eradication of illiteracy and spreading of knowledge to make them enlightened members of society.

2.7 RAJA RAMMOHUN ROY LIBRARY FOUNDATION (RRRLF)

It is a fully financed autonomous organization under the Department of Culture, Government of India. It was set up in May 1972 on the auspicious occasion of the bicentennial birth anniversary of the great Raja who heralded renaissance and modernism, and made special efforts towards the spread of education in the country. The main objective of the Foundation is to promote and support the public library movement in the country by providing adequate library services and popularizing reading habits, particularly in the rural areas, with the active cooperation of the State Library Authorities, UTs and VAs operating in the field of library services.

The Foundation has been operating two types of schemes —Matching and Non-matching — for the development of public libraries.

Matching Schemes: Under this scheme the Foundation provides:

- Assistance towards building up adequate stock of books;
- Assistance towards storage of books;
- Assistance towards organization of seminars, workshops, books exhibitions, training courses, etc.;
- Assistance to State, Central and District Libraries to acquire TV-cum-VCP sets and cassettes for educational purposes; and
- Assistance to libraries below district level for increasing accommodation.

Non-Matching Schemes: Under this scheme the Foundation provides:

- Assistance to State, Central and District libraries towards supply of books through central selection;
- Financial assistance to VAs working in the field of public libraries;
- Assistance to children's libraries and children's section of general public libraries;
- Assistance to public libraries towards celebration of centenary year/125 years/150 years/175 years, etc.;
- Assistance towards organization of seminar/conference by national level library organizations; and
- Assistance towards collection and compilation of library statistics through official and non-official agencies.

The Matching Schemes are operated from the Matching Fund created with contributions from various State Governments (which varies from Rs 1 lakh to Rs 50 lakh depending on its size, population, rate of literacy, existing infrastructure facilities and past utilization) plus an equal share from the Foundation, whereas the Non-matching Schemes are wholly funded by the Foundation.

Besides being a funding body, the Foundation has been functioning, during the year, as a national agency for coordinating, monitoring and developing the public library services all over the country. The Foundation's quarterly newsletter not only highlights its own activities but also disseminate significant news in the field of library services from India and abroad. The Foundation also publishes a bi-annual journal *Granthana* that covers valuable articles from different parts of the country not only on library and information science but also on the ideas and thoughts of Raja Rammohun Roy.

The Foundation with a view to creating a modern, updated information system has set up a project to upgrade its existing computer system by installing office-wide LAN not only for house-keeping jobs but also for a comprehensive information database on public library services in the country.

To encourage the public libraries in the country to render better services with a competitive attitude, the Foundation selects the best State Central Library for a cash award of Rs 1 lakh and 6 best District Libraries from 6 regions of the country for cash award of Rs 50,000 each.

Table 2.1 shows the financial assistance provided by the RRRLF[11] for supply of books to centrally sponsored libraries during the period 1986-87 to 1995-96.

Table: 2.1: Financial Assistance Provided by the RRRLF to Centrally Sponsored Libraries from 1986-87 to 1995-96

Year	*Amount (Rs in lakhs)*	*Number of Libraries (including 25 Mobile Libraries)*
1986-87	0.82	59
1987-88	0.76	48
1988-89	0.31	41
1989-90	0.23	27
1990-91	1.41	105
1991-92	1.38	95
1992-93	5.32	228
1993-94	5.22	214
1994-95	4.93	221
1995-96	4.95	225
Total	25.33	1263

The above statistics indicates that there is significant growth in the financial assistance provided by the RRRLF during the whole decade. As the financial assistance increased, the number of libraries had also increased and the cost of reading and learning materials had also gone up in due course of time. Thus the effect of actual increase in the financial assistance was not much realized.

The Department of Culture, Government of India[12] transferred a scheme to RRRLF to provide assistance to VAs running libraries. The financial assistance rendered by the RRRLF to VAs from 1986-87 to 1995-96 is given in Table 2.2.

Table 2.2: Financial Assistance Provided by the RRRLF to VAs from 1986-87 to 1995-96

Year	*Amount (Rs in lakhs)*	*Number of Beneficiary Libraries*
1986-87	30.55	142
1987-88	22.40	85
1988-89	17.80	57
1989-90	25.90	89
1990-91	07.92	34
1991-92	25.56	82
1992-93	23.16	68
1993-94	19.81	57
1994-95	26.38	73
1995-96	11.81	31
Total	211.29	718

It may be noted that the utilisation of the financial assistance under the scheme was uniform except for the years 1990-91 and 1995-96, which has adversely affected the annual average of the financial assistance rendered. This also indicates that the assistance rendered was for a very small number of VAs as compared to the total number of existing VAs in the country. Even the amount of assistance was also not enough.

The Foundation is engaged in the task of spreading the library movement in small towns and villages with the objectives of developing reading habits among the rural masses. It has assisted more than 25,000 libraries at different levels all over the country during the last two and a half decades. The number of libraries received financial assistance from the Foundation[13] is given in Table 2.3.

Since the Foundation was started functioning in 1972, therefore, number of financial beneficiary libraries was very small. It was increased manifolds within a period of just half decade. At present, a good number of libraries are receiving assistance from RRRLF regularly.

Libraries receiving financial assistance from RRRLF may be categorized in different categories as mentioned in Table 2.4.

Table 2.3: Financial Assistance Provided by the RRRLF to Libraries in Different States and UTs During 1972-97

State/UT	*Number of Libraries during*				
	1972-73	*1979-80*	*1986-87*	*1992-93*	*1996-97*
Andhra Pradesh	27	852	1515	1528	2765
Assam	9	110	145	253	350
Bihar	31	810	1694	1713	4101
Gujarat	18	1115	2154	2155	6714
Haryana	5	30	64	69	80
Himachal Pradesh	9	72	169	177	221
Jammu & Kashmir	14	12	24	28	60
Karnataka	19	113	2134	2140	2296
Kerala	9	1015	1096	2099	5000
Madhya Pradesh	25	1045	2084	2091	3000
Maharashtra	.39	1015	2034	2082	3888
Manipur	4	60	95	107	13
Meghalaya	2	5	7	7	7
Nagaland	2	65	98	141	181
Orissa	13	780	1690	1690	3529
Punjab	11	13	25	25	580
Rajasthan	24	80	119	119	800
Sikkim	4	6	6	6	6
Tamil Nadu	13	760	1486	1540	2547
Tripura	3	20	44	44	220
Uttar Pradesh	54	360	710	718	1624
West Bengal	22	1315	2333	2811	3000
Andaman & Nicobar	—	20	27	40	40
Arunachal Pradesh	9	40	44	77	130
Chandigarh	—	3	5	8	8
Dadra & Nagar Haveli	1	3	3	4	4
Delhi	—	3	3	4	219
Goa	—	66	104	118	118
Lakshadweep Island	—	11	11	11	11
Mizoram	2	45	106	163	181
Pondicherry	2	45	57	58	58
Total	271	10,889	20,086	22,026	41,868

Table 2.4: Type of Libraries Received Financial Assistance from the RRRLF up to 1996-97

Type of Library/Institution	*Number of Libraries*
State Central Libraries	28
Divisional and District Libraries	435
Sub-divisional/Taluka/Tehsil Libraries	501
Town and Rural Libraries	23,859
Mobile Libraries & Book Deposit Centres	784
Nehru Yuvak Kendras	242
Jawahar Bal Bhavans	49
Others	128
Total	26,026

2.8 NATIONAL POLICY ON LIBRARY AND INFORMATION SYSTEM (NAPLIS)

In 1985, a Committee was set up under the Chairmanship of Prof D P Chattopadhyay to formulate a National Policy on Library and Information System (NAPLIS)[14]. The Committee submitted its report in May 1986 after that another Empowered Committee[15] was constituted to examine the practical implications of the Report in all its aspects and to draw up an action plan for its implementation. Again Report was submitted by the Empowered Committee[16] in April 1988 and an Implementation Cell was formed to implement its recommendations within a period of six months. Again, another Working Group, under the Inchargeship of a Joint Secretary to the Government of India in the Department of Culture was constituted to examine its recommendations for implementation. The Working Group submitted its Report in July 1993 and suggested to implement only 29 out of 60 recommendations made by the NAPLIS.

The following are some of the recommendations of NAPLIS related to the public library system:

1. Proposals of maintenance and development of public libraries should preferably be through State Legislative Enactments. The Central Government may revise Model Public Library Bill in the light of the experience gained in recent years. Finances for library development should be found by each state, either from general revenue or from local taxation. Central Government agencies may provide funds under Plan Expenditure.
2. The main thrust should go to rural public library. A village or a cluster of villages with an adequate population should have

community library/rural community centre, which will also serve as an information centre. Resources from various agencies engaged in the public health, adult education, State and Central Government, etc. are to be mobilised to built up and maintain this centre.

3. The Central Government should assist the state governments in the development of public libraries in a larger way than it has done so far. The RRRLF as the national agency for coordinating and assisting the development of public libraries be suitably strengthened enabling it to discharge its responsibilities effectively.
4. It was considered that a few projects to develop standards, guidelines on Model Library Service at several levels may be initiated urgently by the Department of Culture, Government of India.
5. To meet the library needs at the national level, there should be a System of National Library consisting of National Library, Calcutta as the National Library of India, National Depository libraries in Delhi, Bombay and Madras, National Subject Libraries and such other libraries of national importance. These National Libraries should form part of one integrated system.
6. A National Commission on Libraries and Information System or alternatively, it may be named as National Commission on Informatics and Documentation may be constituted by an Act of Parliament to serve under the Ministry of Human Resource Development. The Commission will have representation from appropriate Central and State agencies and could provide guidance and coordinate library development programme in all sectoral areas. This apex body will have the primary responsibility for the implementation of NAPLIS programmes.
7. National Depository Libraries; Connemara Public Library, Chennai; Central Library (Asiatic Society), Bombay; and Delhi Public Library, Delhi should concentrate in different regions intensively upon the development of collections and preservation of Indian culture produced in the languages of the regions concerned, supplementing and complementing the efforts of Indian National Library.
8. The Indian National Bibliography should have a comprehensive coverage about the national output of documents and should be brought out in an updated form on regular basis. This responsibility should be vested in the National Library
9. Government should take steps to create a national awareness of the urgent necessity to preserve the nation's cultural heritage.

National Libraries should carry the responsibility of this preservation and the preservation facilities should be created at the National Libraries. Linkages should be established between libraries, archives and museums for the purpose of national preservation.

10. Ministry of Rural Development has undertaken a plan of building up one Community Centre in every Panchayat Centre. The Department of Culture and the Ministry of Rural Development have agreed to provide library services at each of these Rural Community Centres.
11. An important link should be established between the Community Centre Library and Primary Schools. If the schools do not have libraries of their own, the Community Centre Library should provide children with adequate services.
12. A Community Centre Library should have an important role in Adult Education Programme.
13. A District Library should also provide for more facilities and recreation for the handicapped and under-privileged classes, e.g. literature in Braille.
14. Libraries for special groups should be built in areas of tribal concentration and minority communities to help in developing and sustaining their distinctive cultures. Government will encourage such communities to develop their own libraries through their voluntary efforts.
15. The key role of public libraries as chief sustaining agencies for distant education is to be recognised and they should be adequately equipped with relevant resources, such as publications covering open university and vocational education courses.
16. All public libraries within a state should form part of a network extending from village library through intermediary levels, Community Centre Library, District Library and State Network should be linked up with the national information grid.

2.9 EXPERT GROUP FOR STRENGTHENING OF LIBRARY SYSTEMS IN THE COUNTRY

Government of India, Department of Culture appointed an Expert Group for strengthening the library systems in the country. The Committee submitted its following recommendations to the Government:

1. The Government of India should make it mandatory for all the States and UTs to pass the library legislation. At present only one-third of States/UTs have passed the library legislation. However, in some states such as Kerala, Manipur and Haryana, the State Legislation is not effectively implemented. Hence, the Model Library Act formulated by RRRLF should be adopted on all-India basis.
2. There has always been private initiative for starting the library movement. This movement has to be accelerated by Government support, monitored through the RRRLF, Department of Culture, UGC and other Government agencies, depending on the nature of the libraries.
3. There has to be infrastructural development of all libraries for collection development, preservation, conservation, modernization, resource sharing and human resource development, keeping in view the type of libraries as well as the local needs.
4. The RRRLF may be designated as nodal agency for collection development, modernisation, conservation and preservation and manpower development for public libraries. Financial incentive for enactment of library legislation may be given to each state.
5. Public libraries should take necessary measures such as story telling, book discussions, competitions, book exhibitions, etc. to inculcate reading habits among the members of the community. An apex body for libraries should be established in New Delhi, which will coordinate the activities of the different types of libraries, networks and important institutions in India and abroad. It will also act as the National Referral Centre and serve as the contact point for international organisations and foreign governments. All activities regarding library movement, resource mobilisation from private initiatives will be monitored by the apex body. The activities of the apex body will not in any way overlap those of the National Library and Central Reference Library, Calcutta.
6. Various Friends of Library Groups are functioning in USA and other parts of the world. On the similar lines, Friends of Library Groups be initiated for promotion of public libraries and suitable financial assistance be given to them.
7. Besides recommending the Government grant, the Committee was of the view that the library movement cannot be strengthened without the active involvement of the people and contributions from private enterprises and various institutions — religious, social, cultural, business houses and family donations. In order to

mobilise donations and contributions from these sources, the Government of India should set up a National Culture Fund under the Charitable and Endowments Act, and therefore, such donations and contributions made to this great cause should be eligible for deduction under 80G of Income Tax Act 1961.

The Committee also recommended the adoption of libraries by various business houses, temples, boards and institutions for improvement of library services.

2.10 LIBRARY LEGISLATIONS IN INDIA

Well organized libraries are the need of the hour. After more than five decades of independence, library movement has not yet reached an effective stage. One of the basic reasons is the paucity of funds. Growth and development of libraries are the responsibility of the states as "Public Libraries" are in the "State List" under the Constitution of India. Although the Central Government has also made enormous efforts by establishing many public libraries in the country and these are functioning very well. It is essential for each and every state to enact comprehensive library legislation, which is their prime responsibility. It is the library legislation which defines functions and objectives of libraries. State-wide Public Library Systems can be established in a planned and coordinated manner, good library services can be provided to the users and regular adequate finances can be arranged to the libraries through library legislation.

Dr. S.R. Ranganathan prepared a Model Public Library Act in 1930. Based on this Act, Madras was the first state to adopt Public Libraries Act in 1948, followed by Hyderabad Public Libraries Act (1955), Andhra Pradesh Public Libraries Act (1960), Karnataka Public Libraries Act (1965), Maharashtra Public Libraries Act (1967), West Bengal Public Libraries Act (1979), Manipur Public Libraries Act (1988), Kerala Public Libraries Act (1989), Haryana Public Libraries Act (1989), Mizoram Public Libraries Act (1993) and Goa Public Libraries Act (1994). Majority of these Acts are based on the pattern adopted by Dr. S.R. Ranganathan with some modifications to suit the governments policies. Some of the governments have passed Library Legislations but failed to implement them.

Of the 35 States and UTs in India, only 10 have passed Public Library Act so far. In terms of population, out of 1,027,015,247 people only 425,091,054 (41%) people are enjoying the Library Legislation and remaining 25 States and UTs with a population of 601,924,193 (59%) people are denied this benefit. The statistical break up is given in Table 2.5 and Table 2.6.

Table 2.5: States and UTs Having Library Legislation

State/UT	*Population*
Andhra Pradesh	75,727,541
Goa	1,343,998
Haryana	21,082,989
Karnataka	52,733,958
Kerala	31,838,619
Maharashtra	96,752,247
Manipur	2,388,634
Mizoram	891,058
Tamil Nadu	62,110,839
West Bengal	80,221,171
Total	425,091,054

Table 2.6: States and UTs not Having Library Legislation

State/UT	*Population*
Andaman & Nicobar Islands	356,265
Arunachal Pradesh	1,091,117
Assam	26,638,407
Bihar	82,878,796
Chandigarh	900,914
Chattisgarh	20,795,956
Dadra & Nagar Haveli	220,451
Daman & Diu	158,059
Delhi	13,782,976
Gujarat	50,596,992
Himachal Pradesh	6,077,248
Jammu & Kashmir	10,069,917
Jharkhand	26,909,428
Lakshadweep	60,595
Madhya Pradesh	60,385,118
Meghalaya	2,306,069
Nagaland	1,988,636
Orissa	36,706,920
Pondicherry	973,829
Punjab	24,289,296
Rajasthan	56,473,122
Sikkim	540,493
Tripura	3,191,168
Uttar Pradesh	166,052,859
Uttaranchal	8,479,562
Total	601,924,193

Among all ten Public Library Acts, library cess from surcharge on local property tax is provided by Tamil Nadu, Andhra Pradesh, Karnataka and Haryana to which matching grant is to be given by the State Governments. Maharashtra, West Bengal, Kerala, Manipur, Mizoram and Goa Public Libraries Act do not provide for local library cess. Now it is much overdue for other States and UTs to pass Public Libraries Act and implement them fully in letter and spirit for the development of public libraries.

States and UTs which have library legislation, have shown higher literacy rates than the average national literacy rate (65.4%) except Andhra Pradesh (61.1%). Other nine states are Maharashtra (77.3%), West Bengal (69.2%), Tamil Nadu (73.5%), Karnataka (67.0%), Kerala (90.9%), Mizoram (88.5%), Manipur (68.9%), Haryana (68.6%) and Goa (82.3%). This indicates that there is a direct link between enactment of library legislation and growth of literacy in the states.

2.11 LIBRARY ASSOCIATIONS IN INDIA

A library association is a professional body and not a trade union. Even this is not a group of people who promote their own welfare. Members of the library associations disseminate knowledge and information to the society. The objective of a library association is to strengthen and expand the library movement and not only to assist any particular library or sections of libraries. It basically makes an earnest effort to build up a sense of brotherhood among librarians by cutting across the boundaries of caste, creed, colour and country. It binds people in a self-conscious community devoted to the cultural uplift of their fellowmen, which raises their morale to perform their tasks. It helps devise proper code of conduct based upon professional ethics in the minds to raise the standards of training of librarians to enable them to perform their tasks with greater competence and for the larger benefits of the society.

Library associations discharge their duties by organising local, zonal, national, international seminars, meetings, symposia, round table discussions, workshops, etc. to yield wealth of ideas by publishing library journals, conducting study circles, publicity, exhibitions. These ideas can be used by the planners, policy makers and implementors of the programmes and policies in the country. Library associations work to prepare the taxpayer's mind for accepting the library legislation and also persuade the politicians to include library and literacy movement in their manifesto and set up more public libraries in their constituencies. One of the important functions of the associations is to mobilise public opinion in favour of library and literacy activities for the nation development.

It is quite unfortunate that a little coordination exists between policy makers and these associations. With a lot of persuation and request, policy makers agree to attend the inaugural functions of seminars and conferences and sometimes chair the important or concluding sessions. At the end of seminars or conferences, if some valuable suggestions/recommendations are made and sent for implementation to the same policy maker, it is quite often observed that either recommendations are diluted by constituting an other committee to review these recommendations or no importance is given in implementing them.

There are a number of library associations that exist in the country. Some of them are of national level others are state level associations.

- Andhradesa Library Association (1914)
- Maharashtra Library Association (1921)
- Baroda Library Association
- Bengal Library Association (1925)
- Delhi Library Association
- Government of India Librarians Association (1933)
- Haryana Library Association (1975)
- Indian Association of Special Libraries and Information Centres (IASLIC) (1955)
- Indian Library Association (1933)
- Madras Library Association (1928)
- Medical Libraries Association
- Rajasthan Library Association (1962)
- Society for Information Science
- Uttar Pradesh Library Association (1935)
- Punjab Library Association (1929)
- Assam Library Association (1939)
- Bihar Library Association (1940)
- Utkal Library Association (1944)
- Kerala Granthsala Sangam (1945)
- Madhya Pradesh Library Association (1957)
- Karnataka Library Association (1962)
- Gujarat Granthalaya Sewa Sangh (1970)

There appears to be very little cooperation and coordination among these associations. All library associations are required to work together on common ground to create a climate in which the Central and State Governments should lay down proper library policies, standards for rendering library services and proper code of conducts. Because library association is not merely a forum of librarians, rather it is a platform from where people from various sections of the society, including educationists, writers, authors and those connected with the society, can raise their voice for library movement and force governments to implement policies in favour of societal development. The greater involvement of library associations in literacy movement can bring out fruitful results in enhancing the literacy rates. Because these people closely cooperate and mix up with the local people, talk to them at their door steps, apprise and educate them about the services rendered by the library to the society. These people can create a wholesome atmosphere of a learning society.

REFERENCES

1. UNESCO, Statistics on Libraries, 1966-67, p. 1.
2. RANGANATHAN (S R), Library development plan: Thirty years programme for India, with draft library bills for the Union and constituent States, 1950, University of Delhi, Delhi. p. 273.
3. PRYTHERCH (Ray), *Compiler,* Harrod's librarian's glossary of terms used in librarianship, documentation, book crafts and reference books. (Ed) 6. p. 636.
4. YOUNG (Heartstill) and others, (Ed.) ALA glossary of library and information science, 1983, American Library Association, Chicago, p. 181.
5. REPORT OF ADVISORY COMMITTEE FOR LIBRARIES, 1958, (Ed) 2. 1961, Manager of Publications, Delhi, p. 31.
6. SESSA (Frank B), Public libraries, In. *Encyclopedia of Library and Information Science,* Vol 24, 1978, Marcel Dekker, New York, p. 267.
7. UNESCO, Public Library Manifesto, 1949, UNESCO, Paris.
8. UNESCO, Public Library Manifesto, 1972, UNESCO, Paris
9. IFLA Standards for public libraries, Ed 2, (IFLA Publication. 9), Verlag Dokumentation, Munchen, 1997.
10. KAUL (H K), Barriers in resource sharing in networks, Chapter II, p. 57-8, Ph D Thesis (unpublished), Poona University, Pune, 1996.
11. BHATTACHARJEE (R), Role of Raja Rammohun Roy Library Foundation in the promotion of public library movement in India, *Herald of Library Science,* 38, 1-2; Jan-April, 1999. p. 15.
12. THOMAS (V K), Public library financing - analysis of RRRLF schemes assistance, *Herald of Library Science,* 38, 1-2; Jan-April, 1999; p. 33.
13. *Ibid.* p. 36.
14. Synopsis of Prof. D P Chattopadhyay Committee on NAPLIS, *CLIS Observer,* 15, 1-2; 1998; p. 12.
15. BHATTACHARJEE (R), Role of Raja Rammohun Roy Library Foundation in the promotion of public library movement in India, *Herald of Library Science,* 38, 1-2; Jan-April, 1999, p. 19-20.
16. *Ibid.* p. 20.

Chapter 3

Literacy Status in India

> The only service to be done for our masses is to give them education, to develop their lost individuality. They are to be given ideas; their eyes are to be opened to what is going on in the world around them; and then they will work out their own salvation. —*Swami Vivekananda*

3.1 ORACY AND LITERACY

In ancient days, knowledge and wisdom were communicated through songs, tales and numerous other forms. This oral culture has remained the predominant medium for transmission of knowledge from one generation to other. During those days, reading and writing remained sacred monopoly of a small circle of elites[1]. Thus the knowledge was the intellectual property of a group, race or caste. Access of knowledge was not the right of every one. This created social distance among various classes and communities in the society. Most of the people were added their or oral culture by listening and speaking processes. This system of transfer of knowledge was known as *Sruti* and *Smriti.* It took centuries to shift from oral culture to written culture. It was the system of oral tradition by which knowledge was transmitted from teacher to pupil in an unbroken chain called *Guru Shishya Parampara*.

Invention of printing press, at the end of 15th century created a milestone and gave written culture a distinct edge over oral culture. Thus a long journey of shifting from oracy to literacy entered into a new era. Now the information technology revolution along with the satellite communication revolution has again brought oracy back into reckoning. In fact, many developed countries, including India, are deeply concerned over the declination of reading and writing culture. The oracy can be helpful in educating a person but he cannot become literate without qualifying certain parameters of literacy.

At present, there is no universally agreed upon definition of literacy. The meaning of literacy differs from culture to culture and country to country because the needs and conditions differ widely on the globe. *Dictionary of Education*[2] defines literacy in general sense as "strictly the bare ability to read and write". In 1951, UNESCO Committee[3] proposed the following definition for census purposes.

> "A person is literate who can, with understanding, both read and write a short and simple statement on his everyday life".

Rabindra Nath Tagore defined literacy as:

> "Literacy means enabling the mind to find out that ultimate truth which emancipates us from the bondage of the dust and gives us the wealth, not of things but of inner life, not of power but of love, making the truth its own and giving expression to it".

India Literacy Project[4] (ILP) defines:

> "Literacy is the ability to read forty words per minute, write twenty words per minute, and do two-digit arithmetic."

Literacy is also the first step in march towards change, development and self-reliance. This definition sets the standard of literacy at a very lowest acceptable level. Any literacy statistics based on this kind of definition which had no unsound and unscientific background must be viewed with caution unless actual tests have been conducted, which is neither laid down in the census act nor in a tradition with most of the developing nations of the world.

The academicians have one common approach to define literacy by relating it to a certain level of formal education or to base them on attendance at adult classes. Definitions of this kind are not adequate as they completely overlook the widely observed fact that a person can attend classes and even pass tests and yet be unable to make independent use of literacy. After his formal training is over and also that even when a man has become literate, he can lapse to illiteracy after some time.

Gudschinsky[5] says that:

> "A person is literate who, in a language that he speaks, can read and

> understand if it had been spoken to him, and can write, so that it can be read, as anything he can say".

This definition of literacy lays emphasis on understanding and clears the question of the language in which literacy instruction should be given. Thus, a literate person is one who is able to read with understanding a written passage on any topic that is familiar to him. His reading ability is not limited to the content or subjects covered by the books that were used in the process of his learning to read.

It has been recognised that manpower of any society constitutes the human capital of that society and economic development will take place only when human capital acts upon the material capital in a scientific way and in some definite proportion. It is thus essential that for the development of human capital, at least in developing nations, the ignorance must be done away with so that the individual develops to his fullest capacities and becomes a potential for contributing his full share to the economic development process. In this regard, M.A. Gode[6] says that:

> "Literacy programme unreleased to the working and living conditions of the workers to the challenges of environment and the developmental needs of the country cannot secure an active participation of learners, nor can it be an instrument of development and progress. Thus it is the prime necessity to remove ignorance".

The World Conference on Education for All was organised in Jomtien, Thailand in March 1990 and sponsored by UNESCO, World Bank, UNICEF and UNDP, in which 155 member States participated and emphasised on the basic learning needs. These needs comprise both essential learning tools (such as literacy, oral expression, numeracy and problem solving) and basic learning content (such as knowledge, skills, values and attitudes) required by human beings to be able to survive, to develop their full capacities, to live and work in dignity, to participate fully in development, to improve the quality of their lives, to make informed decisions, and to continue learning. In view of the World Conference[7]:

> "Literacy is a life skill and the primary learning tool for personal and community development and self sufficiency in a rapidly changing and increasingly independent world ..... It is the primary enabling force for all further education. It is a uniquely effective tool for learning, for accessing and processing information, for creating new knowledge, and for participation in one's own culture and the emerging world culture."

According to American National Literacy[8] (ANL) Act 1991:

> "Literacy is an individual's ability to read, write and speak, to compute and solve problems at a level of proficiency necessary to function on the job and in the society to achieve one's goals, and to develop one's knowledge and potential".

It has further divided literacy into three categories: prose, document and quantitative literacy. Prose literacy is defined as the knowledge and skills associated with locating and using information from texts such as editorials, newspaper articles, stories, poems and the like. Document literacy refers to an individual's ability to interpret and use items such as tables, charts, graphs, maps and indexes. Quantitative literacy is determined by ability to perform different arithmetic operations, either alone or sequentially, using information embedded in both prose and document materials.

The Alberta Association of Adult Literacy[9] (AAAL), started in 1981, a non-profit organisation which links approximately 500 members involved in adult literacy and basic education, defines literacy as:

> "The ability to understand and use printed information in daily activities, at home, at work, and in the community — to achieve one's goals and to develop one's knowledge and potential".

The National Adult Education Programme (NAEP) launched on 2 October 1978 defines:

> "Literacy and numeracy, at a level, which would enable learners to continue to learn in a self-reliant manner;
>
> Functional development, functionality being viewed as the role of an individual as a producer and worker, as a member of family and as a citizen in civic and political system;
>
> "Social awareness, of laws and government policies, and the need for poor and non-literate to organize themselves in pursuance of their legitimate interests and for group action".

New Encyclopaedia Britannica[10] defines:

> "A higher level of competence in reading and writing one that qualifies a person to meet many of the practical needs of daily life in his culture or group - has been designated as functional literacy".

Literacy must be related to the practical needs of the learner and his community. Keeping this point in mind, UNESCO Committee[11], in 1962, adopted the following definition:

> "Literacy is not the simple reading of word or a set of associated symbols and sounds, but an act of critical understanding of men's situation in the world. Literacy is not an end in itself but a means of personal liberation and development and extending individuals educational efforts involving overall inter-disciplinary responses to concrete problems".

Further, it defines a functionally literate person as:

> "A person who can, with understanding, both read and write a short simple statement relevant to his everyday life. A person who has acquired all the essential knowledge and skills which enable him to engage in all those activities in which literacy is required for effective functioning in his group and community and whose achievement in reading, writing and numeracy makes it possible to use these skills towards his own and his community's development. In other words, a person who cannot engage in all those activities in which literacy is required for effective functioning of his group and community and also for enabling him to continue to use reading, writing and calculation for his own and community's development".

Here literacy is intimately involved with the individual's own life and with his place in his community. This definition also recognizes that the requirement of literacy varies from society to society.

Kirsch and Jungeblut[12] define:

> "Literacy is not simply ...... a set of isolated skills associated with reading and writing, but more importantly.... The application of those skills for specific purposes in specific contexts.... There is no single measure or specific point on a single scale that separate the 'literate' from the 'illiterate'. Literacy can no longer be defined simply as the ability to sign one's name, completion of a particular year of schooling, or attainment of a specified reading grade level".

Literacy is one infallible medicine for wide-ranging problems such as population growth, social injustice against women and other underprivileged and backward sections of the society, communalism, etc. which are plaguing the country today. It goes beyond alphabetical literacy. A literate person should be able to think and analyse the situation in which he lives and plans for the future. Using the skills of reading and writing is more important than learning the letters of the alphabets.

"None can become literate, learning the letters of the alphabet
Knowledge is not knowing two plus two makes not five but four

Or learning to avoid the thumb and signing the name to pay a debt
Literacy should lift us up, teach us to learn more and more".

It is an essential tool for acquiring the ability to improve his living standards by using whatever knowledge he has gained for further development. Therefore, there is a need to redefine what generally literacy is known today.

"Literacy, a critical factor in knowledge revolution
It's a must if our aim is an improved civilization
Man became a superior animal only when he learned
Think, plan, read, write, use wisely what he earned".

3.2 LITERACY IN INDIA

India is a vast country, with literacy rates ranging from 47.5 per cent (in Bihar) to 90.9 per cent (in Kerala) in different States and Union Territories. India began its existence as an independent country with the ringing words of Pt. Jawaharlal Nehru, its first Prime Minister, that the task ahead included the ending of poverty, ignorance, disease and inequality of opportunity. One of the means adopted for translating this vision into reality was the setting of the target of free and compulsory primary education.

The Directive Principles in Article 45 of the Indian Constitution prescribed that the State shall endeavour to provide, within a period of 10 years from the commencement of this Constitution, for free and compulsory education for all children until they complete the age of 14 years. Yet after more than five and half decades later, the goal of universal basic education remains elusive. Still, there are about 35 million children out-of-school. The promise of basic education made to the future generations in our Constitution is still far from the fulfillment.

At the time of country's independence, Mahatma Gandhi called illiteracy as a sin and shame and pledged countrymen to wipe it out. He said:

"We are all in a movement talks of the mass literacy endeavour sweeping the length and breadth of our country today and particularly of the need to promote the literacy effort on sound lines — the need to development commitment and dedication, to work to achieve goals with a missionary spirit, to build up credibility, to bring in creativity and innovation, to muster youth power, to secure voluntary effort and above all people's participation and support, etc".

Former President of India, Shri K.R. Narayanan[13] addressing to the nation on the eve of Republic Day on 25 January, 1999, said that:

> "Eradication of illiteracy is the need of the hour. Literacy work is not just a service but a duty and commitment enjoined on the literate person, to impart his knowledge to his/her illiterate brethren. We are constitutionally committed under Article 45 to achieve universalisation of elementary education and this was to have been achieved by 1960, which still remains our cherished goal".

Attitudinal change is required in our society and also in the political systems. Shri Atal Bihari Vajpayee, the Prime Minister of India, confessed that:

> "The country cannot excel with half of its population being illiterate. I am not criticizing anybody. We are all to blame for it and we need to sort it out".

Why are we lagging behind in literacy — a basic minimum need for masses in rural and urban areas. On the world scene, on one hand, India can stand proudly shoulder-to-shoulder with the developed countries in the matters of space science, nuclear science and technology, defense research and development, agriculture science and other advanced areas, but in the literacy queue we are far behind other developed countries. At present, India has the largest number of illiterate population in the world (296 million), which exceeds the total population of the United States of America (281 million).

3.3 NEED FOR LITERACY

People are the foundation of any nation. If the foundation is firm and strong, then the nation will enjoy tranquility. In case of our country, where one-third population is illiterate, underfed, under-clothed and under-housed, how the foundation can be made strong. Now, as long as this continues to be true, no one can expect a strong foundation in near future.

India is a democratic country and democracy is by definition a government of the people. This means that the people must contribute both through the electoral process and by intelligent, articulate opinion to the task of exercising political society; a real democratic society with hundred per cent literacy is of prime importance. Success of a democratic country depends upon literate public so that they can understand their duties and powers and may utilize them. The Government of independent India has stressed on the spread of literacy and adult education and felt that the liquidation of mass illiteracy is necessary not only for promoting participation in the working of democratic institutions but also for accelerating other developmental programmes.

Over the years, the scenario has undergone a sea-change. The days of *Sruti* are long over. Tremendous modernization both in the means of communication as well as the content have imparted a new dimension to the entire process. Phenomenal information explosion and diversification in the means of communication have ensured dissemination of news relating to development and growth is not confined to a particular region.

An illiterate person is handicapped and disabled in many ways. He cannot read a newspaper, a classified advertisement, an operational manual of household equipment, street signs, prescription of medicines by a doctor, warning sign or danger label on the goods and medicines, etc. He cannot fill up an application form and so on. These are some of the serious disabilities of an illiterate person. On the other hand, literacy leads to many social benefits, including improvements in standards of hygiene, reduction in infant and child mortality rates, decline in population growth, increase in labour productivity, rise in civic consciousness, greater political empowerment and democratisation, and an improved sense of national unity.

Literacy plays important role in increasing confidence and personality development, making aware of the social responsibility, status in family, educational equality, health and hygiene, empowerment of women. National Family Health Survey Report 1998-99 highlighted impact of women literacy on societal development and says that:

- The fertility rate among illiterate women is 3.47 per cent as compared to 2.64 per cent in literate women;
- Literate women take better care of their health during pregnancy. Over 90 per cent of literate women take tetanus toxide injection as compared to only 55 per cent illiterate women;
- Over 86 per cent literate women take folic acid tablets as compared to 44 per cent illiterate women; and
- Literate women are more aware of AIDS control programme, pulse polio programme, the benefits of small family norms, vaccination and immunization and other health programmes organized by the Government and other health agencies.

The first Five Year Plan document referred to the low percentage of literacy rate in the country and emphasised that the democracy could not take roots with 80 per cent population remaining illiterate. It was further stated that even the constitutional obligation of universalisation of elementary education would be seriously handicapped without an effective support from adult literacy.

Literacy makes a person independent of personal contact. Literacy—reading, writing and arithmetic—can be meaningful and functional in a context where literacy as such is needed, e.g. in urban areas, and where written materials are within reach. Literacy is only one phase in the process of learning throughout life but it is not necessarily the first phase or the first step in a development process. Self-help and income-generation can assume much greater importance in the minds of the learners than mere literacy. Literacy is an essential part of basic services. It is useful to offer literacy instead of food, housing, clean water, electricity or jobs. All these may become uneconomic in due course of time without proper literacy.

While this is particularly evident in the more developed parts of the world, it is not so in the developing ones, where large cross-sections continue to be illiterate. With hardly any access to information, modernization and communication and virtually no access to the irreducible minimum survival tools, they remain helpless victims of poverty, deprivation and exploitation. The benefits of plans and programmes do not percolate to them and they remain cut-off from the mainstream.

Literacy, an important tool for communication, learning and information, is a virtual precondition for an individual's evolution and national development. It promotes objectivity, capacity for clear perception, through logical and coherent analysis. It promotes a sense of history and helps combine individuality with universalisation. In this sense, literacy can be regarded as an inalienable fundamental right.

3.4 LITERACY SKILLS

There are three levels of literacy skills for learners. When learners complete these levels they should have to be masters in the skills mentioned in the following paragraphs.

Basic Level

Reading

- Read newspaper headlines and sub-headings;

- Read and understand posters; and
- Read and recognise figures from 1 to 1000.

Writing

- Write his or her own name and address;
- Communicate in writing, using simple language;
- Write simple letters; and
- Write numerical numbers from 1 to 1000.

Numeracy

- Count and recognise figures from 1 to 1000;
- Add and subtract up to three digits; and
- Understand the principles of simple addition, subtraction, multiplication and division.

Others

- Communicate clearly; and
- Use literacy skills in daily life.

Middle Level

Reading

- Read and comprehend stories, songs, directions, instructions and simple parts of newspapers; and
- Comprehend the main idea of what has been read.

Writing

- Write simple notes and letters; and
- Fill out simple forms and receipts.

Numeracy

- Demonstrate proficiency in addition and subtraction;
- Apply basic skills in multiplication and division;
- Understand basic measurements (money, weight, length, volume); and
- Solve simple numerical problems (family budget and marketing).

Others

- Further improvement in communication and literacy skills.

Self Learning Level

Reading

- Analyse and synthesize main ideas of what he or she has read;
- Discuss with others what he or she has read; and
- Read and interpret simple graphs.

Writing

- Write one to two pages on certain topics;
- Write personal letters, letter of application, report, etc.; and
- Draw graphs and geometric figures.

Numeracy

- Add and subtract large numbers with accuracy and speed;
- Multiply up to five digit numbers and functions; and
- Divide up to three digit numbers and functions.

Others

- Further improvement in communication and literacy skills.

OECD[14] distributes literacy into the following five levels:

Level 1

Very poor skills (e.g. inability to determine the amount of medicine to give to a child from written information).

Level 2

Weak skills (e.g. people who can read, but test poorly and have difficulty in learning new skills).

Level 3

Skill level necessary for copying with the demands of every day life and work in a complex, advanced society and required for successful secondary school completion and college entry.

Level 4 and 5

Command of higher order information processing skills.

3.5 GROWTH OF POPULATION AND LITERACY

Literacy is taken as an important input in overall development of the individuals as well as the nation. In India, data on literacy rate are provided by the population census every ten years. The census[15] held in 2001 indicates the total number of estimated population at 00:00 hours on 1st March 2001 stood at 1027 million comprising 531 million males and 496 million females. It was 16.7 per cent of the world's total population and accounts for meagre 2.42 per cent of the total world geographical area. In an estimation made by the United Nations, the annual growth rate of world population during 1990-2000 was 1.4 per cent. China registered a much lower growth rate (1.00%) of population during the same period, whereas India has registered 1.9 per cent population growth rate during 1991-2001. Estimated global population in 2000 was 6055 million. Estimated population of ten most populous countries of the world along with their reference dates are given in Table 3.1.

Table 3.1: Population Distribution of Ten Most Populous Countries of the World

	Country	*Reference Data*	*Population (in million)*
1.	China	01.02.2000	1,278
2.	India	01.03.2001	1,027
3.	USA	April 2000	281
4.	Indonesia	01.07.2000	212
5.	Brazil	01.07.2000	170
6.	Pakistan	01.07.2000	157
7.	Russian Federation	01.07.2000	147
8.	Bangladesh	01.07.2000	129
9.	Japan	01.10.2000	127
10.	Nigeria	01.02.2000	112

It reveals that India is the second most populous country in the world. It has population more than the combined population of United States of America, Indonesia, Brazil, Pakistan and Russian Federation. As an estimation, the population of India would cross the population of China sometimes during the mid of this century. Data given in the Table 3.1 has been graphically presented in Figure 3.1.

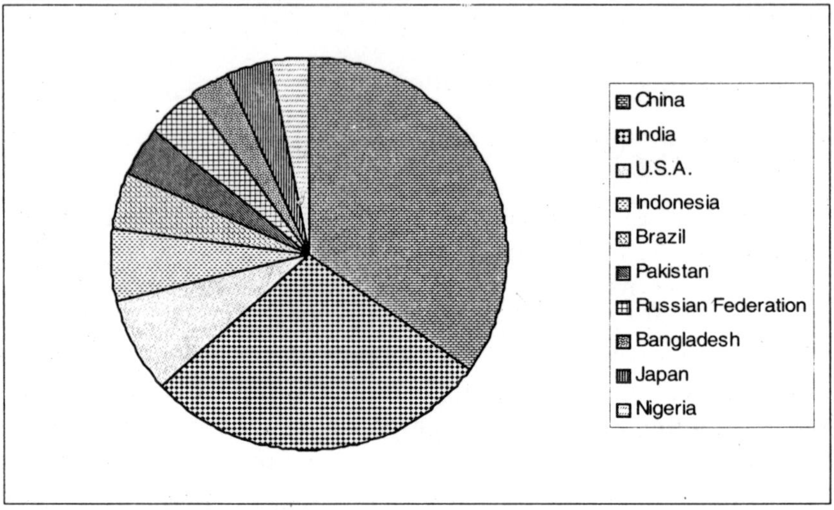

Fig. 3.1: Population Distribution of Ten Most Populous Countries of the World

The total estimated population reported in each census during the 21st century, decadal population growth rate and percentage decadal population growth rate of India over 1901 has been given in Table 3.2.

The graph presented in Figure 3.2 reflects that the estimated population of India at the beginning of 20th century stood at only 238.4 million which has been increased by four times in a period of 100 years and crossed 1027 million at the end of 20th century.

The population growth rate during 1981-91 was more than the estimated population of Bangladesh. The net addition of population during 1981-91 was more than the population of Pakistan whereas, during 1991-2001, it was reached to estimated population of Brazil, the fifth most populous country of the world. For the past three decades, the estimated population of India is increasing with a steady growth rate and adding population of a country every year. It means India has to create extra facilities for education, shelter, health, food, etc for a mass of size of population of a country.

Table 3.3 reflects the selected indicators of percentage decadal population growth rate in 27 States and 8 Union Territories of India during the past two decades (i.e. 1981-1991 and 1991-2001) to analyse the increasing or decreasing trends in population growth.

Table 3.2: Population Growth of India During 1901-2001

Year	Population	*Decadal Growth*		*Progressive Growth Rate over 1901*
		Absolute	*Percent*	(%)
1901	238,396,327	—	—	—
1911	252,093,390	13,697,063	+05.75	05.75
1921	251,321,213	–772,177	–00.31	05.42
1931	278,977,238	27,656,025	+11.00	17.02
1941	318,660,580	39,683,342	+14.22	33.67
1951[1]	361,088,090	42,427,510	+13.31	51.47
1961[1]	439,234,771	8,146,681	+21.64	84.25
1971	548,159,652	108,924,881	+24.80	129.94
1981[2]	683,329,097	135,169,445	+24.66	186.64
1991[3]	843,387,888	163,058,791	+23.86	255.03
2001[4]	1,027,015,247	180,627,359	+21.34	330.80

Notes:

1. In working out 'Decadal Growth' and 'Percentage Decadal Growth' for India 1941-51 and 1951-61 the population of Tuensang district for 1951 (7,025) and the population of Tuensang (83,501) and Mon (5,774) districts for 1961 Census of Nagaland state have not been taken into account as the areas were censused for the first time in 1951 and the same are not comparable.
2. The 1981 census could not be held owing to disturbed conditions prevailing in Assam. Hence the population figures for 1981 of Assam have been worked out by 'interpolation'.
3. The 1991 census could not be held owing to disturbed conditions prevailing in Jammu & Kashmir. Hence the population figures for 1991 of Jammu & Kashmir have been worked out by 'interpolation'.
4. The population of India includes the estimated population of entire Kachchh district, Morvi, Maliya-Miyana and Wankaner talukas of Rajkot district, Jodiya taluka of Jamnagar district of Gujarat State and entire Kinnaur district of Himachal Pradesh where population enumeration of Census of India, 2001, could not be conducted due to natural calamities.

The percentage decadal growth rate of population of various States and UTs in 1981-1991 varied from a lowest 14.3 per cent in Kerala to highest 56.1 per cent in Nagaland. This trend was almost similar during the decade of 1991-2001 i.e. lowest 9.4 per cent in Kerala and highest 64.4 per cent in Nagaland. The per cent decadal growth rate of population has inclined in 9 States and UTs, whereas, it was declined in remaining 26 States and UTs. The total decadal percentage growth rate in population of India as a whole was declined by 2.6 per cent in 1991-2001 as compared to 1981-91.

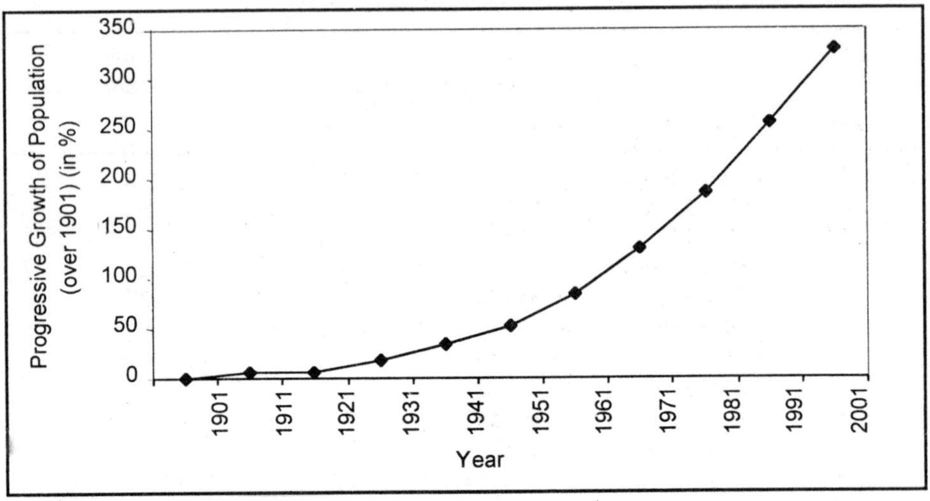

Fig. 3.2: Population Growth of India During 20th Century

To compare the growth rate of population and literacy during the past century, total population of India, its growth rate, progressive growth rate, literacy rate in a particular census year and difference in literacy rates in two consecutive censuses is given in Table 3.4.

The data given in Table 3.4 reveals that there was a sharp growth of population after independence. The average population growth rate from 1901 to 2001 was 15.78 per cent per decade whereas average literacy growth rate during the same period was only 6.01 per cent. A quick look at the overall comparative picture of growth in literacy rates between 1901 and 2001 shows a jump of 60.05 per cent and between 1991 and 2001, it was recorded a sharp growth of 13.19 per cent. It shows that India has made a considerable progress in the field of literacy during the past one decade. This sharp growth looks extraordinary as compared to the decadal literacy growth of previous decades since 1901.

It also shows that up to 1921, population growth rate was not much. Even between the census year 1911 and 1921, population rate was decreased, whereas literacy rate was increased. It has also been observed that the population growth has increased by more than 20 per cent per decade after independence. On the other hand, literacy rate has never gone more than 10 per cent in any decade except during 1991 to 2001. A graph is drawn between census year and literacy rate during 1901-2001 and the same has been presented in Figure 3.3.

Table 3.3: Percentage Decadal Population Growth Rates in States and UTs During 1981-91 and 1991-2001 (Ranked According to Population Growth Rates During 1991-2000)

Rank State	*Growth of Population During* *1981-1991 (in %)*	*1991-2001 (in %)*	*Variation in Decadal Growth Rate (in %)*
INDIA	23.9	21.3	–2.6
1. Nagaland	56.1	64.4	+8.3
2. Dadra & Nagar Haveli	33.6	59.2	+25.6
3. Daman & Diu	28.6	55.6	+27.0
4. Delhi	51.5	46.3	–5.1
5. Chandigarh	42.2	40.3	–1.8
6. Sikkim	28.5	33.0	+4.5
7. Manipur	29.3	30.0	+0.7
8. Meghalaya	32.9	29.9	–2.9
9. Mizoram	39.7	29.2	–10.5
10. Jammu & Kashmir	30.3	29.0	–1.3
11. Bihar	23.4	28.4	+5.1
12. Rajasthan	28.4	28.3	–0.1
13. Haryana	27.4	28.1	+0.7
14. Andaman & Nicobar Islands	48.7	26.9	–21.8
15. Arunachal Pradesh	36.8	26.2	–10.6
16. Uttar Pradesh	25.6	25.8	+0.3
17. Madhya Pradesh	27.2	24.3	–2.9
18. Jharkhand	24.0	23.2	–0.8
19. Maharashtra	25.7	22.6	–3.2
20. Gujarat	21.2	22.5	+1.3
21. Pondicherry	33.6	20.6	–13.1
22. Punjab	20.8	19.8	–1.1
23. Uttaranchal	24.2	19.2	–5.0
24. Assam	24.2	18.9	–5.3
25. Chattisgarh	25.7	18.1	–7.6
26. West Bengal	24.7	17.8	–6.9
27. Himachal Pradesh	20.8	17.5	–3.3
28. Karnataka	21.1	17.3	–3.8
29. Lakshadweep	28.5	17.2	–11.3
30. Orissa	20.1	15.9	–4.2
31. Tripura	34.3	15.7	–18.6
32. Goa	16.1	14.9	–1.2
33. Andhra Pradesh	24.2	13.9	–10.2
34. Tamil Nadu	15.4	11.2	–4.2
35. Kerala	14.3	9.4	–4.9

Note: Ranked according to Population Growth Rates during 1991-2001

Table 3.4: Growth of Population and Literacy in India During 1901-2001

Year	*Population*	*Decadal Growth Rate of Population (%)*	*Progressive Growth Rate of Population (over 1901) (%)*	*Literacy Rate (%)*	*Growth Rate of Literacy (%)*
1901	238,396,327	—	—	05.35	—
1911	252,093,390	+05.75	05.75	05.92	00.57
1921	251,321,213	–00.31	05.42	07.16	01.24
1931	278,977,238	+11.00	17.02	09.50	02.44
1941	318,660,580	+14.22	33.67	16.10	06.60
1951*	361,088,090	+13.31	51.47	18.33	02.23
1961**	439,234,771	+21.64	84.25	28.31	09.98
1971	548,159,652	+24.80	129.94	34.45	06.14
1981***	683,329,097	+24.66	186.64	43.56	09.11
1991#	843,387,888	+23.86	255.03	52.21	08.65
2001	1,027,015,247	+21.34	330.80	65.40	13.19

* Excluding the population of Jammu & Kashmir, Pondicherry and NEFA, Dadra and Nagar Haveli and Diu.
** Excluding the population of Goa, Daman and Diu.
*** Excluding the population of Assam where 1981 Census was not held.
\# Excluding Jammu & Kashmir where 1991 Census was not held.

Notes:
1. The literacy rate for the year 1931 relate to the population aged ten years and above.
2. The literacy rates for the years 1951, 1961, and 1971 relate to the population aged five years and above.
3. The literacy rates for the years 1981, 1991 and 2001 relate to the population aged seven years and above.

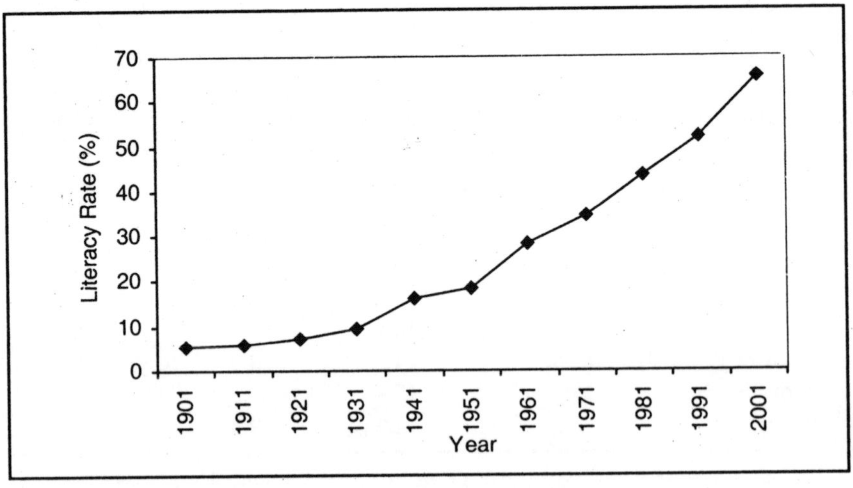

Fig. 3.3: Growth of Literacy of India During 20th Century

The graph shows that the country is, at present, maintaining an annual rate of literacy growth of approximately 1.3 per cent. If this growth rate is maintained constantly, India would reach a level of literacy of 78 per cent by the time of the decennial census of 2011. Assuming that achievable literacy for India means the sustainable threshold level of 75 per cent, then India could be expected to touch this level sometimes between 2007 and 2008. This would be earlier than the previous expectation of around 2011. Literacy position of each State and UT in 2001 census is shown in Figure 3.4

Variation in decadal growth rate of population and decadal growth rate of literacy of India and all its States and UTs between the decades 1981-1991and 1991-2001 is presented in Table 3.5. The data is tabulated in order of increasing growth rate of population during 1991-2001.

There is a declined trend on growth of population of States and UTs during the period 1991-2001 as compared to 1981-1991. Although the population of India is increasing but the rate of growth has been slowed down. On one side, the population of Daman and Diu recorded the highest growth rate of 27 per cent and on the other side, Andaman & Nicobar has not only arrested its growth rate but also declined it by 21.8 per cent. Similarly, comparison of literacy rates between two decades reveals that Rajasthan, newly created state of Chattisgarh, Madhya Pradesh, etc. have made significant contribution in increasing literacy, whereas much literate States and UTs like Kerala, Mizoram, Chandigarh, Lakshadweep, etc. have not made much progress in this regard.

3.6 MALE-FEMALE LITERACY RATES

Literacy implies a process of awareness and empowerment combined with the delivery of practical knowledge and skill-training. This is more true for programmes for girls and women. For them, literacy programmes are often the only systematically organised form of education, which makes them aware of their strength and potential. Therefore, many literacy programmes are turned out to be the women's development programmes. It is quite obvious that the literacy of parents and especially mothers has consequences for the education of their children.

Women are playing vital role in developing the nation. Educated woman makes her family educated and once families become educated, the continuous progress of the society and ultimately the nation can be obtained. For this, conducting adult and continuing education programmes for women are essential.

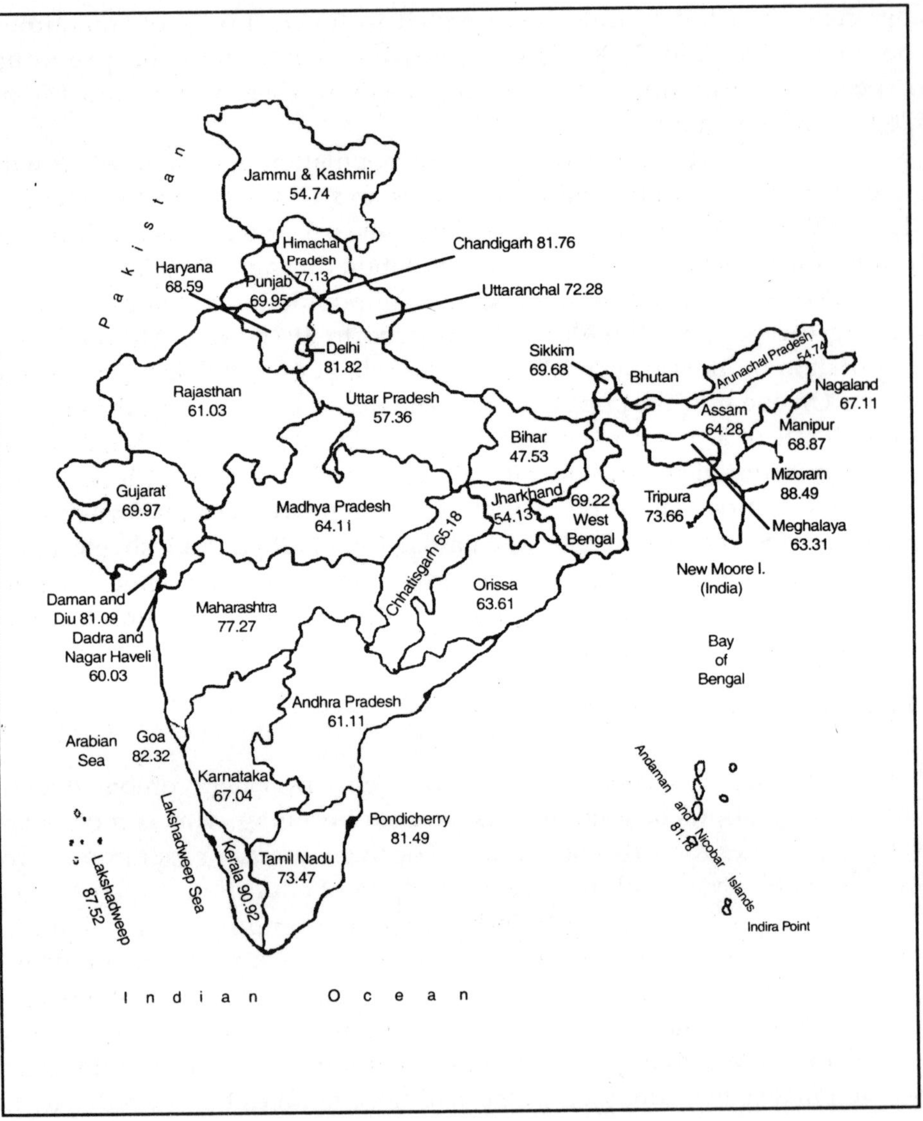

Fig. 3.4: Literacy Status of States and UTs in 2001

Table 3.5: Percentage Decadal Population Growth Rates and Decadal Literacy Growth Rates in States and UTs During 1981-91 and 1991-2001

Rank	*State*	*Variation in Decadal Growth Rate of Population (in %) 1991-2001 compared to 1981-1991*	*Variation in Decadal Growth Rate of Literacy (in %) 1991-2001 compared to 1981-1991*
	INDIA	–2.5	13.4
1.	Nagaland	+8.3	5.5
2.	Dadra & Nagar Haveli	+25.6	19.3
3.	Daman & Diu	+27.0	9.9
4.	Delhi	–5.1	6.5
5.	Chandigarh	–1.8	4.0
6.	Sikkim	+4.5	12.7
7.	Manipur	+0.7	9.0
8.	Meghalaya	–2.9	14.2
9.	Mizoram	–10.5	6.2
10.	Jammu & Kashmir	–1.3	NA
11.	Bihar	+5.1	10.0
12.	Rajasthan	–0.1	22.5
13.	Haryana	+0.7	12.7
14.	Andaman & Nicobar Islands	–21.8	8.2
15.	Arunachal Pradesh	–10.6	13.2
16.	Uttar Pradesh	+0.3	16.7
17.	Madhya Pradesh	–2.9	19.4
18.	Jharkhand	–0.8	12.7
19.	Maharashtra	–3.2	12.4
20.	Gujarat	+1.3	8.4
21.	Pondicherry	–13.1	6.8
22.	Punjab	–1.1	11.4
23.	Uttaranchal	–5.0	14.5
24.	Assam	–5.4	11.4
25.	Chattisgarh	–7.7	22.3
26.	West Bengal	–6.9	11.5
27.	Himachal Pradesh	–3.3	13.2
28.	Karnataka	–3.9	11.0
29.	Lakshadweep	–11.3	5.7
30.	Orissa	–4.1	14.5
31.	Tripura	–18.6	13.2
32.	Goa	–1.2	6.8
33.	Andhra Pradesh	–10.3	17.0
34.	Tamil Nadu	–4.2	10.8
35.	Kerala	–4.9	1.1

Note: Ranked according to Population Growth Rates during 1991-2001

Besides the fact that India has the world's largest number of professionally qualified women, more number of female doctors, surgeons, scientists and professors than the United States of America, and more number of working women than any other country in the world, it has the largest number of illiterate women in the world.

According to the last census held in 2001, the percentage of female literacy rate in the country was 54.20 per cent. The female literacy rate has increased from 0.60 per cent in 1901 to 54.20 per cent in 2001. The male literacy rate increased from 9.83 per cent in 1901 to 65.40 per cent in 2001. The female literacy rate was 11.20 per cent less than the country's overall literacy rate in 2001, whereas male literacy rate was 10.50 per cent higher than the country's literacy rate in the same census. The growth of male-female literacy rate in the 20th century is given in Table 3.6 and the same has been presented graphically in Figure 3.5.

Table 3.6: Growth of Male, Female and Total Literacy Rate in India During 1901-2001

Year	*Person*	*Male*	*Female*	*Gap in M-F Literacy Rate*
1901	05.35	09.83	00.60	09.23
1911	05.92	10.56	01.05	09.51
1921	07.16	12.21	01.81	10.40
1931	09.50	15.59	02.93	12.66
1941	16.10	24.90	07.30	17.60
1951*	18.33	27.16	08.86	18.30
1961**	28.31	40.40	15.34	25.06
1971	34.45	45.95	21.97	23.98
1981***	43.56	56.37	29.75	26.62
1991#	52.21	64.13	39.29	24.84
2001	65.40	75.90	54.20	21.70

* Excluding the population of Jammu & Kashmir, Pondicherry and NEFA, Dadra, Nagar Haveli and Diu.

** Excluding the population of Goa, Daman and Diu.

*** Excluding the population of Assam where 1981 Census was not held.

Excluding the population of Jammu & Kashmir where 1991 Census was not held.

Notes:

1. The literacy rate for the year 1931 relate to the population aged ten years and above.
2. The literacy rates for the years 1951, 1961, and 1971 relate to the population aged five years and above.

The literacy rates for the years 1981, 1991 and 2001 relate to the population aged seven years and above. The female literacy rate was increased by 9.54 per cent during 1981-1991, whereas the male literacy rate rose by 7.76 per cent during the same period. The female literacy rate during 1991-2001 was increased by 14.91 per cent whereas male literacy rate for the same period has risen by 13.19 per cent. Thus the faster rate of growth of literacy among females has not only been maintained but slightly enhanced. The credit goes to various literacy programmes for their special emphasis on women's participation in these programmes. Hence, the female literacy rate has actually increased more than the male literacy rate.

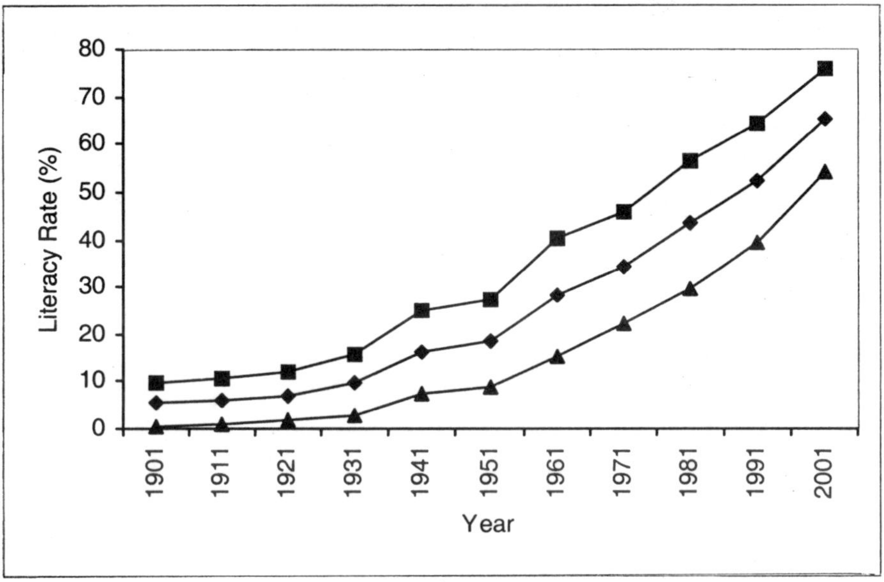

Fig. 3.5: Growth of Male and Female Literacy Rates in India During 20th Century

The variation of total literacy rate during the past one decade has been made more clear in Tables 3.7, 3.8 and 3.9 where literacy rate of males, females and total literacy rate have been tabulated for further analysis.

It is significant to note that Kerala, Mizoram and Lakshdweep occupied first, second and third positions respectively in 1991 census and retained the same positions in 2001 census also. Chandigarh has slipped down from 4th to 6th rank after one decade. Goa has jumped forward from 5th to 4th rank. Other States and UTs like Rajasthan, Madhya Pradesh, Uttaranchal, Chattisgarh, Andhra Pradesh, Uttar Pradesh, Orissa, Dadra & Nagar Haveli, Arunachal Pradesh and Jharkhand, where literacy rates were less than 50 per cent, have done significant progress in 2001. Bihar is the only state where literacy rate has not crossed half mark till now. This variation has been presented graphically in Figure 3.6.

Table 3.7: Variation of Total Literacy Rates in States and UTs During 1991-2001

	State/UT	*Total Literacy Rate (in %)*		
		2001	*1991*	*Variation*
	INDIA	65.4	52.0	13.4
1.	Jammu & Kashmir	54.5	NA	–
2.	Chattisgarh	65.2	42.9	22.3
3.	Rajasthan	61.0	38.6	22.5
4.	Madhya Pradesh	64.1	44.7	19.4
5.	Uttaranchal	72.3	57.8	14.5
6.	Uttar Pradesh	57.4	40.7	16.7
7.	Andhra Pradesh	61.1	44.1	17.0
8.	Orissa	63.6	49.1	14.5
9.	Dadra & Nagar Haveli	60.0	40.7	19.3
10.	Haryana	68.6	55.9	12.7
11.	Himachal Pradesh	77.1	63.9	13.2
12.	Tripura	73.7	60.4	13.2
13.	Meghalaya	63.3	49.1	14.2
14.	Maharashtra	77.3	64.9	12.4
15.	Sikkim	69.7	56.9	12.7
16.	Arunachal Pradesh	54.7	41.6	13.2
17.	Jharkhand	54.1	41.4	12.7
18.	West Bengal	69.2	57.7	11.5
19.	Tamil Nadu	73.5	62.7	10.8
20.	Punjab	70.0	58.5	11.4
21.	Karnataka	67.0	56.0	11.0
22.	Assam	64.3	52.9	11.4
23.	Manipur	68.9	59.9	9.0
24.	Bihar	47.5	37.5	10.0
25.	Daman & Diu	81.1	71.2	9.9
26.	Andaman & Nicobar Islands	81.2	73.0	8.2
27.	Gujarat	70.0	61.6	8.4
28.	Lakshadweep	87.5	81.8	5.7
29.	Pondicherry	81.5	74.7	6.8
30.	Goa	82.3	75.5	6.8
31.	Delhi	81.8	75.3	6.5
32.	Mizoram	88.5	82.3	6.2
33.	Nagaland	67.1	61.7	5.5
34.	Chandigarh	81.8	77.8	4.0
35.	Kerala	90.9	89.8	1.1

Table 3.8: Variation of Male Literacy Rates in States and UTs During 1991-2001

	State/UT	*Male Literacy Rate (in %)*		
		2001	*1991*	*Variation*
	INDIA	76.9	64.1	12.8
1.	Jammu & Kashmir	65.8	NA	—
2.	Chattisgarh	77.9	58.1	19.8
3.	Rajasthan	76.5	55.0	21.5
4.	Madhya Pradesh	76.8	58.5	18.3
5.	Uttaranchal	84.0	72.8	11.2
6.	Uttar Pradesh	70.2	54.8	15.4
7.	Andhra Pradesh	70.9	55.1	15.7
8.	Orissa	76.0	63.1	12.9
9.	Dadra & Nagar Haveli	73.3	53.6	19.8
10.	Haryana	79.3	69.1	10.2
11.	Himachal Pradesh	86.0	75.4	10.6
12.	Tripura	81.5	70.6	10.9
13.	Meghalaya	66.1	53.1	13.0
14.	Maharashtra	86.3	76.6	9.7
15.	Sikkim	76.7	65.7	11.0
16.	Arunachal Pradesh	64.1	51.5	12.6
17.	Jharkhand	67.9	55.8	12.1
18.	West Bengal	77.6	67.8	9.8
19.	Tamil Nadu	82.3	73.8	8.6
20.	Punjab	75.6	65.7	10.0
21.	Karnataka	76.3	67.3	9.0
22.	Assam	71.9	61.9	10.1
23.	Manipur	77.9	71.6	6.2
24.	Bihar	60.3	51.4	9.0
25.	Daman & Diu	88.4	82.7	5.7
26.	Andaman & Nicobar Islands	86.1	79.0	7.1
27.	Gujarat	80.5	73.4	7.1
28.	Lakshadweep	93.2	90.2	3.0
29.	Pondicherry	88.9	83.7	5.2
30.	Goa	88.9	83.6	5.2
31.	Delhi	87.4	82.0	5.4
32.	Mizoram	90.7	85.6	5.1
33.	Nagaland	71.8	67.6	4.1
34.	Chandigarh	85.7	82.0	3.6
35.	Kerala	94.2	93.6	0.0

The higher visible improvement of male literacy rate during 1991-2001 is for Rajasthan where it has moved forward by 21.5 per cent followed by Chattisgarh, Dadra & Nagar Haveli, Madhya Pradesh, Andhra Pradesh and Uttar Pradesh which show an improvement of 19.8 per cent, 19.8 per cent, 18.3 per cent, 15.7 per cent, and 15.4 per cent respectively. Since Kerala has already reached the saturation point of literacy, therefore, increase in male literacy was recorded as minimum of 1.1 per cent only. The variation of male and female literacy has been presented graphically in Figure 3.6. The variation of female literacy rates in States and UTs during 1991-2001 has been tabulated in Table 3.9.

Table 3.9: Variation of Female Literacy Rates in States and UTs During 1991-2001

	State/UT	*Female Literacy Rate (in %)*		
		2001	*1991*	*Variation*
	INDIA	54.2	39.3	14.9
1.	Jammu & Kashmir	41.8	NA	—
2.	Chattisgarh	52.4	27.5	24.9
3.	Rajasthan	44.3	20.4	23.9
4.	Madhya Pradesh	50.3	29.4	20.9
5.	Uttaranchal	60.3	41.6	18.6
6.	Uttar Pradesh	43.0	24.4	18.6
7.	Andhra Pradesh	51.2	32.7	18.5
8.	Orissa	51.0	34.7	16.3
9.	Dadra & Nagar Haveli	43.0	27.0	16.0
10.	Haryana	56.3	40.5	15.8
11.	Himachal Pradesh	68.1	52.3	15.8
12.	Tripura	65.4	49.7	15.8
13.	Meghalaya	60.4	44.9	15.6
14.	Maharashtra	67.5	52.3	15.8
15.	Sikkim	61.5	46.8	14.7
16.	Arunachal Pradesh	44.2	29.7	14.6
17.	Jharkhand	39.4	25.5	13.9
18.	West Bengal	60.2	46.6	13.7
19.	Tamil Nadu	64.6	51.3	13.2
20.	Punjab	63.6	50.4	13.1
21.	Karnataka	57.5	44.3	13.1
22.	Assam	56.0	43.0	13.0
23.	Manipur	59.7	47.6	12.1
24.	Bihar	33.6	22.0	11.6
25.	Daman & Diu	70.4	59.4	11.0
26.	Andaman & Nicobar Islands	75.3	65.5	9.8
27.	Gujarat	58.6	48.9	9.7
28.	Lakshadweep	81.6	72.9	8.7
29.	Pondicherry	74.1	65.6	8.5
30.	Goa	75.5	67.1	8.4
31.	Delhi	75.0	67.0	8.0
32.	Mizoram	86.1	78.6	7.5
33.	Nagaland	61.6	54.8	6.9
34.	Chandigarh	76.7	72.3	4.3
35.	Kerala	87.9	86.2	1.7

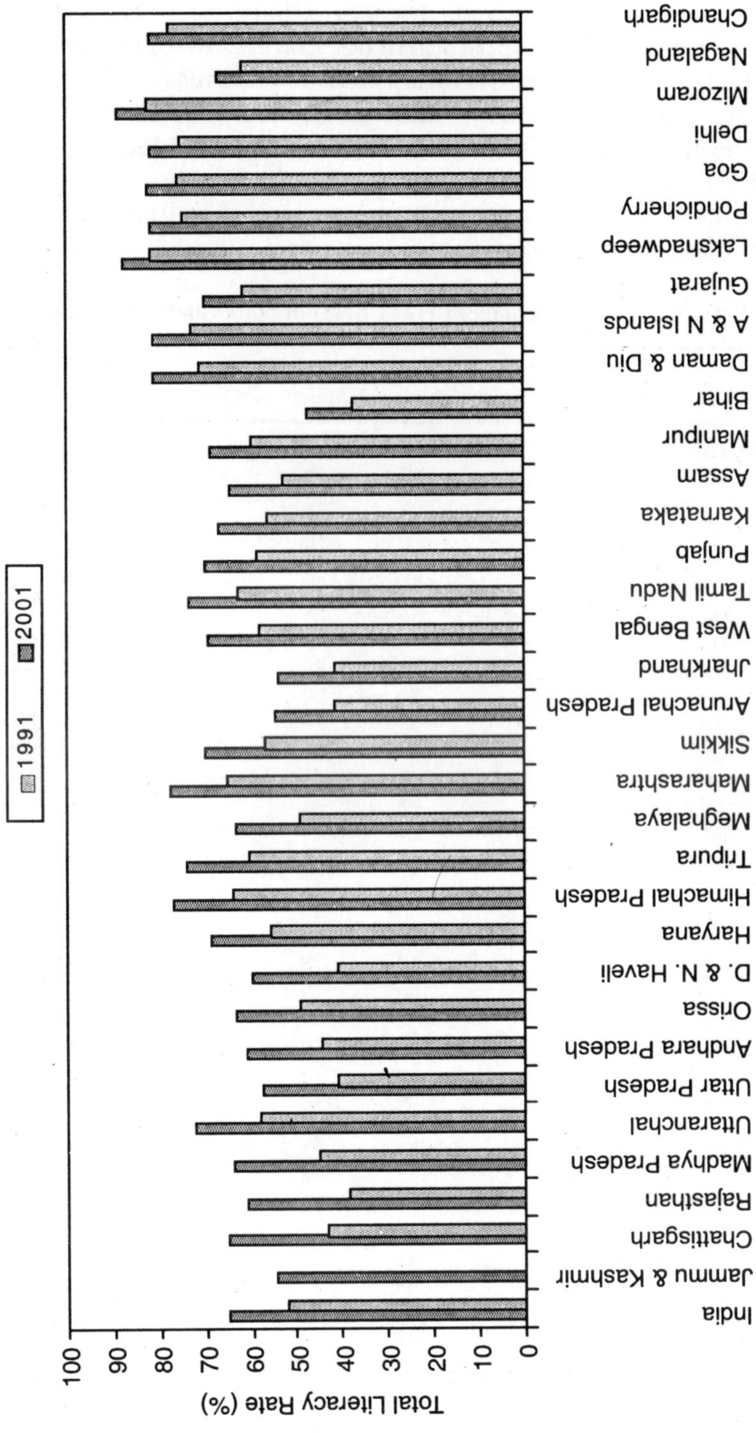

Fig. 3.6: Variation of Total Literacy Rates in States and UTs During 1991-2001

On the same pattern of male literacy, Chattisgarh and Rajasthan occupied the first and second position of decadal growth of female literacy respectively. These states have recorded creditable increase of 24.9 per cent and 23.9 per cent respectively. Madhya Pradesh, Uttaranchal, Uttar Pradesh, Andhra Pradesh, Orissa and Dadra & Nagar Haveli are the other States and UTs made significant improvement in decadal female literacy growth. Again, Kerala has shown minimum increase in literacy of 1.7 per cent during the same period.

Table 3.10: Variation in Male-Female Literacy Rates of States and UTs in 2001

Rank	*State/UT*	*Literacy Rate (in %)*			*Gap in M-F Literacy Rate*
		Females	*Males*	*Persons*	
	INDIA	54	76	65	22
1.	Kerala	88	94	91	6
2.	Mizoram	86	91	89	5
3.	Lakshadweep	82	93	88	11
4.	Chandigarh	77	86	82	9
5.	Goa	76	89	82	13
6.	Andaman & Nicobar Islands	75	86	81	11
7.	Delhi	75	87	82	12
8.	Pondicherry	74	89	81	15
9.	Daman & Diu	70	88	81	18
10.	Himachal Pradesh	68	86	77	18
11.	Maharashtra	68	86	77	18
12.	Tripura	65	81	74	16
13.	Tamil Nadu	65	82	73	17
14.	Punjab	64	76	70	12
15.	Nagaland	62	72	67	10
16.	Sikkim	61	77	70	16
17.	Meghalaya	60	66	63	6
18.	Uttaranchal	60	84	72	24
19.	West Bengal	60	78	69	18
20.	Manipur	60	78	69	18
21.	Gujarat	59	81	70	22
22.	Karnataka	57	76	67	19
23.	Haryana	56	79	69	23
24.	Assam	56	72	64	16
25.	Chattisgarh	52	78	65	26
26.	Andhra Pradesh	51	71	61	20
27.	Orissa	51	76	64	25
28.	Madhya Pradesh	50	77	64	27
29.	Rajasthan	44	76	61	32
30.	Arunachal Pradesh	44	64	55	20
31.	Dadra & Nagar Haveli	43	73	60	30
32.	Uttar Pradesh	43	70	57	27
33.	Jammu & Kashmir	42	66	54	24
34.	Jharkhand	39	68	54	29
35.	Bihar	34	60	48	26

Note: Ranked according to Female Literacy Rate

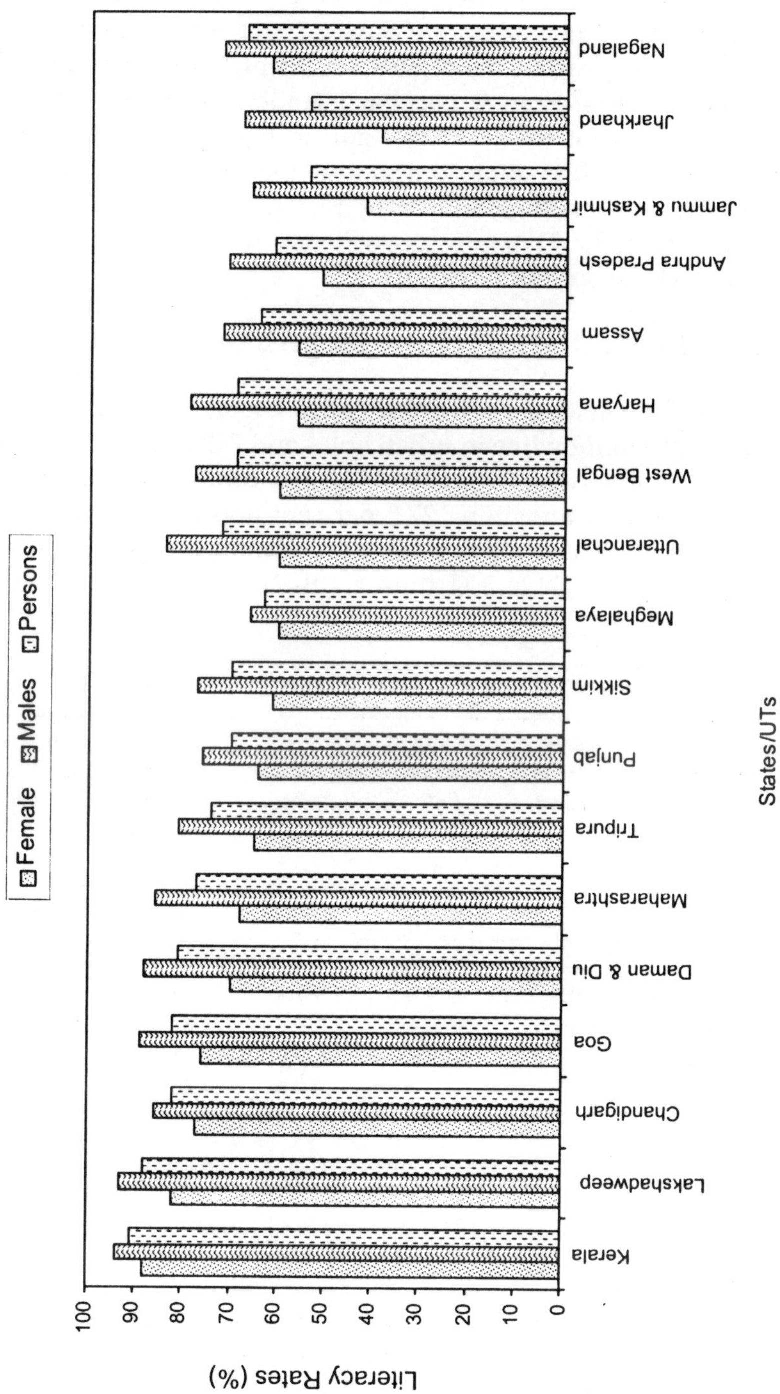

Fig. 3.7: Male, Female and Total Literacy Rates in States and UTs in 2001

Table 3.10 reveals that the country has observed only 5 per cent gap in male-female literacy rate in Mizoram during 2001 followed by Kerala and Meghalaya 6 per cent each, Chandigarh 9 per cent, Nagaland 10 per cent, Lakshadweep and Andaman & Nicobar Islands 11 per cent each, Delhi and Punjab 12 per cent each. Overall gap in male-female literacy was observed 22 per cent. It is important to note that relatively more literate States and UTs have less male-female literacy gap as compared to lesser literate States and UTs. This gap has widened more in northern states, particularly in Hindi speaking region.

3.7 RURAL-URBAN DISTRIBUTION OF LITERACY

According to last census held in 2001, out of total population of 1027 million, about 285 million live in urban areas and 742 million live in rural areas. In other words, we can say that 72.2 per cent population of India live in rural areas and remaining 27.2 per cent population live in urban areas. Therefore, we have to pay more attention for the improvement in literacy in rural areas. Table 3.11 presents the rural-urban literacy rates from 1961 to 2001.

Table 3.11: Rural-Urban Distribution of Total Literacy in India During 1961-2001

Year	*Urban Literacy Rate*	*Increase in Urban Literacy Rate*	*Rural Literacy Rate*	*Increase in Rural Literacy Rate*	*Difference in Urban-Rural Literacy Rate*	*Increase in Urban-Rural Literacy Rate*
	(A)	(B)	(C)	(D)	(A-C)	(B-D)
1961	54.4%	—	22.5%	—	31.9%	—
1971	60.2%	5.8%	27.9%	5.4%	32.3%	+0.4%
1981	67.2%	7.0%	36.0%	8.1%	31.2%	–1.1%
1991	73.1%	5.9%	44.5%	8.5%	28.6%	–2.6%
2001	80.1%	7.0%	59.2%	14.7%	20.9%	–7.7%

Notes:

1. The literacy rates for the years 1961 and 1971 relate to the population aged five years and above.
2. The literacy rates for the years 1981, 1991 and 2001 relate to the population aged seven years and above.

The average increase in literacy rate from 1961 to 2001 was not more than 7 per cent in urban areas during any decade, whereas, it was reached to 14.7 per cent in the rural areas during 1991-2001. The urban-rural difference in literacy rates has also shown a mark decline in the successive years. This difference was 31.9 per cent in 1961, which was reduced to 20.9 per cent in 2001. The rapidity of growth of literacy in rural areas was more during 1991-2001 as compared to any previous decades.

A big difference was found between male and female literacy rates in rural and urban areas in every State and UTs of the country. Even in certain states, this margin was found almost double. To know the status of male, female and total literacy rate in urban and rural areas in the country, an analysis for the year 1991 and 2001 is given in Table 3.12.

Almost in every State and UT, the literacy rate in urban areas was higher than the rural areas as per Census Reports of 1991 and 2001. Women belonging to the rural areas were found to be the most backward as far as literacy is concerned. Female literacy rate in the rural areas of Rajasthan was just 11.59 per cent in 1991 hich increased to 37.74 per cent in 2001. In the same state, urban female literacy rate was two times higher than the female literacy rate in rural areas. Similar situation was in Haryana, where urban female literacy rate was almost double the literacy rate of rural female. The case of Delhi was quite different from these two states. Here difference in urban-rural literacy rate in female was just 7 per cent and urban-rural male literacy rate was just 0.23 per cent in 2001. The basic reason for thin literacy rate in rural areas may be due to the lack of adult education centres, learning materials, awareness of benefits of being literate and educated citizen. In urban areas, schools and other academic institutions are at the approachable distance. Another reason for low literacy may be the poor economic conditions and unemployment of people living in the rural areas.

3.8 GROWTH OF LITERACY RATE IN INDIA DURING PAST TWO DECADES

India is a vast country, with varying levels of economic and human development performance among its various States and UTs. As such, to get a better picture of India's literacy and educational progress, one needs to have a desegregated profile by State and UT. The literacy position of States and UTs during the census held in 1981, 1991 and 2001 are given in Table 3.13, Table 3.14 and Table 3.15 respectively. Overall picture of decadal growth of literacy in 1981-1991 and 1991-2001 with their rankings are given in Table 3.16 and 3.17 respectively.

Table 3.12: Rural-Urban Distribution of Male, Female, and Total Literacy Rates in States and UTs in 1991and 2001

State/UT		Literacy Rate (in %)					
		Person 1991	Person 2001	Male 1991	Male 2001	Female 1991	Female 2001
1. Andhra Pradesh	Rural	35.74	55.33	47.28	66.13	23.92	44.36
	Urban	66.35	76.39	75.87	83.21	56.41	69.34
	Total	44.09	61.11	55.13	70.85	32.72	51.17
2. Arunachal Pradesh	Rural	37.02	48.34	47.00	58.09	25.31	37.56
	Urban	71.59	78.82	77.99	85.61	62.23	70.60
	Total	41.59	54.74	51.45	64.07	29.69	44.24
3. Assam	Rural	49.32	60.92	58.66	69.02	39.19	52.25
	Urban	79.39	85.76	84.37	89.88	73.32	81.03
	Total	52.89	64.28	61.87	71.93	43.03	56.03
4. Bihar	Rural	33.83	44.42	48.31	57.70	17.95	30.03
	Urban	67.89	72.71	77.72	80.80	55.94	63.30
	Total	38.48	47.53	52.49	60.32	22.89	33.57
5. Goa	Rural	72.31	79.65	81.71	87.69	62.87	71.55
	Urban	80.10	85.03	86.33	90.06	73.38	79.65
	Total	75.51	82.32	83.64	88.88	67.09	75.51
6. Gujarat	Rural	53.09	58.53	66.84	70.71	38.65	45.75
	Urban	76.54	79.24	84.56	85.46	67.70	72.23
	Total	61.29	66.43	73.13	76.46	48.64	55.61
7. Haryana	Rural	49.85	63.82	64.78	76.13	32.51	49.77
	Urban	73.66	79.89	81.96	86.58	64.06	72.05
	Total	55.85	68.59	69.10	79.25	40.47	56.31
8. Himachal Pradesh	Rural	61.86	74.38	73.89	83.58	49.79	65.23
	Urban	84.17	89.59	88.97	92.49	78.32	85.91
	Total	63.86	75.91	75.36	84.57	52.13	67.08
9. Karnataka	Rural	47.69	59.68	60.30	70.63	34.76	48.50
	Urban	74.20	81.05	82.04	86.85	65.74	74.87
	Total	56.04	67.04	67.26	76.29	44.34	57.45
10. Kerala	Rural	88.92	90.05	92.91	93.54	85.12	86.79
	Urban	92.25	93.38	95.58	96.07	89.06	90.87
	Total	89.81	90.92	93.62	94.20	86.17	87.86
11. Madhya Pradesh	Rural	35.87	58.10	51.04	72.10	19.73	42.96
	Urban	70.81	79.67	81.32	87.78	58.92	70.62
	Total	44.20	64.08	58.42	76.50	28.85	50.55
12. Maharashtra	Rural	55.52	70.84	69.74	82.17	40.96	59.12
	Urban	79.20	85.76	86.41	91.42	70.87	79.25
	Total	64.87	77.27	76.56	86.27	52.32	67.51
13. Manipur	Rural	55.79	65.33	67.64	74.50	43.26	55.88
	Urban	70.53	80.04	82.11	88.72	58.67	71.47
	Total	59.89	68.87	71.63	77.87	47.60	59.70
14. Meghalaya	Rural	41.05	57.00	44.83	59.90	37.12	54.02

Table 3.12 *contd.*

State/UT		*Literacy Rate (in %)* *Person* 1991	*Person* 2001	*Male* 1991	*Male* 2001	*Female* 1991	*Female* 2001
	Urban	81.74	87.12	85.72	98.90	77.32	84.30
	Total	49.10	63.31	53.12	66.14	44.85	60.41
15. Mizoram	Rural	72.47	80.46	77.36	84.38	67.03	76.17
	Urban	93.45	96.35	95.15	96.97	91.61	95.69
	Total	82.27	88.49	85.61	90.69	78.60	86.13
16. Nagaland	Rural	57.23	62.99	63.42	67.73	50.36	57.87
	Urban	83.10	85.95	85.94	89.01	79.10	82.09
	Total	61.65	67.11	67.62	71.77	54.75	61.92
17. Orissa	Rural	45.46	60.44	60.00	73.57	30.79	47.22
	Urban	71.99	80.95	81.21	88.32	61.18	72.68
	Total	49.09	63.61	63.09	75.95	34.68	50.97
18. Punjab	Rural	52.77	65.16	60.71	71.70	43.85	57.91
	Urban	72.08	79.13	77.26	82.97	66.12	74.63
	Total	58.51	69.95	65.66	75.63	50.41	63.55
19. Rajasthan	Rural	30.37	55.92	47.64	72.96	11.59	37.74
	Urban	65.33	76.89	78.50	87.10	50.24	65.42
	Total	38.55	61.03	54.99	76.46	20.44	44.34
20. Sikkim	Rural	54.39	67.67	63.44	75.11	44.06	59.05
	Urban	80.89	84.82	85.19	88.61	74.90	80.19
	Total	56.94	69.68	65.70	76.73	46.76	61.46
21. Tamil Nadu	Rural	54.59	66.66	67.18	77.47	41.84	55.84
	Urban	77.99	82.07	86.06	88.40	69.61	75.64
	Total	62.66	73.47	73.75	82.33	51.33	64.55
22. Tripura	Rural	56.08	70.23	67.07	78.89	44.33	61.05
	Urban	83.09	89.51	89.00	93.51	76.93	85.36
	Total	60.44	73.66	70.58	81.47	49.65	65.41
23. Uttar Pradesh	Rural	36.66	53.68	52.05	68.01	19.02	37.74
	Urban	61.00	70.61	69.98	78.13	50.38	62.05
	Total	41.60	57.36	55.73	70.23	25.31	42.97
24. West Bengal	Rural	50.50	64.06	62.05	73.75	38.12	53.82
	Urban	75.27	81.63	81.19	86.49	68.25	76.14
	Total	57.70	69.22	67.81	77.58	46.56	60.22
25. Andaman & Nicobar Islands	Rural	69.73	78.55	75.99	83.90	61.99	72.23
	Urban	81.69	86.48	86.59	90.35	75.08	81.65
	Total	73.02	81.18	78.99	86.07	65.46	75.29
26. Chandigarh	Rural	59.12	76.23	65.67	81.54	47.83	67.17
	Urban	79.87	82.36	84.09	86.16	74.57	77.53
	Total	77.81	81.76	82.04	85.65	72.34	76.65
27. Dadar & NagarHaveli	Rural	37.00	52.24	50.04	67.13	23.30	34.08
	Urban	78.44	85.25	86.35	91.57	68.42	75.67
	Total	40.71	60.03	53.56	73.32	26.98	42.99

Table 3.12 *contd.*

State/UT		Literacy Rate (in %) Person 1991	Person 2001	Male 1991	Male 2001	Female 1991	Female 2001
28. Daman & Diu	Rural	61.55	78.31	75.23	86.48	46.70	63.31
	Urban	81.61	85.96	91.14	92.72	72.35	79.14
	Total	71.20	81.09	82.66	88.48	59.40	70.37
29. Delhi	Rural	66.90	78.75	78.46	87.15	52.15	68.23
	Urban	76.18	82.04	82.39	87.38	68.54	75.49
	Total	75.29	81.82	82.01	87.37	66.99	75.00
30. Lakshadweep	Rural	78.89	86.39	88.66	92.56	68.72	79.86
	Urban	83.99	88.89	91.31	93.85	76.11	83.60
	Total	81.78	87.52	90.18	93.15	72.89	81.56
31. Pondicherry	Rural	65.36	74.28	76.44	83.87	53.96	64.63
	Urban	79.88	85.05	87.70	91.40	71.98	78.78
	Total	74.74	81.49	83.68	88.89	65.63	74.13
32. Jammu & Kashmir	Rural	—	48.22	—	60.34	—	35.09
	Urban	—	72.17	—	80.30	—	62.22
	Total	—	54.46	—	65.75	—	41.82
33. Uttaranchal	Rural	—	68.95	—	82.74	—	55.52
	Urban	—	81.50	—	87.21	—	74.77
	Total	—	72.28	—	84.01	—	60.26
34. Jharkhand	Rural	—	46.26	—	61.57	—	30.33
	Urban	—	79.86	—	87.73	—	70.71
	Total	—	54.13	—	67.94	—	39.38
35. Chattisgarh	Rural	—	60.93	—	74.58	—	47.41
	Urban	—	81.08	—	89.87	—	71.63
	Total	—	65.12	—	77.86	—	52.28
36. India	Rural	44.69	59.21	57.87	71.18	30.62	46.58
	Urban	—	80.06	—	86.42	—	72.99
	Total	52.21	65.20	64.13	75.64	39.29	54.03

Notes:
1. Census was not held in Jammu & Kashmir in 1991.
2. The literacy rates for the years 1991 and 2001 relate to the population aged five years and above.
3. States of Bihar, Uttar Pradesh and Madhya Pradesh also include data for Jharkhand, Uttaranchal and Chattisgarh, respectively.

Source: Census of India 1991 and 2001

Kerala, Chandigarh, Mizoram, Delhi, Lakshadweep, Goa, Pondicherry, Andaman & Nicobar Islands, Daman & Diu and Maharashtra occupied first ten ranks of males, females and total literacy during 1981. Arunachal Pradesh, Jammu & Kashmir, Rajasthan, Bihar, Uttar Pradesh and Dadra &

Nagar Haveli were the States and UTs where literacy rate was found much below than the average national literacy rate.

Table 3.13: Ranking of Literacy Rates in States and UTs in 1981

Sl. No.	*State/UT*	*Literacy Rate (in %) and Rank*					
		Person	*(Rank)*	*Male*	*(Rank)*	*Female*	*(Rank)*
1.	Andhra Pradesh	35.66	(25)	46.83	(26)	24.16	(25)
2.	Arunachal Pradesh	25.55	(32)	35.12	(32)	14.02	(31)
3.	Assam*	—	—	—	—	—	—
4.	Bihar	32.05	(30)	46.60	(28)	16.52	(30)
5.	Goa	65.71	(6)	76.01	(7)	55.17	(6)
6.	Gujarat	52.21	(12)	65.14	(12)	38.46	(14)
7.	Haryana	43.88	(20)	58.51	(19)	26.93	(23)
8.	Himachal Pradesh	51.18	(13)	64.27	(13)	37.72	(16)
9.	Jammu & Kashmir	32.68	(29)	44.18	(31)	19.55	(27)
10.	Karnataka	46.21	(19)	58.73	(17)	33.17	(20)
11.	Kerala	81.56	(1)	87.73	(1)	75.65	(1)
12.	Madhya Pradesh	34.23	(26)	48.42	(24)	19.00	(28)
13.	Maharashtra	55.83	(10)	69.65	(10)	41.01	(10)
14.	Manipur	49.66	(16)	64.15	(14)	34.67	(19)
15.	Meghalaya	42.05	(22)	46.65	(27)	37.17	(17)
16.	Mizoram	74.26	(3)	79.36	(3)	68.61	(3)
17.	Nagaland	50.28	(14)	58.58	(18)	40.39	(12)
18.	Orissa	40.97	(24)	56.45	(21)	25.14	(24)
19.	Punjab	48.17	(18)	55.56	(22)	39.70	(13)
20.	Rajasthan	30.11	(31)	44.74	(29)	14.00	(32)
21.	Sikkim	41.59	(23)	53.00	(23)	27.38	(22)
22.	Tamil Nadu	54.39	(11)	68.05	(11)	40.43	(11)
23.	Tripura	50.11	(15)	61.49	(15)	38.01	(15)
24.	Uttar Pradesh	33.35	(27)	47.45	(25)	17.19	(29)
25.	West Bengal	48.65	(17)	59.93	(16)	36.07	(18)
26.	Andaman & Nicobar Islands	63.19	(8)	70.29	(9)	53.19	(7)
27.	Chandigarh	74.81	(2)	78.89	(5)	69.31	(2)
28.	Dadar & Nagar Haveli	32.70	(28)	44.64	(30)	20.37	(26)
29.	Daman & Diu	59.91	(9)	74.47	(8)	46.50	(9)
30.	Delhi	71.94	(4)	79.28	(4)	62.60	(4)
31.	Lakshadweep	68.42	(5)	81.24	(2)	55.32	(5)
32.	Pondicherry	65.14	(7)	77.09	(6)	53.03	(8)
33.	Uttaranchal	—	—	—	—	—	—
34.	Chattisgarh	—	—	—	—	—	—
35.	Jharkhand	—	—	—	—	—	—
	INDIA	43.67	(21)	56.50	(20)	29.85	(21)

* Census was not conducted in 1981 in Assam.

Notes: 1. Source: Census of India 1981

2. Literacy rate for 1981 census relate to the population of 7+ years

Table 3.14: Ranking of Literacy Rates in States and UTs in 1991

		Literacy Rate (in %) and Rank					
Sl. No.	*State/UT*	*Person*	*(Rank)*	*Male*	*(Rank)*	*Female*	*(Rank)*
1.	Andhra Pradesh	44.09	(27)	55.13	(27)	32.72	(26)
2.	Arunachal Pradesh	41.59	(29)	51.45	(32)	29.69	(27)
3.	Assam	52.89	(22)	61.87	(24)	43.03	(22)
4.	Bihar	38.48	(32)	52.49	(31)	22.89	(31)
5.	Goa	75.51	(5)	83.64	(5)	67.09	(5)
6.	Gujarat	61.29	(14)	73.13	(13)	48.64	(16)
7.	Haryana	55.85	(21)	69.10	(16)	40.47	(23)
8.	Himachal Pradesh	63.86	(11)	75.36	(11)	52.13	(12)
9.	Jammu & Kashmir*	—	—	—	—	—	—
10.	Karnataka	56.04	(20)	67.26	(19)	44.34	(21)
11.	Kerala	89.81	(1)	93.62	(1)	86.17	(1)
12.	Madhya Pradesh	44.20	(26)	58.42	(25)	28.85	(28)
13.	Maharashtra	64.87	(10)	76.56	(10)	52.32	(11)
14.	Manipur	59.89	(16)	71.63	(14)	47.60	(17)
15.	Meghalaya	49.10	(24)	53.12	(30)	44.85	(20)
16.	Mizoram	82.27	(2)	85.61	(3)	78.60	(2)
17.	Nagaland	61.65	(13)	67.62	(18)	54.75	(10)
18.	Orissa	49.09	(25)	63.09	(23)	34.68	(25)
19.	Punjab	58.51	(17)	65.66	(21)	50.41	(14)
20.	Rajasthan	38.55	(31)	54.99	(28)	20.44	(32)
21.	Sikkim	56.94	(19)	65.74	(20)	46.69	(18)
22.	Tamil Nadu	62.66	(12)	73.75	(12)	51.33	(13)
23.	Tripura	60.44	(15)	70.58	(15)	49.65	(15)
24.	Uttar Pradesh	41.60	(28)	55.73	(26)	25.31	(30)
25.	West Bengal	57.70	(18)	67.81	(17)	46.56	(19)
26.	Andaman & Nicobar Islands	73.02	(8)	78.99	(9)	65.46	(8)
27.	Chandigarh	77.81	(4)	82.04	(7)	72.34	(3)
28.	Dadar & Nagar Haveli	40.71	(30)	53.56	(29)	26.98	(29)
29.	Daman & Diu	71.20	(9)	82.66	(6)	59.40	(9)
30.	Delhi	75.29	(6)	82.01	(8)	66.99	(6)
31.	Lakshadweep	81.78	(3)	90.18	(2)	72.09	(4)
32.	Pondicherry	74.74	(7)	83.68	(4)	65.63	(7)
33.	Uttaranchal	—	—	—	—	—	—
34.	Chattisgarh	—	—	—	—	—	—
35.	Jharkhand	—	—	—	—	—	—
	INDIA	52.21	(23)	64.13	(22)	39.29	(24)

* Census was not conducted in 1991 in Jammu & Kashmir.

Notes: 1. Source: Census of India 1991

2. Literacy rate for 1991 census relate to the population of 7+ years

Again Kerala, Mizoram, Lakshadweep, Chandigarh, Goa, Delhi, Pondicherry, Andaman & Nicobar Islands, Daman & Diu and Maharashtra occupied first ten ranks of males, females and total literacy rate during 1991. The only difference was that Chandigarh slipped down from 2nd to 4th position, Delhi from 4th to 6th position. On the contrary, Mizoram jumped forward from 3rd to 2nd, Lakshadweep from 5th to 3rd position and Goa from 6th to 5th position. Bihar, Arunachal Pradesh, Rajasthan, Dadra & Nagar Haveli, Uttar Pradesh and Meghalaya have not made much progress in this regard.

Table 3.15: Ranking of Literacy Rates in States and UTs in 2001

		Literacy Rate (in %) and Rank					
Sl. No.	*State/UT*	*Person*	*(Rank)*	*Male*	*(Rank)*	*Female*	*(Rank)*
1.	Andhra Pradesh	61.11	(28)	70.85	(29)	51.17	(26)
2.	Arunachal Pradesh	54.74	(32)	64.07	(34)	44.24	(30)
3.	Assam	64.28	(24)	71.93	(27)	56.03	(24)
4.	Bihar	47.53	(35)	60.32	(35)	33.57	(35)
5.	Goa	82.32	(4)	88.88	(5)	75.51	(5)
6.	Gujarat	69.97	(15)	80.50	(15)	58.60	(21)
7.	Haryana	68.59	(20)	79.25	(16)	56.31	(23)
8.	Himachal Pradesh	77.13	(11)	86.02	(10)	68.08	(10)
9.	Jammu & Kashmir	54.46	(33)	65.75	(33)	41.82	(33)
10.	Karnataka	67.04	(22)	76.29	(23)	57.45	(22)
11.	Kerala	90.92	(1)	94.20	(1)	87.86	(1)
12.	Madhya Pradesh	64.11	(25)	76.80	(20)	50.28	(28)
13.	Maharashtra	77.27	(10)	86.27	(8)	67.51	(11)
14.	Manipur	68.87	(19)	77.87	(17)	59.70	(20)
15.	Meghalaya	63.31	(27)	66.14	(32)	60.41	(17)
16.	Mizoram	88.49	(2)	90.69	(3)	86.13	(2)
17.	Nagaland	67.11	(21)	71.77	(28)	61.92	(15)
18.	Orissa	63.61	(26)	75.95	(23)	50.97	(27)
19.	Punjab	69.95	(16)	75.63	(25)	63.55	(14)
20.	Rajasthan	61.03	(29)	76.46	(22)	44.34	(29)
21.	Sikkim	69.68	(17)	76.73	(21)	61.46	(16)
22.	Tamil Nadu	73.47	(13)	83.33	(13)	64.55	(13)
23.	Tripura	73.66	(12)	81.47	(14)	65.41	(12)
24.	Uttar Pradesh	57.36	(31)	70.23	(30)	42.98	(32)
25.	West Bengal	69.22	(18)	77.58	(19)	60.22	(19)
26.	Andaman & Nicobar Islands	81.18	(8)	86.07	(9)	75.29	(6)
27.	Chandigarh	81.76	(6)	85.65	(11)	76.65	(4)
28.	Dadra & Nagar Haveli	60.03	(30)	73.32	(26)	42.99	(31)
29.	Daman & Diu	81.09	(9)	88.40	(6)	70.37	(9)
30.	Delhi	81.82	(5)	87.37	(7)	75.00	(7)
31.	Lakshadweep	87.52	(3)	93.15	(2)	81.56	(3)
32.	Pondicherry	81.49	(7)	88.89	(4)	74.13	(8)
33.	Uttaranchal	72.28	(14)	84.01	(12)	60.26	(18)
34.	Chattisgarh	65.18	(23)	77.86	(18)	52.40	(25)
35.	Jharkhand	54.13	(34)	67.94	(31)	39.38	(34)
	INDIA	65.49	(22)	75.9	(24)	54.2	(24)

Note: 1. Literacy rate for 2001 census relate to the population of 7+ years
Source: Census of India 2001

First time in 2001, census was held in three newly created states of Chattisgarh, Jharkhand and Uttaranchal. This time again first top ten positions were occupied by Kerala, Mizoram, Lakshadweep, Goa, Delhi, Chandigarh, Pondicherry, Andaman & Nicobar Islands, Daman & Diu and Maharashtra in total literacy rate in 2001. UT of Chandigarh again slipped down from 4th to 6th position. On the other hand, Goa jumped forward from 5th to 4th position and Delhi from 6th to 5th position. Bihar was the least literate state, followed by Jharkhand, Jammu & Kashmir, Arunachal Pradesh, Uttar Pradesh, Dadra & Nagar Haveli, etc. Data given in Table 3.15 is presented graphically in Figure 3.7.

Decadal growth rates of literacy of States and UTs during past two decades i.e. 1981-1991 and 1991-2001, have been reflected in Table 3.16 and Table 3.17 respectively.

There were 23 States and UTs, which had higher literacy growth rate than the national average growth rate during 1981-1991. Arunachal Pradesh was the top ranker among all States and UTs in overall as well as male literacy rate during 1981-1991. Sikkim scored the second position in this literacy rank list. Delhi, Haryana and Rajasthan were at the 27th, 5th and 18th positions respectively. Arunachal Pradesh, Sikkim, Lakshadweep, Himachal Pradesh, Haryana, Nagaland, Daman & Diu, Punjab, Tripura, Manipur were the States and UTs which had made significant contribution in improvement of total literacy rate in during 1981-1991. Madhya Pradesh and Rajasthan were the exceptions which were ranked 7th and 5th in increasing of male literacy rate. Status of Bihar was not improved during this period.

Rajasthan, Madhya Pradesh, Dadra & Nagar Haveli, Andhra Pradesh, Uttar Pradesh, Orissa, Meghalaya, Himachal Pradesh, Tripura, Arunachal Pradesh were the first top ten States and UTs which improved their literacy rates during the past one decade. In terms of female literacy, Haryana has made significant improvement and ranked at 8th place. Bihar was again far away from the race of literacy. On the other hand, Rajasthan has done remarkable improvement in this direction which may be due to various literacy and educational programmes. States and UTs like Kerala, Chandigarh, Lakshadweep, Pondicherry, where literacy rates were above the average national literacy rate, have reached near saturation and consequently they have very little for improvement in literacy.

A comparative decadal growth of male, female and total literacy rates of States and UTs has been given in Figure 3.8.

Table 3.16: Decadal Growth of Literacy Rates in States and UTs During 1981-91

Sl. No.	State/UT	Person	(Rank)	Male	(Rank)	Female	(Rank)
		Literacy Rate (in %) and Rank					
1.	Andhra Pradesh	08.43	(19)	08.30	(14)	08.56	(23)
2.	Arunachal Pradesh	16.04	(1)	16.33	(1)	15.67	(3)
3.	Assam*	—	—	—	—	—	—
4.	Bihar	06.43	(26)	05.89	(26)	06.36	(28)
5.	Goa	09.80	(13)	07.63	(19)	11.92	(11)
6.	Gujarat	09.08	(15)	07.99	(17)	10.18	(19)
7.	Haryana	11.97	(5)	10.59	(4)	13.54	(6)
8.	Himachal Pradesh	12.68	(4)	11.09	(3)	14.41	(4)
9.	Jammu & Kashmir*	—	—	—	—	—	—
10.	Karnataka	09.83	(12)	08.53	(13)	11.17	(14)
11.	Kerala	08.25	(21)	05.89	(26)	10.52	(17)
12.	Madhya Pradesh	09.97	(11)	10.00	(7)	09.85	(20)
13.	Maharashtra	09.04	(17)	06.91	(21)	11.31	(13)
14.	Manipur	10.23	(10)	07.48	(20)	12.93	(7)
15.	Meghalaya	07.05	(25)	06.47	(24)	07.68	(25)
16.	Mizoram	08.01	(23)	06.25	(25)	09.99	(19)
17.	Nagaland	11.37	(6)	09.04	(9)	14.36	(5)
18.	Orissa	08.12	(22)	06.64	(22)	09.54	(21)
19.	Punjab	10.34	(8)	10.10	(6)	10.71	(16)
20.	Rajasthan	08.44	(18)	10.25	(5)	06.44	(27)
21.	Sikkim	15.35	(2)	12.74	(2)	19.31	(1)
22.	Tamil Nadu	08.27	(20)	05.70	(27)	10.90	(15)
23.	Tripura	10.33	(9)	09.09	(8)	11.64	(12)
24.	Uttar Pradesh	08.25	(21)	08.28	(15)	08.12	(24)
25.	West Bengal	09.05	(16)	07.88	(18)	10.49	(18)
26.	Andaman & Nicobar Islands	09.83	(12)	08.70	(12)	12.27	(10)
27.	Chandigarh	03.00	(28)	03.15	(28)	03.03	(30)
28.	Dadra & Nicobar Haveli	08.01	(23)	08.92	(11)	06.61	(26)
29.	Daman & Diu	11.29	(7)	08.19	(16)	12.90	(8)
30.	Delhi	03.35	(27)	02.73	(29)	04.39	(29)
31.	Lakshadweep	13.36	(3)	08.94	(10)	16.77	(2)
32.	Pondicherry	09.60	(14)	06.59	(23)	12.60	(9)
33.	Uttaranchal	—	—	—	—	—	—
34.	Chattisgarh	—	—	—	—	—	—
35.	Jharkhand	—	—	—	—	—	—
	INDIA	07.54	(24)	07.63	(19)	09.44	(22)

*Census was not conducted in Assam in 1981 and in Jammu & Kashmir in 1991.

Note: The literacy rate for 1981 census and 1991 census relate to the population of 7+ years.

Table 3.17: Decadal Growth of Literacy Rates in States and UTs During 1991-2001

		Literacy Rate (in %) and Rank					
Sl. No.	*State/UT*	*Person*	*(Rank)*	*Male*	*(Rank)*	*Female*	*(Rank)*
1.	Andhra Pradesh	17.02	(4)	15.72	(4)	18.45	(3)
2.	Arunachal Pradesh	13.15	(10)	12.62	(8)	14.55	(13)
3.	Assam	11.39	(15)	10.06	(13)	13.00	(18)
4.	Bihar	09.05	(19)	07.90	(19)	10.68	(21)
5.	Goa	06.81	(24)	05.24	(26)	08.42	(27)
6.	Gujarat	08.68	(21)	07.37	(21)	09.96	(22)
7.	Haryana	12.74	(11)	10.15	(12)	15.84	(8)
8.	Himachal Pradesh	13.27	(8)	10.66	(11)	15.95	(7)
9.	Jammu & Kashmir*	—	—	—	—	—	—
10.	Karnataka	11.00	(16)	09.03	(18)	13.11	(17)
11.	Kerala	01.11	(31)	00.58	(32)	01.69	(32)
12.	Madhya Pradesh	19.91	(2)	18.38	(3)	21.43	(2)
13.	Maharashtra	12.40	(12)	09.71	(16)	15.19	(11)
14.	Manipur	08.98	(20)	06.24	(23)	12.10	(19)
15.	Meghalaya	14.21	(7)	13.02	(6)	15.56	(10)
16.	Mizoram	06.22	(27)	05.08	(28)	07.53	(29)
17.	Nagaland	05.46	(29)	04.15	(29)	07.17	(30)
18.	Orissa	14.52	(6)	12.86	(7)	16.29	(5)
19.	Punjab	11.44	(14)	09.97	(14)	13.14	(16)
20.	Rajasthan	22.44	(1)	21.47	(1)	23.90	(1)
21.	Sikkim	12.74	(11)	10.99	(9)	14.77	(12)
22.	Tamil Nadu	10.81	(17)	09.58	(17)	13.22	(15)
23.	Tripura	13.22	(9)	10.89	(10)	15.76	(9)
24.	Uttar Pradesh	15.76	(5)	14.50	(5)	17.67	(4)
25.	West Bengal	11.52	(13)	09.77	(15)	13.66	(14)
26.	Andaman & Nicobar Islands	08.16	(22)	07.08	(22)	09.83	(23)
27.	Chandigarh	03.95	(30)	03.61	(30)	04.31	(31)
28.	Dadra & Nagar Haveli	19.32	(3)	19.76	(2)	16.01	(6)
29.	Daman & Diu	09.89	(18)	05.74	(24)	10.97	(20)
30.	Delhi	06.53	(26)	05.36	(25)	08.01	(28)
31.	Lakshadweep	05.74	(28)	02.97	(31)	09.47	(24)
32.	Pondicherry	06.75	(25)	05.21	(27)	08.49	(26)
33.	Uttaranchal	—	—	—	—	—	—
34.	Chattisgarh	—	—	—	—	—	—
35.	Jharkhand	—	—	—	—	—	—
	INDIA	07.54	(23)	07.63	(20)	09.44	(25)

* Census was not conducted in Jammu & Kashmir in 1991.

Note: The literacy rate for 1991 and 2001 census relate to the population of 7+ years.

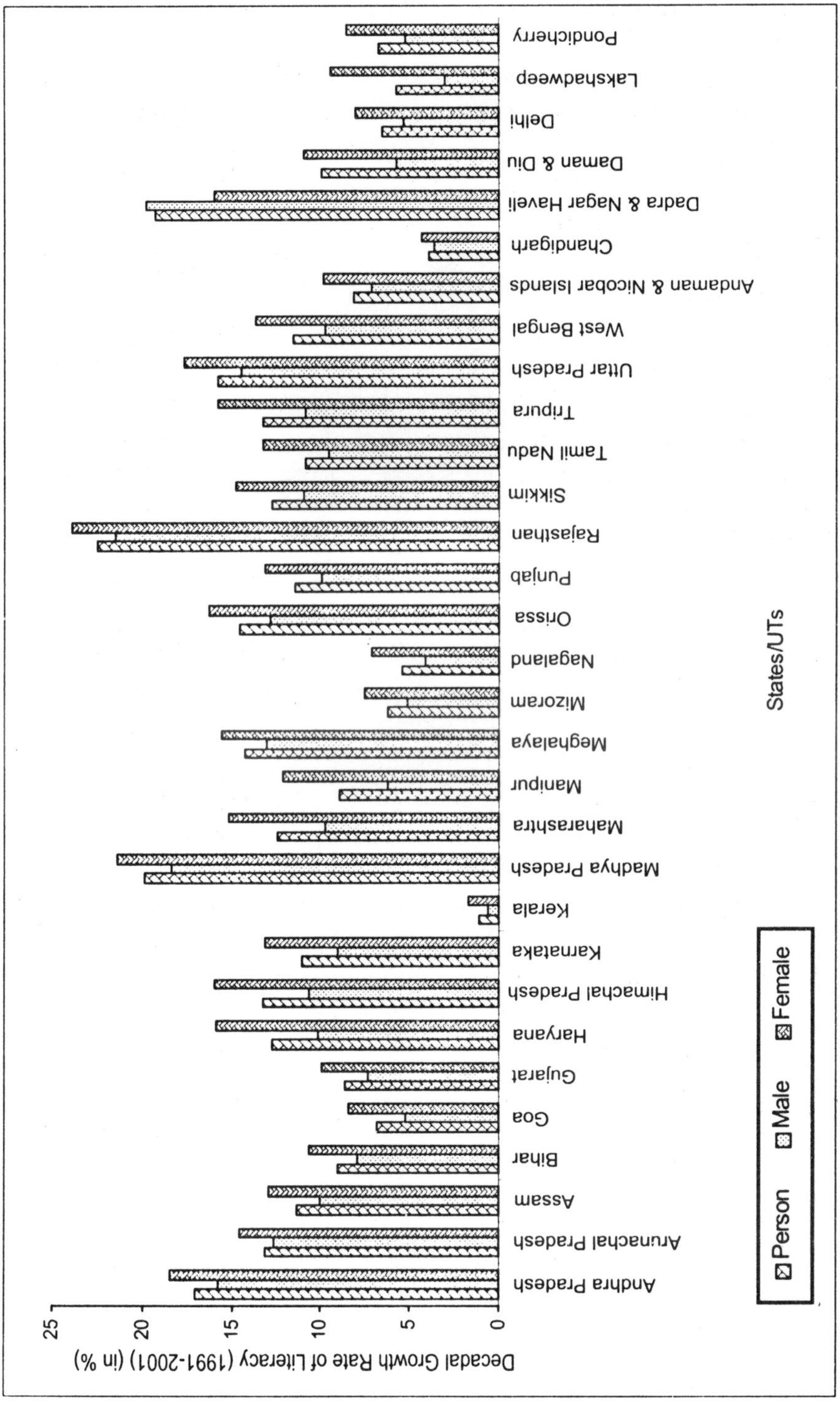

Fig. 3.8: Decadal Growth of Male, Female, and Total Literacy Rates in States and UTs During 1991-2001

3.9 LITERACY RATE OF GENERAL CATEGORY

There are substantial literacy gaps across major social groups in rural and urban areas in India as a whole. The overall literacy rate for persons aged 7 years and above varies from 38.48 per cent to 89.81 per cent for General Category as given in Table 3.18.

Table 3.18: Literacy Rates of General Category in States and UTs in 1991

		Literacy Rate (in %) and Rank					
Sl No.	*State/UT*	*Person*	*(Rank)*	*Male*	*(Rank)*	*Female*	*(Rank)*
1.	Kerala	89.81	(1)	93.62	(1)	86.17	(1)
2.	Mizoram	82.27	(2)	85.61	(3)	78.60	(2)
3.	Lakshadweep	81.78	(3)	90.18	(2)	72.89	(3)
4.	Chandigarh	77.81	(4)	82.04	(7)	72.34	(4)
5.	Goa	75.51	(5)	83.64	(5)	67.09	(5)
6.	Delhi	75.29	(6)	82.01	(8)	66.99	(6)
7.	Pondicherry	74.74	(7)	83.68	(4)	65.63	(7)
8.	Andaman & Nicobar Islands	73.02	(8)	78.99	(9)	65.46	(8)
9.	Daman & Diu	71.20	(9)	82.66	(6)	59.40	(9)
10.	Maharashtra	64.87	(10)	76.56	(10)	52.32	(11)
11.	Himachal Pradesh	63.86	(11)	75.36	(11)	52.17	(12)
12.	Tamil Nadu	62.66	(12)	73.75	(12)	51.33	(13)
13.	Nagaland	61.65	(13)	67.62	(18)	54.75	(10)
14.	Gujarat	61.29	(14)	73.13	(13)	48.64	(16)
15.	Tripura	60.44	(15)	70.58	(15)	49.65	(15)
16.	Manipur	59.89	(16)	71.63	(14)	47.60	(17)
17.	Punjab	58.51	(17)	65.66	(21)	50.41	(14)
18.	West Bengal	57.70	(18)	67.81	(17)	46.56	(19)
19.	Sikkim	56.94	(19)	65.74	(20)	46.69	(18)
20.	Karnataka	56.04	(20)	67.26	(19)	44.34	(21)
21.	Haryana	55.85	(21)	69.10	(16)	40.47	(23)
22.	Assam	52.89	(22)	61.87	(24)	43.03	(22)
23.	**INDIA**	**52.21**	**(23)**	**64.13**	**(22)**	**39.29**	**(24)**
24.	Meghalaya	49.10	(24)	53.12	(30)	44.85	(20)
25.	Orissa	49.09	(25)	63.09	(23)	34.68	(25)
26.	Madhya Pradesh	44.20	(26)	58.42	(25)	28.85	(28)
27.	Andhra Pradesh	44.09	(27)	55.13	(27)	32.72	(26)
28.	Uttar Pradesh	41.60	(28)	55.73	(26)	25.31	(30)
29.	Arunachal Pradesh	41.59	(29)	51.45	(32)	29.69	(27)
30.	Dadra & Nagar Haveli	40.71	(30)	53.56	(29)	26.98	(29)
31.	Rajasthan	38.55	(31)	54.99	(28)	20.44	(32)
32.	Bihar	38.48	(32)	52.49	(31)	22.89	(31)
33.	Jammu & Kashmir*	—	—	—	—	—	—

* Census was not conducted in Jammu & Kashmir in 1991.
Source: Census of India 1991

Kerala has been at the top rank with total literacy rate just below 90 per cent. This state has retained its rank in male and female literacy rates. Bihar, Rajasthan, Dadra & Nagar Haveli, Arunachal Pradesh and Uttar Pradesh were far away from the average national literacy of General Category.

3.10 LITERACY RATE OF SCHEDULED CASTES

After independence, Government of India started paying attention to the literacy of SCs and STs. These constitute about 20 crore i.e., 24.34 per cent of the total population of the country. The SCs alone constitute 16.33 per cent of the total population. Overall literacy rate among SCs vary from 20 per cent to 80 per cent, as shown in Table 3.19.

There were 22 States and UTs in the country, which have literacy rates among SCs higher than the national average literacy rate in 1991. Table 3.19 shows that Kerala again retained its position on top by being with overall 79.66 per cent literacy rate among SCs. Mizoram and Daman & Diu were the first rankers in female and male literacy in 1991 census. Among all States and UTs, only Mizoram has female literacy rate higher than the male literacy rate by 3.71 per cent. Bihar stood at the bottom with overall literacy rate of 19.49 per cent and Rajasthan being close to it having 26.29 per cent rate of literacy. Literacy rate among SC females in Rajasthan was 8.31 per cent as compared to 42.38 per cent of males literacy rate. Delhi and Haryana were still above the overall average literacy rate of India with seventh and twenty-first rank respectively. Literacy rates among SCs in Bihar, Madhya Pradesh, Rajasthan and Uttar Pradesh (BIMARU) were not satisfactory. These four states along with Orissa and Andhra Pradesh constitute majority of SCs population, and if they do not improve they will drag India down with them. The literacy rates of SCs in these six states are lower than the average national literacy rate.

A scheme of Special Educational Development Programme for SC Girls belonging to very low literacy level was introduced during 1996-97 on pilot basis with a view to provide a package of educational inputs through residential schools for SC girls in areas of very low SC female literacy where traditions and environment are not conducive to their learning. The schools are intended to supplement the existing measures to impart and consolidate literacy and to promote quality education to such girls who are first generation learners in areas of low literacy. Grant-in-aid under the scheme comprises of the package of Rs.11,340 per student in class I only, which includes direct facilities to the students as well as cost towards infrastructure, staff and other running cost. No fees, charges or contributions are recovered from the students. The scheme is implemented by the Zila Parishads (District level Panchayats) of the concerned district. The Zila Parishads are required to send their proposals to the Ministry, through their state governments.

Table 3.19: Literacy Rates of Scheduled Castes in States and UTs in 1991

		Literacy Rate (in %) and Rank					
Sl. No.	*State/UT*	*Person*	*(Rank)*	*Male*	*(Rank)*	*Female*	*(Rank)*
1.	Kerala	79.66	(1)	85.22	(3)	74.31	(2)
2.	Daman & Diu	79.18	(2)	91.85	(1)	67.62	(3)
3.	Mizoram	77.92	(3)	77.54	(4)	81.25	(1)
4.	Dadra & Nagar Haveli	77.64	(4)	88.03	(2)	66.61	(4)
5.	Gujarat	61.07	(5)	75.47	(5)	45.54	(8)
6.	Goa	58.73	(6)	69.55	(7)	47.51	(5)
7.	Delhi	57.60	(7)	68.77	(8)	43.82	(10)
8.	Arunachal Pradesh	57.27	(8)	66.25	(10)	41.42	(15)
9.	Tripura	56.66	(9)	67.25	(9)	45.45	(9)
10.	Maharashtra	56.46	(10)	70.45	(6)	41.59	(14)
11.	Manipur	56.44	(11)	65.28	(12)	47.41	(6)
12.	Pondicherry	56.26	(12)	66.10	(11)	46.28	(7)
13.	Chandigarh	55.44	(13)	64.74	(14)	43.54	(11)
14.	Assam	53.94	(14)	63.88	(15)	42.99	(12)
15.	Himachal Pradesh	53.20	(15)	64.98	(13)	41.02	(16)
16.	Sikkim	51.03	(16)	58.69	(16)	42.77	(13)
17.	Tamil Nadu	46.74	(17)	58.36	(17)	34.89	(17)
18.	Meghalaya	44.27	(18)	54.56	(18)	31.19	(18)
19.	West Bengal	42.21	(19)	54.55	(19)	28.87	(20)
20.	Punjab	41.09	(20)	49.82	(24)	31.03	(19)
21.	Haryana	39.22	(21)	52.06	(21)	24.15	(22)
22.	Karnataka	38.06	(22)	49.69	(25)	25.95	(21)
23.	INDIA	37.41	(23)	49.91	(23)	23.76	(23)
24.	Orissa	36.78	(24)	52.42	(20)	20.74	(25)
25.	Madhya Pradesh	35.08	(25)	50.51	(22)	18.11	(26)
26.	Andhra Pradesh	31.59	(26)	41.88	(27)	20.92	(24)
27.	Uttar Pradesh	26.85	(27)	40.80	(28)	10.69	(27)
28.	Rajasthan	26.29	(28)	42.38	(26)	08.31	(28)
29.	Bihar	19.49	(29)	30.64	(29)	07.07	(29)
30.	Jammu & Kashmir*	—	—	—	—	—	—
31.	Nagaland**	—	—	—	—	—	—
32.	Andaman & Nicobar Islands	—	—	—	—	—	—
33.	Lakshadweep**	—	—	—	—	—	—

* Census was not held in Jammu and Kashmir in 1991

** Scheduled Castes population do not exist

Source: Census of India 1991

As per 1981 census, 48 districts situated in Bihar, Madhya Pradesh, Rajasthan and Uttar Pradesh had been identified where percentage of literate SC girls was less than 2 per cent. The details of such districts are given in the following Table 3.20.

Table 3.20: List of Districts Having Scheduled Caste Female Literacy Rates Below 2 per cent in 1981

Sl. No.	*District*	*Literacy Rate (in %)*	*Sl. No.*	*District*	*Literacy Rate (in %)*
Bihar					
1.	Giridih	1.81	24.	Ganganagar	1.92
2.	Darbhanga	1.79	25.	Bharatpur	1.85
3.	Muzaffarpur	1.74	26.	Tonk	1.82
4.	Hazaribagh	1.73	27.	Pali	1.82
5.	Gopalganj	1.64	28.	Sawai Madhopur	1.68
6.	Gaya	1.61	29.	Bhilwara	1.31
7.	Purnia	1.52	30.	Churu	0.91
8.	Palamanu	1.29	31.	Nagaur	0.75
9.	Paschim Champaran	1.24	32.	Jaisalmer	0.62
10.	Purba Champaran	1.24	33.	Jalor	0.51
11.	Nawada	1.18	34.	Barmer	0.51
12.	Madhubani	1.09	**Uttar Pradesh**		
13.	Saharsa	1.07	35.	Deoria	1.93
14.	Sitamarhi	0.89	36.	Rai Bareli	1.92
Madhya Pradesh			37.	Lalitpur	1.77
15.	Guna	1.91	38.	Sitapur	1.64
16.	Satna	1.90	39.	Badaun	1.62
17.	Chhatarpur	1.83	40.	Pratapgarh	1.61
18.	Panna	1.46	41.	Banda	1.60
19.	Rajgarh	1.29	42.	Barabanki	1.48
20.	Shahapur	1.28	43.	Kheri	1.43
21.	Rewa	1.14	44.	Mirzapur	1.41
22.	Sidhi	0.58	45.	Basti	1.39
			46.	Sultanpur	1.14
Rajasthan			47.	Gonda	0.85
23.	Sikar	1.95	48.	Behraich	0.78

Source : Census of India 1981

3.11 LITERACY RATE OF SCHEDULED TRIBES

The Scheduled Tribes in Bihar were more literate than in Orissa, Madhya Pradesh, Rajasthan and Andhra Pradesh. Rajasthan was far behind from average national literacy rate and ranked 26th among STs category, as shown in Table 3.21. Kerala, which stood first in tha total literacy rate of General and SC categories, has slipped to fifth position in literacy rate of ST category.

Table 3.21: Literacy Rates of Scheduled Tribes in States and UTs in 1991

		Literacy Rate (in %) and Rank					
Sl. No.	*State/UT*	*Person*	*(Rank)*	*Male*	*(Rank)*	*Female*	*(Rank)*
1.	Mizoram	82.71	(1)	86.66	(2)	78.70	(1)
2.	Lakshadweep	80.58	(2)	89.50	(1)	71.72	(2)
3.	Nagaland	60.39	(3)	66.27	(4)	54.51	(3)
4.	Sikkim	59.01	(4)	66.80	(3)	50.37	(5)
5.	Kerala	57.22	(5)	63.38	(7)	51.07	(4)
6.	Andaman & Nicobar Islands	56.62	(6)	64.16	(5)	48.74	(6)
7.	Manipur	53.63	(7)	62.39	(9)	44.48	(7)
8.	Daman & Diu	52.91	(8)	63.58	(6)	41.49	(9)
9.	Assam	49.16	(9)	58.93	(10)	38.98	(10)
10.	Himachal Pradesh	47.09	(10)	62.74	(8)	31.18	(11)
11.	Meghalaya	46.71	(11)	49.78	(14)	43.63	(8)
12.	Goa	42.91	(12)	54.43	(11)	29.01	(12)
13.	Tripura	40.37	(13)	52.88	(12)	27.34	(13)
14.	Maharashtra	36.79	(14)	49.09	(15)	24.03	(16)
15.	Gujarat	36.45	(15)	48.25	(16)	24.20	(15)
16.	Karnataka	36.01	(16)	47.95	(17)	23.57	(17)
17.	Uttar Pradesh	35.70	(17)	49.95	(13)	19.86	(19)
18.	Arunachal Pradesh	34.45	(18)	44.00	(18)	24.94	(14)
19.	**INDIA**	**29.60**	**(19)**	**40.65**	**(20)**	**18.19**	**(20)**
20.	Dadra & Nagar Haveli	28.21	(20)	40.75	(19)	15.94	(21)
21.	Tamil Nadu	27.89	(21)	35.25	(23)	20.23	(18)
22.	West Bengal	27.78	(22)	40.07	(21)	14.98	(22)
23.	Bihar	26.78	(23)	38.40	(22)	14.75	(23)
24.	Orissa	22.31	(24)	34.44	(24)	10.21	(25)
25.	Madhya Pradesh	21.54	(25)	32.16	(26)	10.73	(24)
26.	Rajasthan	19.44	(26)	33.29	(25)	04.42	(27)
27.	Andhra Pradesh	17.16	(27)	25.25	(27)	08.68	(26)
28.	Jammu & Kashmir*	—	—	—	—	—	—
29.	Haryana**	—	—	—	—	—	—
30.	Punjab**	—	—	—	—	—	—
31.	Chandigarh**	—	—	—	—	—	—
32.	Delhi**	—	—	—	—	—	—
33.	Pondicherry**	—	—	—	—	—	—

* Census was not held in Jammu and Kashmir in 1991

** Scheduled Tribes population do not exist

Source: Census of India 1991

There were no STs found in Punjab, Chandigarh, Pondicherry, Delhi and Haryana as per census report 1991. Literacy rate among ST women was just 4.42 per cent as compared to 33.29 per cent male in the same category in Rajasthan. Overall literacy rate of STs was found to be lowest 17.16 per cent in Andhra Pradesh followed by 19.49 per cent in Rajasthan, 21.54 per cent in Madhya Pradesh, 22.31 per cent in Orissa and 26.78 per cent in Bihar. It means BIMARU states have to make more improvement in increasing male and female literacy rates of STs.

3.12 CONCLUSION

India has missed all the targets on hundred per cent literacy. As per our constitution, it was to be completed by 1961. The UNESCO wanted the same task to be completed by the end of the 20th century. India has missed all set goals and there was no repercussion from the political systems. Unless we make a firm commitment of making India a fully literate nation within a specified time schedule, the objective may not be achieved even through the next generation. We have just to go on counting number of illiterates in every census. Now we must understand that:

> "The West became rich through industry, West Asia through oil. It is now India's chance to arrive using the mind".

REFERENCES

1. CIPOLLA (Carlo M), Literacy and development in the west, Penguine Book Co Ltd., England, 1969, p. 8.
2. *Dictionary of Education*, Mc-Graw Hill Book Company, New York, 1959, p. 323.
3. UNESCO, The experimental world literacy programme: a critical assessment, UNESCO, Paris, 1976.
4. http://www.ilpnet.org/projects.asp
5. SONAL SINGH and SURINDER SINGH, *Role of librarianship in eradication of illiteracy*. In Libraries and information services in the electronic information era. Seminar papers presented in the Fourth All India Library Conference held at Hyderabad during 25-28 February 1999. p. 23.
6. *Ibid*. p. 23.
7. WORLD DECLARATION on Education for all and framework for action to meet basic learning needs. Documents adopted at the world conference on Education for All: Meeting basic learning needs. UNESCO, Thailand, 1990, p. 134.
8. http://www.epionline.org/illiteracy04.htm

9. http://www.nald.ca/province/alt/aaal/aboutaaa.htm
10. New Encyclopaedia Britannica – Micropaedia: Encyclopaedia Britannica Inc. Chicago. 1982. p. 261.
11. UNESCO, Literacy as a factor in development, UNESCO, Paris, 1965.
12. KIRSCH (I) and JUNGEBLUT (A), Literacy: Profiles of America's young adults, Final Report of the National Assessment of Educational Progress, Educational Testing Service, New Jersey, 1986.
13. GOVIL (Adarsh N) and AMBILI (KS), *Eradication of illiteracy in the electronic information era.* In Libraries and information services in the electronic information era. Seminar papers presented in the Fourth All India Library Conference held at Hyderabad during 25-28 February 1999. p. 41.
14. Literacy and information age, OECD, Paris, 2000.
15. http://www.censusindia.net/popu1.htm

Chapter 4

Literacy Programmes in India

Ask not what your country can do for you; ask what you can do for your country.

—*John F. Kennedy*

4.1 INTRODUCTION

The importance of literacy was realized in 19th century as an instrument for socio-economic development of the country. Social reformer Raja Rammohun Roy did much in this direction. In 1825 he established Vedanta College, a centre for both western and Indian learning. Great scholar Ishwar Chandra Vidyasagar introduced western education system and opened a college for non-Brahmins. Dayanand Saraswati established first college in 1886 in Lahore. Sir Syed Ahmed Khan and Mahamana Madan Mohan Malviya founded Aligarh Muslim University and Benaras Hindu University respectively. But all these were for higher education and learning only.

The Father of Nation, Mahatma Gandhi, uttered the following historic words with a lot of anguish:

"It is a matter of sin and shame that millions in India continue to be illiterate, they have to be liberated".

After that a series of mass campaigns for total literacy as well as adult literacy programmes were launched. Before independence, the following isolated, scattered but result- oriented programmes were launched with limited coverage:

- Dr. Syed Mahmud launched literacy campaign in Bihar.

- Bombay Adult Education Committee under the chairmanship of Shri B. G. Kher launched literacy movement in Bombay city.
- Mysore University launched literacy campaign in 1940.
- Dr Frank Laubach inspired a large number of teachers in Monga in Punjab and launched a campaign for *"each one teach one"*, which gave rise to literacy in almost all the districts of the state.
- Granthshala Movement in Kerala and Village Library Movement in several parts of the country were launched for post-literacy and continuing education.
- Shri Chakravarthy Rajgopalachari, the then Chief Minister of Tamil Nadu, wrote a primer for neo-literates known as *"Thambee Va"* and also short stories for new literates *"Kuttikathaiagal"*.

Similarly, other intellectuals like Smt Durgabai Deshmukh, Shri J. P. Naik, Dr. Frank Laubach, Sir M. Visvesvarya, Dr Weathy Fisher, Dr Mohan Singh Mehta and Dr. S. R. Ranganathan had also made huge efforts in this direction.

4.2 FIVE YEAR PLANS AND LITERACY

At the time of independence, Indian leaders felt that literacy and education must be given top priority in nation-building process and, therefore, suggested that a minimum 10 per cent of total plan outlay should be reserved exclusively for education. The Planning Commission was set up in March 1950 to propose the most effective and balanced utilization of the nation's resources within the context of the fundamental rights and of the directive principles of state policy and of the declared objective of the government to promote a rapid rise in the standard of living of the people by efficient exploitation of the resources of the country, increasing production and offering opportunities to all for employment in the service of the community.

With each successive Five Year Plan, the percentage allocated to education kept on shrinking. The First Five Year Plan saw 7.22 per cent of the total outlay going for education, the Second 6.2 per cent. By the Fourth Plan, this has fallen down to 5.2 per cent. Sixth Plan saw this dip to 3.3 per cent. In the Seventh Plan, education got 3.9 per cent but only 3.3 per cent was spent. The share of elementary education has sharply reduced during this Plan. During the First Plan period, money spent on elementary education accounted for 55 per cent of all the money spent on education as a whole. By the Seventh Plan its share has fallen down to 34 per cent with a decrease of 20 per cent.

During First Five Year Plan 1951-56, little emphasis was given on right to education and economic and social aspects of planning. However, literacy was not considered as the prime factor for economic development of the country. In this Plan, it was realised to have community development programme with education as one of its main lines of activity because full development of a community is possible only if it has a strong educational base. This was termed as social education. Its necessity was felt that before any programme of the state is launched, the people should be so educated in regard to it that their instinct to help themselves is fully aroused and they are anxious to receive the programme and do their utmost in its execution. Literacy was one part of the social education together with health, recreation, home life of the adults, their economic life and citizenship training. It implied an all-comprehensive programme of community uplift through community action. No provision was made for the libraries in this Plan.

The process initiated in the First Five Year Plan was further carried out in the Second Five Year Plan. But the literacy was again not given the prime importance in this Plan too. However, it was stated that the country had a large manpower resource, which was not being utilised fully and emphasis was given to formal education. During this Plan, about 35,000 Adult Education Centres were opened which could have imparted literacy to 773,000 adults.

Not much emphasis was given to education of non-literate adults in the Third Five Year Plan. However, goal was set for good life for the masses of the Indian people in this Plan. For the first time, poverty was called a curse and prime cause of social and economic backwardness. Education was termed as social service like health, sanitation, water supply and housing.

In the Fourth Five Year Plan, there was no reference to the education of non-literate adults. The Plan document quotes Article 45 of the Constitution about the free and compulsory schooling and Article 46 for the promotion of the educational and economic interest of the weaker sections of the society. Emphasis was laid down on social justice and equality, social welfare, welfare and development of the backward classes.

Only one sentence on non-formal education, referring to the renewal of existing programme, was given in the Fifth Five Year Plan. Growth, modernisation, self-reliance and social justice were the main objectives of the Sixth Plan. There was no reference to the literacy or library except that appropriate education will be used for promoting the active involvement of all sections of the people in the process of development. The focus was given on 15-35 years age group education with the aim of raising level of productivity in the economy. In this document, messages of health and biology of reproduction were introduced as the part of adult education. A sum of Rs 60 crore was allocated in the Central Plan for adult education. Again library was not mentioned in the Plan document.

The goal for the Seventh Five Year Plan was to virtually eliminate poverty and illiteracy by the year 2000 and adult literacy programme were to be pursued with the objective of covering all illiterates in the age group of 15-35 years by 1990. For the first time, a bold initiative was taken and a long term strategy was framed for adult literacy programme. The document emphasised educated people as instruments of progress of the country. A sum of Rs 130 crore was allocated in the Central Plan towards mass movement programme of adult education.

Eighth Five Year Plan realised that only healthy and educated people can contribute to human well-being. Priority was given to human development and eradication of illiteracy programme. In the process of development *"people must operate and government must cooperate"* policy was adopted in this Plan. Education was treated as an investment in the process of development. The responsibility of the government was to provide basic education, which helps development of human capital. The document emphasised the planning and structuring of education system to cultivate necessary calibre, skills and value systems. It framed a long term development perspective of fulfilling the social and human aspirations of the people, meeting the essential requirements of living, raising income levels and improving their quality of life. The target of this Plan was to achieve 100 per cent literacy in the age group of 15-35 years. Another objective of Eighth Five Year Plan was to cover 345 districts and make 100 million people functionally literate.

The Ninth Five Year Plan document states that the objective of the Plan is to focus on growth with social justice and equality. Emphasis was given to Universal Primary Education. In order to promote literacy and education, government has proposed to formulate and implement plans to gradually increase expenditure on education up to 6 per cent of the GDP and to achieve total literacy by the year 2005. Good efforts have been made to implement all programmes/schemes to achieve the goal of literacy.

Tables 4.1 and 4.2 provide expenditure on literacy programmes during Eighth and Ninth Five Year Plans respectively.

The status of expenditure shows that the funds allocated for the purpose was not fully utilized in any financial year during both the Five Year Plans. During Eighth Five Year Plan, only 74 per cent funds were utilised and this percentage of utilisation was almost similar in the next Plan.

Table 4.1: Expenditure on Literacy Programmes During Eighth Five Year Plan (1992-93 to 1996-97)

Year	*Allocation (Rs in crore)*	*Expenditure (Rs in crore)*	*Utilised funds (in % of allocation)*
1992-93	120.00	97.58	81.32
1993-94	177.97	166.39	93.49
1994-95	214.00	206.90	96.69
1995-96	234.00	143.93	61.51
1996-97	224.50	103.12	45.93
TOTAL	970.47	717.92	73.98

Table 4.2: Expenditure on Literacy Programmes During Ninth Five Year Plan (1997-98 to 2001-2002)

Year	*Allocation (Rs in crore)*	*Expenditure (Rs in crore)*	*Utilised funds (in % of allocation)*
1997-98	127.00	79.74	62.79
1998-99	93.97	72.23	76.86
1999-2000	110.00	87.07	79.15
2000-2001	120.00	108.16	90.13
2001-2002	200.00	—	—
TOTAL	650.97	—	—

4.3 PANCHAYATI RAJ INSTITUTIONS (PRIs)

The enactment of Constitution (73rd Amendment) Act, 1992, provides constitutional status to the Panchayati Raj Institutions (PRIs). Except Jammu & Kashmir and NCT of Delhi, all other States and UTs have enacted the necessary legislation pertaining to PRI. As a result, village level, intermediate level and district level panchayats have been constituted. These panchayats are being manned by about 34 lakh elected representatives at all levels. Each State and UT which has population more than 20 lakh has three tier system i.e. Village Panchayat, Intermediate Panchayat and District Panchayat. A conference of the State Ministers of Panchayati Raj was held on 11 July 2001 at New Delhi, in which a Task Force was set up to suggest the measures of administrative decentralisation of funds, functions and functionaries with regard to the "Matters" listed in the XIth Schedule of the Constitution ***(Appendix 'B')***. The Report submitted by the Task Force in August 2001 suggested identification of activities, tasks and responsibilities to be assigned to different tiers of panchayats for each of the 29 Subjects mentioned in the Constitution. Out of them only poverty alleviation, adult and non-formal education and libraries are being covered in Table 4.3.

Table 4.3: Activity Mapping among District Panchayat, Intermediate Panchayat and Gram Panchayat

Activity	*Distribution of Functions*		
	District Panchayat (DP)	*Intermediate Panchayat (IP)*	*Gram Panchayat (GP)*
Item No 16: Poverty Alleviation Programmes			
Planning and implementation of Poverty Alleviation Programmes.	Scrutiny and consolidation of IPs for poverty alleviation programmes; approval and allocation of funds; infrastructure development.; technical assistance to IPs and GPs; supervision and review of schemes and programmes; and coordination with other departments.	Technical and managerial assistance to GPs to implement schemes; preparation of plans; collection, distribution and evaluation of data; review the plans of GPs; integration of other schemes with poverty alleviation programmes; and provide technical approval to GPs.	Identification of beneficiaries under SSY and other schemes; implementation of JGSY, SSY and other employment generation schemes; to report the IPs and DPs; to ensure proper utilisation of funds allocated for the purpose.
Wage Employment Programmes.	Preparation, formulation, assigning, approval and sanction of projects to IPs, GPs and NGOs; release of funds; inspection, monitoring and supervision of the progress; reporting to the Government.	Formulating projects with IPs funds; scrutinising, providing approval and technical assistance to GPs projects; inspection of projects; feedback to DP for utilisation of funds. Procurement and supply of material for projects.	Assisting in identification of labourers in village through Gram Sabha; to ensure employ-ment to all in village; monitoring and supervision of quality of works and assets.
Item No 19: Adult Education and Non-formal Education			
Planning and Implementation of Adult Education, Non-formal Education and Total Literacy Campaign (TLC).	Identification of suitable locations for establishing adult education centres selection of volunteers supervisors; acquiring literacy materials; organising TLCs, monitoring and supervising activities.	Implementation of adult education and non-formal education programme and TLCs; distribution of materials to these centres; monitoring and supervising functions and activities.	Mobilising people for participation in adult education and TLC campaign; supervising and assisting in functioning of the centres.
Item No 20: Libraries			
Establishment and maintenance of libraries.	Planning for establishment of new libraries and improving the existing libraries; procuring library materials; maintenance of libraries.	Providing assistance in maintenance and functioning of libraries.	Providing assistance in construction of library building; arrangement of funds; managing library activities.

Table 4.4: Transfer of Funds, Functions and Functionaries to Panchayats

Activity	*Powers*	*Staff and Org Support*	*Funds*
District Panchayats			
Item No 16: Poverty Alleviation Programmes			
Planning and implementation of Poverty Alleviation Programmes. Wage Employment (JRY, IJRY, ESA)	Planning and implementation of poverty alleviation programmes by CEO; DRDA Cell to assist DPs For implementation of SGSY, IAY, etc; limited power to transfer officials; communication with the Government.	CEO is to be assisted by DRDA Staff of DPs and subordinate staff.	Grants from the Government and local resources including District Plan Funds.
Item No 19: Adult Education and Non-formal Education			
Planning and Implementation of Adult Education, Non-formal Education and Total Literacy Campaign.	CEO, to be the controlling officer of the District Education Officer for tour diaries, attendance, etc., limited powers to recommend transfer of officials; and communication with the Government.	District Education Officer to be the member/invitee for discussions on department's schemes; assistance from subordinate staff.	Grants from Government for district level schemes and local resources including District Plan Funds.
Item No 20: Libraries			
Establishment and maintenance of libraries.	CEO to be the controlling officer of the district level librarians for tour diaries, etc.; limited power to recommend transfer of officials and communication with the Government.	District level librarians to be the member /invitee for discussions on department's schemes; to be assisted by the subordinate staff.	Grants from the Govt. for district level schemes and local resources including District Plan Funds.
Intermediate Panchayats			
Item No 16: Poverty Alleviation Programmes			
Planning and implementation of Poverty Alleviation Programmes Wage Employment	EO/BDO to be the controlling officer; redeployment of departmental staff within the block;	EO/BDO will be responsible for planning and implementation for all the schemes; to be	Grants from Government, DPs and local resources including District Plan Funds

Table 4.4 (*Contd.*)

Activity	*Powers*	*Staff and Org Support*	*Funds*
(JGSY,ESA, Food for Work).	to recommend DP for inter-block transfer; to take action on complaint against GP; all communication from GP to DP through IP.	assisted by the deptt officials; to execute IP's and DP's decisions.	
Item No 19: Adult Education and Non-formal Education			
Planning and implementation of Adult Education, Non-formal Education and Total Literacy Campaign.	EO/BDO to be the controlling officer of all departmental officers in Block for tour diaries, attendance, etc; redeployment of staff within the Block; to recommend DP for Inter-Block transfer of officials; and communication from GP to DP through IP.	Block Education Officer will be responsible for planning and implementation of schemes; assistance from subordinate staff; Departmental Officials to execute the IP's and DP's decisions on schemes.	Block Education Officer will be responsible for planning and implementation of schemes; assistance from subordinate staff; Departmental Officials to execute the IP's and DP's decisions on schemes.
Item No 20: Libraries			
Establishment and maintenance of libraries.	EO/BDO to be the controlling officer of all departmental officials in the Block for tour diaries, etc; limited power to recommend transfer of officials and communication from GP to DP through IP.	Librarian at Block level will be responsible for planning and implementation of all schemes; to be assisted by the subordinate staff; to execute decisions of IP's and DP's on the schemes.	Grants from the Govt., DPs for Block level schemes; local resources including District Plan Funds.
Gram Panchayats			
Item No 16: Poverty Alleviation Programmes			
Planning and implementation of Poverty Alleviation Programmes; (JRY, IJRY, ESA prioritisation of food for work)	Power to check attendance of all GP, IPs, DPs and DPCs and local level officials; allocation of work within the GP; to recommend transfer; to inform IP about complaint received	DP/IP level senior most line functionary to attend the GP meetings; Plan and implement the rural development programmes for creating of village level infrastructure	Grants from IPs, DPs and DPCs and local resources

Table 4.4 (*Contd.*)

Activity	*Powers*	*Staff and Org Support*	*Funds*
Item No 19: Adult Education and Non-formal Education			
Planning and implementation of Adult Education, Non-formal Education and Total Literacy Campaign.	Power to check attendance of all GP level officials; allocation of work within the GP; to recommend transfer; to inform IP about complaint received.	DP/IP level senior most line functionary to attend the GP meetings; selection of teachers and supervision for this purpose.	Funds from IPs, DPs and DPCs and local resources.
Item No 20: Libraries			
Establishment and maintenance of libraries.	Power to check attendance of all GP level officials; allocation of work within the GP; to recommend transfer; to inform IP about complaint received.	DP/IP level senior most line functionary to attend the GP meetings; maintenance of village level libraries.	Funds from IPs, DPs; united from DPCs; local resources.

The Task Force suggested that there was an urgent need to rationalise all the schemes related to XIth Schedule of the Constitution, implemented by the Central or State Governments and a proportion of funds allocated to the schemes should be transferred to the PRIs. A sum of Rs. 31,575.87 crore for the 26 schemes/programmes of Central Ministries and Rs 40,818.65 crore for the 32 schemes/programmes of the State Governments were allocated during the Annual Plan 2000-2001 under the Subjects mentioned in the XIth Schedule of the Constitution.

4.4 NATIONAL LITERACY MISSION (NLM)

The National Literacy Mission[1] was launched by the then Prime Minister of India, late Shri Rajiv Gandhi, at Vigyan Bhavan, New Delhi on 5th May 1988. Its objective was to achieve a sustainable threshold level of 75 per cent literacy rate by 2005 AD. It was launched with a clear vision of literate society and an action programme to start a mass movement to mobilise volunteers for literacy work to impart functional literacy to adult illiterate persons in the age group of 15-35 years within a definite time frame. This age group was selected by the NLM, because they are both in the productive and reproductive period of life. In case they had earlier missed opportunity to become literate, or were denied access to mainstream formal education, NLM offers them another chance. Later, the scope of the programme has been enlarged to include people in the age group of 9 to 14 years, in the areas not covered by the non-formal education programme, to ensure that the benefits of NLM are made available to the out-of-school children as well. Special care has been taken to bring disadvantaged groups, like women, SCs, STs and other backward classes into the programme.

At the time of launching of the programme, the target was to reach 80 million illiterates by 1995. The NLM programme is based on extensive collaboration among the government, VAs, and the community. Further, the objective of the programme was changed to make all young illiterates functionally literate by the year 2001, which was again found quite difficult to achieve.

As far as structure is concerned, the NLM has a three-tiered structure. At the apex, the National Literacy Mission Authority, supported by the Directorate of Adult Education, controls the programme at the national level. The State Literacy Mission Authority directs activities at the state level, supported by the Directorate of Adult Education. The Zilla Saksharata Samiti (ZSS) helps in making the programme a reality in districts and villages all over India. In urban areas, Nagar Palikas are being encouraged to take up the challenge.

The ZSS is registered under the Registration of Societies Act as independent and autonomous body, to provide a forum for individuals and organisations to work together. The leadership to the ZSS is provided by the District Collector. All sections of society are thus duly represented in the planning and implementation of the programme. Under the literacy campaign, funds are released by the NLM directly to the district. While the pattern of sharing is usually in the proportion of 2:1 between Central and State Governments, and in the case of tribal sub-plan districts, the pattern of sharing is 4:1. NLM aims to launch literacy campaigns in different districts according to the needs of that area. While these campaigns vary a great deal in their details, these have certain common features, such as:

- Creating a conducive environment for motivating learners;
- Training an army of instructors;
- Preparing, producing and disseminating teaching materials;
- Organizing literacy classes; and
- Monitoring and evaluating the whole operation.

The NLM seeks to impart functional literacy to all illiterates by:

- Creating an environment conducive to teaching-learning process;

- Providing good and relevant teaching-learning materials and facilitating teaching-learning by good training, media and communication;
- Improving the pace of learning and injecting confidence among the learners about their potential to learn and by ensuring that the process is not drudgery;
- Integrating basic literacy with post-literacy and continuing education; and
- Developing the quality of human resources at all levels of functionaries through orientation and training.

The NLM seeks to impart functional literacy to illiterates in the age group of 15-35 years through:

- Self-reliance in reading, writing and numeracy (3 R's);
- Participating in the development process;
- Skill improvement to improve economic status and general well-being; and
- Imbibing values such as national integration, conservation of environment, gender equality and observance of a small family norms, etc.

The NLM seeks to achieve these objectives by:

- Creating conducive environment for teaching-learning process, provision of good and relevant teaching–learning materials and facilitating it by good training, media and communication; and
- Improving the pace of learning and injecting confidence among the learners about their potential to learn.

The project places great emphasis on the training of key resource persons. Volunteer teachers are given a full year's training before they join the literacy campaign.

Due to enormous efforts made in this area, the NLM won the UNESCO's prestigious Noma Literacy Prize[2] for 1999. The award was given in recognition of the NLM's initiative of the campaign as the dominant strategy for the eradication of illiteracy. NLM's effort was also recognised in prompting activities towards national integration, conservation of the environment, promotion of the women's equality and the preservation of the family customs and traditions.

In its endeavour to achieve the set goals, The NLM faces the following challenges:

The Hindi Heartland: The four Hindi-speaking states — Bihar, Madhya Pradesh, Rajasthan and Uttar Pradesh (BIMARU) account for half of the India's illiterate population. The large number of illiterate population and, therefore, the relatively small number of educated population from where volunteers are drawn, as well as socio-economic backwardness of these states, combine to make the achievement of literacy difficult in these areas.

Regional Disparity: There are large regional disparities among the states, the districts in a state, the males and females, and the tribal and non-tribal areas. These disparities create localised hurdles in the smooth running of the literacy campaigns.

Community Involvement: Literacy campaigns are successful when the community is actively involved and, in fact, accepts its responsibility for effective managing and supervising the programme. As per the available information, the NLM has been able to make the following achievements:

1. Literacy campaigns have been launched in 574 districts, out of which 302 districts have moved into the first phase of imparting basic literacy skills and are now implementing PLCs, 112 districts have entered into the continuing education phase.
2. Literacy projects sanctioned so far under all the schemes of NLM are estimated to cover 150 million neo-literates in the age group of 9-35 years.
3. Of them, nearly 125 million learners have been enrolled under literacy campaigns and more than 12 million volunteers have participated in this mission.
4. Over 92 million illiterates have already been made literate under various programmes.
5. About 61 per cent learners are female and 39 per cent are male.
6. About 23 per cent learners belong to SC and 13 per cent belong to ST catergories.
7. Twenty two states and four UTs have been covered under its literacy campaigns.

The cumulative number of literacy volunteers mobilised since the launching of literacy campaigns exceeds 12 million. The main strength of these literacy campaigns has been their success in inculcating a volunteering spirit among people. A multimedia approach is adopted to recruit them from within the district. Puppet shows, *Kala Jathas* (cultural groupes, including folk artists), school teachers and volunteers cover the entire district, informing and motivating people to learn and create a supportive environment for learning. The literacy campaigns thus represent the largest ever civil mobilization in the history of the country.

After the 73rd Constitutional Amendment, the responsibility of adult education now rests with Zilla Parisad/Zilla Panchayats. Steps have been taken to orient the elected representatives of the Panchayati Raj Institutions to the literacy programmes and to integrate the Panchayati structure more meaningfully with ZSS. In newly formed districts, representation of Panchayati Raj Institutions at various levels is being ensured, and in the ZSSs of Panchayati Raj, the representatives are being given orientation and sensitisation through workshops held by the State Resource Centres (SRC) and the National Literacy Resource Centre (NLRC). The NLRC was set up by the NLM at the Lal Bahadur Shastri Academy of Administration at Mussoorie for a period of five years from 1998-99 to 2002-2003. The Centre organises training and orientation programmes for district level mission leaders and various district functionaries of ZSS and Panchayati Raj Institutions, apart from preparing various case studies and video documentations. During the past couple of years, the NLRC has carried out the following activities:

Orientation of District Teams: Organised two workshops covering all districts of Uttar Pradesh, three workshops covering all districts of Rajasthan, and one workshop for 20 districts of Madhya Pradesh.

Case Studies/Documentation: Conducted case studies of two districts and prepared audio-visual documentation for TLC and PLC.

Regional Workshops: Organised workshop on PLC and CEP in Dumka, Bihar and Adult Numeracy and Folk Muths in Chennai.

Publications: Brought out publications—*Saksharata Samvaad, Saksharata Aayee Cycle Par Sawaar, Zillah Ki Kahaani Apni Zubaani,* and Handbook of Numeracy Counts.

Thematic Workshops/Seminars: Conducted a number of seminars and workshops for resource persons and participants on various topics related to literacy.

4.5 TOTAL LITERACY CAMPAIGN (TLC)

A literacy miracle took place in Ernakulam[3], a small district in Kerala, during the late 1980s. It took just one year to teach 185,000 illiterates in the district to read, write, add, subtract, multiply and divide. Every one in the district is totally literate by now. This is not an isolated experience. Many other districts in various states and UTs are getting similar benefits from the NLM. The campaigns are implemented by ZSS specially constituted under the District Collectors. Membership of ZSS is drawn from all sections of the society. In most districts, the ZSS conceived ephemeral mass mobilisation strategies in the form of *Jathas*, which moved along village roads communicating the message through songs and dance. Campaigns are implemented through direct funding to the ZSS by the Central and State Governments. The focus of TLCs has now been shifted to the Hindi speaking areas where bulk of illiterate population resides. The costing norm for a TLC budget is at the rate of Rs 65 a learner. About 55 per cent goes towards training materials and teaching-learning aids, 35 per cent for programme management, such as honorariums to the volunteer programme managers, and 10 per cent to the environment-building measures. But the actual cost of a TLC tends to exceed the norm of Rs 65 per learner. It goes up to about Rs 180 per learner.

It is, however, unfortunate that TLC seems to have lost tempo in the last few years despite initial success in the states like Kerala, Andhra Pradesh, West Bengal, Tamil Nadu, Gujarat and Maharashtra. The programme seems to suffer mainly from lack of innovative projects, absence of effective post-literacy follow-up, under-utilisation of funds and poor management of schemes by the State Governments. The scheme is also having lack of accountability.

The TLC model has now been accepted as a dominant strategy of eradication of adult illiteracy by all States/UTs in India. This strategy has been reviewed and endorsed by the National Development Council (NDC) and also by the Conference of Chief Ministers of States[4] convened by the Prime Minister on February 15, 1994. As a follow-up of the conference, another meeting of the Chief Ministers of Bihar, Madhya Pradesh, Rajasthan and Uttar Pradesh (BIMARU) was held in Bhopal[5] on 1st July 1994 and recommended as follows:

- The four states will accord priority to primary education and literacy programmes. Expenditure cuts due to economy measures will not apply to these programmes. During the currency of the plan period, efforts will be made to enhance allocations to 6 per cent of the Gross National Product (GNP) for the promotion of education. For the implementation of primary education and the literacy programmes by State Governments, services of talented and dedicated officers will be made available for a sufficient period. The District Collectors of the TLC districts would not be disturbed during the implementation of the programme except in extreme public exigency.

The TLCs have such features as make them unique and distinguish them from other government programmes:

- These campaigns are area-specific, time-bound, volunteer-based, cost-effective and outcome-oriented. The thrust in TLCs is on attainment of predetermined norms of literacy and numeracy.
- The campaigns are implemented through district level literacy committees, which are registered under the Registration of Societies Act as independent and autonomous bodies to provide a unified umbrella under which a number of individuals and organisations work together.
- The campaign approach to total literacy is characterised by large scale mobilisation through a multifaceted communi-cation strategy. The success of the campaign rests substantially on the effectiveness with which all sections of society are mobilized.
- No targets are fixed from the top. The targets emanate from the grassroots level on the basis of a detailed door-to-door survey conducted by the volunteers.
- The campaign is delivered through volunteers who work without any expectation of reward or incentive.
- The management information system in a campaign is based on the twin principles of participation and correction. It has to be accountable and credible and not merely enrollment-oriented.
- To enable every learner to achieve measurable levels of literacy, the new pedagogy known as Improved Pace and Content of Learning (IPCL). It has been translated into a set of multigrade and integrated teaching-learning materials and training.
- Training of all functionaries involved in the campaign is significant to the success of the campaign. Training has to be primer-specific, participative, communicative and a tool of continuous correction, upgradation and human resource development.
- Though the TLC is meant to impart functional literacy, it also disseminates a 'basket' of other socially relevant messages such as enrollment and retention of children in school, immunization, propagation of small family norms, promotion of maternity and child care; women's equality and empowerment, peace and communal harmony, etc.

In 1993, Government of India constituted an Expert Committee under the Chairmanship of Prof Arun Ghosh[6], a former member of Planning Commission. The Committee undertook the evaluation of the TLCs and submitted its report in 1994. The Committee recommended:

- To stop formal declaration of total literacy achievements by the states/districts.

- Results of the final evaluation to be shared with the people.
- Target of 80 per cent success is unrealistic and 55 per cent to 60 per cent success to be considered as good progress.
- To enhance the involvement of Panchayati Raj Institutions and the elected representatives of Gram Panchayats and Panchayat Samitis.
- To decentralise the procedure for sanction of the project.
- To tighten the evaluation procedures.
- To cover the age-group of 9-14 also under TLCs, where non-formal education is not in operation.

The Committee observed the following strengths and weaknesses of TLCs:

Strengths:

- TLC is more of a movement than a programme.
- There has been an overwhelming impact of TLCs on women.
- The TLCs have led to a positive impact on caste and communal relations.
- The TLCs have generated a demand for primary education.
- TLCs have activated concerns for developing a humane society.
- They have led to sensitization of the bureaucracy.
- The launching of TLCs has placed literacy high on national agenda.

Weaknesses:

- The quality of teaching has suffered in some places where there has been excessive preoccupation with literacy skills alone.
- Fragile literacy skills need to be consolidated through more effective post-literacy measures.
- Some campaigns have been launched without adequate preparation.

Several doubts had been created in the past and even now that the efforts made by these campaigns would be fruitful or not. Now it has become clear with the participation of the Government, volunteers, beneficiaries and other creative forces in full dedication towards making India a fully literate nation. As more and more people would join the campaign, the bureaucracy would get closer to the people; it would become more positive, sensitive and empathetic. A distinguished historian and member of National Literacy Mission Authority (NLMA), when visited a literacy programme in a district in West Bengal, expressed his views as:

"It was a perfect coordination between the administration and the Panchayat. In that district, when our team visited, we noticed that District Collector and Sabhadhipati of Zilla Parishad were working in unison. The District Collector and his team became whole time worker. It was for the first time, we noticed, the entire district administration went to the people instead of people coming to them. It was a unique exposure for them and they enjoyed it. The District Collector was walking through the muddy roads, his hair greyed with the dust. There was hardly any difference between a political worker, a volunteer and an administrator."

Energetic District Collectors, representatives of PRIs and their team members in the other districts are also following the same path for achieving the goals and removing any doubt about the success of the campaign.

4.6 POST-LITERACY PROGRAMME (PLP)

The aim of the post-literacy programme[7] is to consolidate the basic literacy skills of reading, writing, numeracy and problem-solving. While at the same time, transforming the neo-literates into educated whole persons, who are a productive socio-economic asset to the community. The programme envisages making such persons willing and able to participate actively and productively in our nation's development. The post-literacy programme is designed to serve:

- Neo-literates in the age group of 9-14 years who have completed the basic literacy course under TLC;
- Neo-literates in the age group of 15-35 years;
- Semi-literates/drop-outs from the basic literacy phase;
- Drop-outs from primary schools; and
- Pass-outs from non-formal education programmes.

As per the definition of post-literacy, the key aim of PLP is to ensure that participants have become functionally literate. The ultimate aim of post-literacy programme is to help participants to become true autonomous learners in the broadest and the best sense. Some of the goals of post-literacy programme are:

- To prevent regression to literacy;
- To enroll drop-outs and enable non-achievers to upgrade their literacy skills;
- To improve literacy skills to self-reliant level of learning;

- To enable learners to use literacy skills in day-to-day life;
- To enable learners to acquire skills for economic self-reliance; and
- To promote collective action and facilitate take-off to continuing education.

The following are some of the salient features of PLP:

- It is treated as a preparatory stage for continuing education;
- Unlike TLC, it is not regarded as campaign but as a programme;
- Duration of PLP is restricted to 365 days only;
- Duration is reckoned from the date of receipt of funds from the Government of India; and
- No extension of time-unspent balance is refunded at the end of one year from the date of receipt of funds from Government of India.

The following are some of the outcomes of the PLCs:

- The decision to continue literacy efforts in the Mission is fully justified;
- Low-cost education, as imparted under the NLM, can prove extremely effective;
- Stress on girls is paying dividends; and
- The campaign approach has proved its worth and TLCs should now be followed by intensive PLPs and CEPs.

4.7 CONTINUING EDUCATION PROGRAMME (CEP)

Literacy provides an entry point to the world of letters and through the world of letters to the world of communication and information. It is a basic step towards adult education, which is a process of lifelong learning. The enthusiasm and confidence generated among the learners in the districts which have successfully completed both the TLC as well as the PLC phases, clearly points towards the need to sustain the educational process and to provide learning opportunities on a continuing basis. The access to the world of letters and skills acquired by the neo-literates need to be further reinforced and widened so as to enable them to fully play the crucial role for their own personal, social and economic problems, application and utilization of literacy skills acquired by the neo-literates often remains a difficult proposition. The literacy processes have creative energies of the people, which must be sustainable to enable the people to realise their potential, to help themselves and achieve self-reliance. Hence, the crucial importance of creating satisfactory arrangements for continuing education of all learners.

Continuing education is also an indispensable aspect of the strategy of human resource development and of the goal of creation of a learning society. Formal education as an instrument of human resource development is not really effective in remedying the structural inequalities in the society. Continuing education, which provides a second chance to those who missed formal education and is responsive to learners' needs, directly addresses itself to structural inequalities. Only continuing education can bring about full development of human resources. Since continuing education is the opportunity to engage in now emerging as the main component of the broader view of education as a whole.

Continuing education includes post-literacy for neo-literates and school drop-outs for retention of literacy skills, continuation of learning beyond elementary literacy and application of this learning for improving their living conditions. But continuing education goes beyond post-literacy and it includes all of the learning opportunities all people want or need outside of basic literacy, education and primary education. In continuing education, human resource development becomes the focus of attention. Thus, it is also an essential extension of literacy to promote human resource development.

In a public meeting held at Kozhikode[8] on 18 April 1999, Ms Chelakkodan Ayisha, a 60 years old lady, declared Kerala as a fully literate state. She was also one among the 12.2 lakh people who became literates under the mass literacy campaign called *Akshara Keralam*. Kerala's literacy rate was 89.81 per cent as per Census Report 1991. This was increased to 93 per cent in 1997, which was close to the UNESCO guidelines of 95 per cent for total literacy. Just after eight years Kerala has lost its glory. Its literacy rank has slipped from first to fourth place after Andaman (97%), Lakshadweep (96%) and Mizoram (95%). It happened because 5 lakhs, out of 12.2 lakhs neo-literates in Kerala have relapsed into illiteracy and now they have become neo-illiterates. The same situation may occur in other states also if no continuous efforts are made to sustain literacy acquired over the period of time. Thus, there is, need of the hour to have CEPs for permanent solution of slipping of neo-literates back into the net of illiteracy.

The NLM has launched a specific programme to cater to the continuing education needs of millions of neo-literates emerging from the successful completion of PLPs in several districts all over the country. This programme has come into force from January 1, 1996. CEP had been launched in more than 65 districts of the country by the end of February 1999. The following are some of the factors, which led to the launching of CEP:

- After the successful implementation of TLCs in many States/Uts, millions of illiterates have joined the rank of neo-literates;
- The products of NFE centres, school drop-out and out-of-school children and adolescents have also joined the category of neo-literates;
- The efforts of VAs and other institutions led to increased number of neo-literates;
- The potential need of neo-literates is to retain and augment their literacy skills;
- To enable neo-literates to further extend and continue their learning activities; and
- To upgrade innovative skills among neo-literates.

The following target groups have been taken for the CEP:

- Neo-literates;
- School drop-outs;
- Out-of-school youth/children;
- Residual illiteracy; and
- General public.

The main objectives of the CEP include the following:

- Provision of facilities for retention of literacy skills and continuing education to enable the learners to continue their learning beyond basic literacy;
- Creating scope for application of functional literacy for improvement of living conditions and quality of life;
- Dissemination of information on development programmes as well as widening and improving participation of traditionally deprived sections of the society;
- Creation of awareness about national concerns such as national integration, conservation and improvement of the environment, gender equality, observance of small family norms, etc. and sharing of common problems of the community;
- Improvement of economic conditions and general well-being as well as improvement of productivity by organizing short-duration

of life for purposes of planning and programme design, the various quality of life indicators can broadly be categorized as biological, social, economic, humanistic and environmental. Its role is to facilitate positive societal change with respect to these indicators through education. However, it may not be possible to address to all aspects of quality of life through educational programmes alone. The objective of QLIPs is, therefore, mainly to educate people and help groups to learn and act on how to improve their quality of life. QLIPs, therefore, need to be designed with clearly defined targets which may be achievable through training, community education and action projects.

These programmes are capable of delivery through a multi-sectoral approach since many sectors of the government may be concerned with development programmes covering different elements of quality of life such as family welfare, health, nutrition, drinking water, sanitation, population education, environment, social services, communal harmony, transportation, etc. The target for QLIPs is a specific community group or all adult citizens in a specific area. The delivery systems are of a broad outreach and sufficiently flexible to accommodate a variety of presentation methods. The methods of delivery may include structured courses conducted through learning centres or distance education techniques, public education campaigns, carefully sequenced information disseminated through mass media, self-learning, printed materials, etc. QLIPs are primarily concerned with bringing about societal changes. These are project-and action-oriented and have a specified time-frame. Further, being essentially educational programmes, only those aspects of quality of life which can be addressed using the methodologies of adult education are involved.

Individual Interest Promotion Programmes (IIPPs): These programmes aim to provide opportunity for individuals to participate and learn about their chosen social, cultural, spiritual, health, physical and artistic interests. In contrast to QLIPs, which aim to establish a common base line of effective living for all citizens, the objective of IIPPs is to provide learning experience to promote and improve individual interests of all adults, but especially people such as youth, women and the elderly people in rural areas. The focus of IIPPs is on personal development by providing opportunities for promotion of specialized individual interests which may lead to improvement in the quality of human resources of the society.

Planning and implementation of IIPPs involve designing and providing of appropriate courses, which cater to the genuine needs of local adult community. These courses are developed for the purpose to include a wide variety of learning programmes which encourage people to constructively utilize their leisure time and also simultaneously facilitate self-actualisation and life improvement. The categories of individual interests, which catered to through these programmes, include leisure time interests such as sports or hobbies; interests such as art, painting, drawing, traditional music, dance, drama, etc; interests catering to promotion of self-reliance such as dress-making, sewing, knitting, healthy cooking, repair of agricultural machinery and electrical appliances, first-aid, self-defence for women etc. and; personal development and self-actualization interests such as meditation, creative writing, speed reading, public speaking, leadership skills, etc. The main thrust in the administration of such programmes is on encouraging the provision of as wide a range of learning activities as possible to cater to highly diverse interests in society. This is significant since one of the major objectives of IIPPs is to enrich life by enabling individuals to work towards personal goals and gain a sense of fulfillment and achievement.

The IIPPs are provided by a variety of agencies. Since many agencies are involved in providing special interest activities, an important administrative role is to ensure that such agencies are known to the potential beneficiaries and to facilitate establishment of a networking and coordination mechanism to obtain cooperation of all such agencies in implementation of the IIPPs in specified areas. IIPPs are delivered by any of the methods available for other types of CEPs i.e. contact sessions at learning centres, individual self-paced learning, distance education or by a combination of any of these. Group discussions, practical workshops, study tours and visits are also effectively utilized as alternative delivery systems for such programmes.

The principle objective of establishment of CECs is to provide a window or a focal service point where diverse kinds of CEPs and activities are taken up to provide opportunities for life-long learning to all sections of the population. The functions of CEC would include:

Evening Class for upgradation of literacy and numeracy skills to organize for 3-4 hours once a week. The learners have the option to come for an hour or so at the time of their convenience on that day.

Library and Reading Room for which books are purchased from the non-recurring and recurring provisions; copies of old journals are maintained and useful booklets relating to development programmes are published by concerned agencies. Wall papers and newspapers, appropriate for adult learners, informative and entertaining journals, developmental literature etc. are also made available.

Charcha Mandal (Discussion Group) for discussion on common problems. This forum is utilized for quality of life improvement and individual interest programmes.

Training Programmes of simple and short duration relating to subjects such as health and family welfare, new developments in agriculture and animal husbandry, conservation of energy, improved *Chulha,* etc. CECs also help the local youth to benefit from various vocational training programmes. Income generation programmes, which help participants acquire or upgrade their vocational skills and enable them to conduct income generating activities. These are made available in structured packages.

Sports and Adventurous Activities are organized in the areas of indigenous sports, walking excursions, cycling trips in groups, etc.

Recreational and Cultural Activities are also organized, particularly traditional and folk forms of art, rural theatre, puppetry, etc. under this programme.

Information Window for securing information on various developmental programmes. Information and material suitable for neo-literates are procured from the concerned development agencies.

A Communication Centre where community radio, audio/video cassettes player-cum-recorders are provided.

State level agencies like State Resource Centres (SRCs) in collaboration with the Central Directorate of Adult Education and National Open School provide technical and academic resource support of ZSS for implementation of CEPs. The areas covered by such resource support would include:

- Designing and development of curriculum framework and learning materials for various types of CEPs;
- Preparing multimedia packages for short duration vocational training courses;
- Developing training modules and materials for functionaries at various levels;
- Organising training modules and materials for functionaries at various levels;
- Organizing orientation courses and training programmes for Key Resource Persons;
- Production of books suitable for CEC libraries;
- Production of video/audio cassettes and other audio-visual materials;
- Research and evaluation; and
- Providing other professional support for implementation of CEPs.

In order to help the neo-literates to reach some level of equivalency with formal system, the SRCs, in collaboration with National Open School, develop structured graded materials in regional languages. The SRCs also assist ZSS in conducting evaluation tests at the end of the courses and in certifying the successful completion of graded courses.

The CECs are established under the schemes, which are intended to be permanent centre for life long education. Establishment and running of CECs obviously require financial support throughout the course of their existence. While the Central Government provides financial assistance for initial establishment and running of CECs, in the longer run all such CECs have to become self-sustaining. The scheme, therefore, envisages provision of financial assistance from the Central Government for a limited period of five years. The funding of CEPs has two components:

(a) Financial assistance for establishment and running of the CECs based on a uniform pattern comprising of non-recurring provision of Rs. 10,000 per CEC, which is admissible in the first year only, and a recurring provision of Rs 10,000 per CEC per year. The corresponding provision for the Nodal CEC is Rs 20,000 each for non-recurring and recurring per Nodal CEC.
(b) Financial assistance for talking up innovative target-specific functional programmes and continuing education activities. This also includes the requirements for meeting the organizational and managerial expenses of the ZSS.

The CEPs under the scheme are provided financial assistance on 100 per cent basis by the Central Government for the first three years from the date of issue of formal sanction by the SLMA/State Government. For the next two years, the extent of Central assistance is limited to 50 per cent and the remaining 50 per cent is to be shared by the State Government. After a period of five years, the Central Government does not extend any financial assistance for continued running of established CECs. The State Government then takes over the responsibility for continued running of CECs through PRIs or other local bodies. The State Governments are also required to give their consent to this pattern of funding before sanctioning of CE projects in the State.

Government of India had approved a *new "Scheme of Continuing Education for Neo-literates"* during the year 1995-96. The scheme broadly laid down the broad programmes, which can be taken up under the CE Scheme. To firm up the guidelines for the successful implementation of the scheme two important workshops were conducted, one at Hyderabad from 26th June to 28th June, 1996 and another at Ahmedabad from 3rd December to 5th December, 1996. Based upon the discussions, the following guidelines were emerged for implementing the Scheme of Continuing Education for Neo-literates.

- One CEC is to be established for each village to serve around 500 neo-literates in a population of about 1500-2000. Since the emphasis is more on creating CECs for the neo-literates, the number of CECs may be arrived at taking the norm of CECs for 500 neo-literates excluding the population criteria of 1500 to 2000 mentioned there in. However, for the thin populated areas, hill track, tribal and desert areas, special concessions are to be given for establishment of CEC.
- The role of NGOs in the implementation of the scheme is recognized and it is proposed to involve them on a large scale in the implementation of this scheme. Sufficient provision is being made under the VAs scheme of the Adult Education Bureau. Wherever the VAs have set up or going to set up and run the CECs, the ZSS will not duplicate by setting up the CECs.
- For running the CE schemes, there is a need for proper resource support at all levels. At national level, the necessary resource support is provided by the Directorate of Adult Education as well as the NIAE. At the State level, the necessary support is provided by the SRCs. Since the activities of the continuing education would encompass coordination with the activities of different departments and NGOs, it is required that Departments of Rural Development, Women & Child Welfare, Social Welfare, Health & Family Planning should be properly represented in the SLMA for utilizing their expertise in formulating the CEPs. Interested NGOs should be brought on the ZSS. To get their active cooperation, the DRUs as part of the DIETS should provide necessary resource support at the district level. The SVs, wherever they are established, may provide necessary vocational training support for the CEP. So also it has been proposed under the Department of Rural Development should also be properly utilized for providing the resource support for vocational training programme.

4.8 VOLUNTARY AGENCIES (VAs)

The involvement of government is not enough to reach the goal of literacy. Voluntary Agencies[9] (VAs) or NGOs have to play very crucial role in fulfilling the set objectives. VAs are aware of the grassroots reality of literacy because they are nearer to the community. They can interact with the State Government machinery and provide them guidance and support and also create friendly learning environment. Their involvement in the mass movement for socio-cultural development activities, right from the planning stage to execution has been well recognised. NLM has fully recognized the need and importance of getting VAs extensively involved in the implementation of all its programmes and schemes. At present more than six hundred VAs are involved in implementing the literacy programmes by running adult education centres. Millions of students from academic institutions participate in the literacy mission when asked for. To ensure extensive involvement of VAs, universities and other academic institutions in the literacy campaign, the NLM has strengthened the scheme of assistance to these bodies in adult education and has also made other provisions for assistance to NGOs. The scheme of providing assistance to VAs in the field of adult education was designed and started in the First Five Year Plan and was modified and continued in subsequent plans. The modified scheme described as *"Central Scheme of Assistance to Voluntary Agencies"* came into operation under the NLM in 1988. There are three main components of the scheme:

- Grants to VAs for undertaking projects of basic literacy and other projects for achievements of objectives of NLM;
- Grants to open and operate Literacy Resource Centres; and
- Grants to institutions for evaluation of literacy/adult education programmes.

The activities for which grants are admissible to the VAs under this scheme include:

- Taking responsibility for eradication of illiteracy and running of PLPs and CEPs in well-defined areas;
- Organising programmes of vocational and technical education for neo-literates, undertaking resource development activities;
- Innovation experimentation, learner evaluation and action research; and
- Conducting evaluation studies, organising symposia and conferences and publication of books, periodicals, newspapers, etc.

A large number of Literacy Resource Centres have been functioning in the country since 1976. These Centres cater to the needs of neo-literates of a well defined area. Each State/UT is served by one or more than one Resource Centres. These are functioning under the universities or the VAs. A list of existing Resource Centres is given at ***Appendix 'C'***. The basic functions of these Centres are:

- To prepare teaching, learning and training materials for literacy programmes;
- To train literacy functionaries;
- To conduct action research; and
- To evaluate and monitor literacy projects.

4.9 INDIA LITERACY PROJECT (ILP)

India Literacy Project[10] is a registered non-profit organisation in the United States of America (USA). It was founded in 1990 by a nuclear scientist, Dr Parameshwar Rao. He was trained in USA and returned to India in 1967. He dedicated his life to improving the lives of poor in rural India. He realised that literacy was necessary prerequisite if the villagers were to absorb the knowledge, he wished to impart to them. Dr Rao observed that:

- Literacy literally is the first step on the road to change the development;
- There is a strong correlation between female literacy and population growth;
- A participative democracy requires a literate population. If people are not literate, they are easily marginalised;
- A strong nation requires strong social, political and economic foundations. To build them, the people have to be educated, or at the very minimum, made literate; and
- Each neo-literate's boost in self-confidence is a heart-warming testimonial to the power of literacy.

Today ILP is an active organisation with more than thousand volunteers in USA. It does not presently have a registered Chapter in India, although a group of volunteers help ILP to fund projects and monitor them. At present ILP supports many projects in India and has its presence in most of the states.

ILP has a noble goal of making India 100 per cent literate by the year 2020. Having recognised the problems associated with illiteracy, it actively seeks to spread awareness, identify organisations in India working for the cause of literacy and to raise funds to support these organisations. The funds are raised by organising cultural events, pursuing corporate contributions, selling T-shirts and greeting cards, etc. ILP estimates that on an average US $30 is needed to literate one person in India.

4.10 SANKALP

A group of students at IOWA State University, USA has formed a like-minded social group known as Sankalp in 1995 to contribute to the process of social development in India with special emphasis on empowering through literacy. The basic aim of this group is to support and empower illiterate masses living in India through literacy so that they may get a chance to break away from the current situation and give them opportunity to affect positive change in their lives. To fight illiteracy, the Sankalp has adopted the following approaches:

- Create awareness in locals and non-locals about the problems of illiteracy and other related issues in India;
- Sponsor and nurture literacy projects in India on sustained basis;
- Create awareness about the work done by the various organizations in India and in the USA to tackle this problem effectively; and
- Establish network and collaborate with other such organizations.

Sankalp has good contact with the other organizations in India and provides support to the following projects:

1. Rishi Valley Education Project, Chittoor, Andhra Pradesh;
2. Alternative India Development, West Singh Bhum District, Bihar;
3. Marr-Munning Ashram, Koraput, District Jeypore, Orissa.

The Sankalp has established good examples for other such organizations in raising funds through the following activities:

1. Sale of Indian handicrafts;
2. Penny collection;
3. Can redemption drive;
4. Individual donation;
5. Sale of Indian music CDs; and
6. Sale of Indian greeting cards made by the students.

4.11 UNESCO

UNESCO has consistently supported the need for researching and promoting literacy projects, programmes and campaigns with a developmental aim, in the context of its commitment to life-long education. The commitment of UNESCO, to adult learning and the leading role it has played in the promotion of adult education, has been in clear evidence over the last five decades.

During 1955-56, UNESCO was making efforts to produce reading materials for neo-literates. The news and information column of UNESCO Bulletin states that one of the projects included in UNESCO's programme is concerned with the problem of producing reading materials for new literate. It was decided to concentrate UNESCO's activities on this question in four countries — Burma, Ceylon, India and Pakistan. In order to develop the programme effectively, a Regional Meeting of Experts on the Production of Reading Materials for New Literates was held from 11 to 18 June 1956 in Murree, West Pakistan. The meeting emphasised that libraries had an important role to play in facilitating the distribution of suitable reading materials and encouraging new literates to continue their efforts so that reading became easy and natural.

The Fifth International Conference on Adult Education held in Hamburg, Germany in July, 1997 marked a turning point for adult learning and for the role expected to be played by UNESCO and its member-countries in this fast growing field. It demonstrated the extent to which adult education has become the key to the future. The new concept of adult education presents a challenge to existing practices because it calls for effective networking within the formal and non-formal systems, and for innovation, creativity and flexibility. Adult literacy, broadly conceived as the basic knowledge and skills needed by all in a rapid changing world, is a fundamental right. Literacy is also a catalyst for participation in social, cultural, political and economic activities and for learning throughout life.

UNESCO, International Literacy Institute (University of Pennsylvania, USA) and the NLM of India organised a major literacy meeting, the Second Asia Regional Literacy Forum, in February 1998 in New Delhi to consider innovations and professionalisation in adult literacy. The forum reviewed literacy problems within the complex diversity of Asia's pluralistic society, rejected the *"one size fits all"* approach for literacy eradication, and addressed the new demands on literacy skills. Literacy and linguistics, ethnic and cultural diversity in Asia and technological innovations were among the many issues discussed.

Over the years, UNESCO has been collaborating with the NLM for the celebration of International Literacy Day and in sponsoring publications on education and literacy. In collaboration with the State Resource Centre for Adult and Non-formal Education, Jamia Millia Islamia, New Delhi, the UNESCO has launched an innovative programme to provide new reading-learning materials to all those who have been declared newly literate at the end of a TLC. A pilot project, which is limited to specific areas in Delhi, has been launched to reach all neo-literates through the postal system. They will receive periodic news/information sheets. Each neo-literate is required to respond on a pre-paid reply card. The periodic material will build on the basic skills already acquired by the neo-literates. The scheme allows the neo-literates to continue their education even when the campaign is over.

4.12 ADULT EDUCATION PROGRAMME (AEP)

The progress of a nation mostly depends on the rate of literacy of that nation. Higher illiteracy rate is the main cause of poverty, growth of population and many other problems of our country. In Indian families, the adults have dominant positions where they take most of the family decisions. So it can be very well stated that adults play an important role in the development of the nation. Society is run by the adults who make decisions. The decision made by them directly affects the nature of our life in the present, and also in the future. Therefore, adult should be educated or at least should be made literate. Taking this into consideration, the concept of adult education comes forward.

The aim of adult education is to create an educated mind among the adult illiterates. The adult education activities include night schools, lectures, group discussions, film shows and arranging talks on topics of interest to the various sections of the society, organising readings, holding exhibitions and presenting educative themes through films, radios, televisions, etc.

Eradication of illiteracy has been one of the major national concerns of the Government of India since Independence. The need for a literate population and universal education for all children in the age group of 6-14 years was recognized as a crucial input for nation building and was given due consideration in the Constitution as well as in the successive Five Years Plans. A number of significant programmes have been taken up since Independence to eradicate illiteracy among adults.

The Directorate of Adult Education, in the Department of Education, Ministry of Human Resource Development, has been functioning as the

National Resource Centre for Adult Education and Literacy Programmes in the country. It is the functional arm of the NLM, which is responsible for monitoring and evaluation of various schemes and programmes launched under the aegis of the Mission. It is also entrusted with the task of developing model teaching learning materials for the learners and neo-literates and harnessing all kinds of media facilities for furtherance of the objectives of the NLM. It provides professional, academic and technical guidance for the effective functioning of the Shramik Vidyapeeths. It also implements UNFPA assisted project, *"Population Education and Development in Post-literacy and Continuing Education"* through SRCs. The Centres are actively involved in printing and publishing of different literacy campaigns stories and also in coordination, collaboration and networking with all Resource Centres and other organisations/agencies. The Central Government, through its various policies/plans/programmes, provides adequate funds for adult education. The outlays of adult education have increased from Rs 5 crore in the First Five Year Plan to Rs 1807.64 crore in the Eighth Five Year Plan. Table 4.5 gives a quick view of the expenditure occurred on adult education during the past five Five Year Plans and Table 4.6 gives data about the funds released to the States and UTs for AEP from 1995-96 to 2000-2001.

Table 4.5: Expenditure on Adult Education

Plan Period		*Expenditure (Rs in crore)*	*Percentage Variation in Successive Plans (in %)*	*Percentage Variation over Ist Five Year Plan (in %)*
First Plan	(1951-1956)	50 (3.5%)	—	—
Second Plan	(1956-1961)	40 (1.6%)	–20%	–20%
Third Plan	(1961-1966)	20 (0.3%)	–50%	–60%
Fourth Plan	(1969-1974)	59 (0.1%)	+195%	+18%
Fifth Plan	(1974-1979)	326 (0.3%)	+453%	+552%
Eighth Plan	(1992-1997)	1807	+454%	+3514%

Note: Figures in parentheses are percentage of total allocation on education.

Low priority was given to the adult education programmes in the first four Plans. In the First Five Year Plan, the expenditure was only Rs 50 crore which declined to Rs 40 crore in the Second Plan and further declined to Rs 20 crore in the Third Plan. The allocation witnessed marked increase after the Sixth Plan and now it accounts for nearly 9 per cent of the Plan allocation to education.

Table 4.6: Funds Released to the States and UTs for Adult Education Programme from 1995-96 to 2000-2001

(Rs in Lakhs)

States/UTs	*1995-96*	*1996-97*	*1997-98*	*1998-99*	*1999-00*	*2000-01*	*Total*
Andaman & Nicobar Islands	8.12	12.56	—	5.81	—	—	26.49
Andhra Pradesh	884.21	1081.06	922.55	114.52	872.24	626.97	4501.55
Arunachal Pradesh	25.63	20.72	3.67	—	—	—	50.02
Assam	361.09	194.29	86.97	195.61	332.99	166.15	1337.10
Bihar	1977.84	1062.52	446.98	347.39	241.21	419.99	4495.93
Chattisgarh	—	—	—	—	—	10.00	10.00
Chandigarh	20.12	41.37	20.00	57.86	14.60	26.00	179.95
Daman & Diu	0.50	—	—	—	0.80	—	1.30
Dadra & Nagar Haveli	—	—	—	—	—	—	—
Delhi	322.58	158.57	173.87	32.25	138.20	186.82	1012.29
Goa	5.95	3.32	0.56	4.61	—	—	14.44
Gujarat	262.98	458.78	112.34	105.25	806.84	1002.90	2749.09
Haryana	175.31	57.12	77.50	55.50	89.40	103.67	558.50
Himachal Pradesh	26.43	49.18	112.82	63.86	40.52	59.85	352.66
Jammu & Kashmir	132.70	50.47	38.20	130.04	59.00	73.13	483.36
Jharkhand	—	—	—	—	—	55.00	55.00
Karnataka	319.58	350.16	303.29	84.39	581.06	2537.23	4175.71
Kerala	7.00	537.97	15.35	48.34	369.35	706.25	1684.26
Lakshadweep	1.62	4.32	—	3.21	—	—	9.51
Madhya Pradesh	977.67	548.53	459.47	636.25	231.54	343.10	3196.56
Maharashtra	1153.63	432.82	746.29	467.71	526.85	317.00	3644.31
Manipur	17.62	20.63	17.94	25.55	8.70	2.61	93.05
Meghalaya	127.74	112.46	16.85	16.00	12.50	25.50	311.05
Mizoram	2.29	0.57	34.23	49.52	—	59.40	146.01
Nagaland	47.81	56.90	32.34	27.89	—	—	164.94
Orissa	801.36	310.13	196.62	206.91	301.77	202.28	2019.07
Pondicherry	—	—	18.24	—	—	31.92	50.16
Punjab	370.34	135.00	211.14	42.98	58.33	80.76	898.55
Rajasthan	1681.76	1304.62	820.35	359.73	1124.96	419.90	5711.32
Sikkim	—	11.22	—	—	—	—	11.22
Tamil Nadu	1212.48	261.21	554.00	120.17	169.97	212.50	2530.33
Tripura	0.10	4.73	27.00	61.32	10.00	30.50	133.65
Uttar Pradesh	1888.01	943.27	537.23	728.37	739.94	872.82	5709.64
Uttaranchal	—	—	—	—	—	59.02	59.02
West Bengal	308.40	728.11	502.82	1937.06	357.00	708.15	4541.54
TOTAL	13,120.87	8,952.62	6,488.44	5,928.10	7,087.77	9,339.42	50,917.22

Among all States and Uts, Rajasthan has received maximum share of funds for AEPs, followed by Uttar Pradesh, West Bengal, Andhra Pradesh,

Bihar, Karnataka, Maharashtra, Madhya Pradesh, etc. Maximum allocation of funds was released during 1995-96 and went on decreasing till 1998-99 which further increased in the successive years. By the end of 2000-2001, Government had released over Rs 50,000 crore for AEPs to all 35 States and UTs.

4.12.1 National Adult Education Programme (NAEP)

The first nation-wide attempt at eradication of illiteracy was made through the National Adult Education Programme launched on 2nd October 1978. It was a massive programme, which aimed at educating 100 million non-literate adults in the age group of 15-35 years within a time frame of five years i.e. 1978-1983.

The objectives of the NAEP were not merely to impart literacy in the conventional sense, but also to provide learners with functional awareness which were conceived as three integral components of the skills of reading, writing and numeracy. Functionality implied the skills acquired with a view to promote efficiency of the neo-literate. The social awareness component aimed at knowing, understanding and taking action on issues, which affect the individuals, community and society.

The programme became a victim of its own hierarchy and out-moded rules and procedures. It failed to inspire the policy formulators and implementors, opinion moulders and representatives of people, etc.

4.12.2 State Adult Education Programme (SAEP)

The State also took up Centre-based projects under the State Plan Funds on the lines of RELPs.

4.13 GRAM SHIKSHAN MOHIM

The Mohim (movement) for literacy in the rural areas was started in 1959 in Satara district of Maharashtra, and was later extended to other 25 districts of the state. The programme aimed at imparting basic literacy skills within a period of about four months and by 1963, it spread to all districts of the State. In these 25 districts, the annual average figure of persons becoming literate increased from 3,000 in 1959 to 109,000 in 1961. A total of 1,008,000 persons in the age group of 14-50 years in 1,109 villages of the state were made literate. It aimed at total eradication of illiteracy and retention of literacy by providing library services and other reading and learning materials for all round development of villages through social education centres. The enthusiasm and tempo generated by the Mohim could not, however, be sustained due to lack of adequate back up support and services, particularly in the field of post-literacy and continuing education and there was large scale relapse of neo-literates to the net of illiteracy.

4.14 ELEMENTARY EDUCATION PROGRAMME

In spite of considerable progress made in Universalisation of Elementary Education (UEE), ensuring access to good quality learning environment for children in the age group of 6-14 years remains a daunting task. According to Sixth All India Educational Survey Report 1993, a total 11,574 rural habitations were indicated as schoolless habitations. At primary stage, the estimated number of out of school children was about 3 crore and the number at upper primary stage was about 3.31 crore. The drop-outrates were still high at 36.3 per cent for primary school children and 52.7 per cent for upper primary classes.

At the same time, expenditure on elementary education was increased steeply during Sixth, Seventh and Eighth Five Year Plans. It had gone up from Rs 841.74 crore in Sixth Plan to Rs 10,556.50 crore in Eighth Plan. The increase was more than eleven times. Central Sector expenditure on elementary education was increased from 8.65 per cent in Sixth Plan to 23.25 per cent in Seventh Plan and it was further risen to 42.63 per cent during Eighth Plan period, but the share of the states decreased from 91.35 per cent in Sixth Plan to 57.37 per cent in Eighth Plan. Now State Governments are becoming more and more dependent on the Central Government for financial assistance in providing basic education, which is not a healthy sign. Details of expenditure occurred on elementary education during 1980-2002 is given in Table 4.7.

Table 4.7: Expenditure on Elementary Education

Year	*Expenditure (Rs in crore)*
1980-1985	842
1985-1990	2,855
1992-1997	10,557
1998-1999	4,045
1999-2000	4,385
2000-2001	4,950
2001-2002*	5,919

* Budget estimate

Surprisingly, our achievements in the field of primary and upper primary (known as elementary) are not commensurate with the level of plan investments made during last three plans. Rate of increase in the number of schools (primary and upper primary) from Sixth to Seventh Plan is 4.98 per cent and it has further gone up to 17.07 per cent during Eighth Plan period. Number of teachers has registered an increase of 8.75 per cent between Sixth and Seventh Plan, which has further risen to 17.23 per cent at the end of Eighth Plan.

The task of UEE could not be completed because of inadequate funds. It is often said that the proportion of national income devoted to education in India is small in comparison with that of advanced countries of the world.

4.15 EDUCATION FOR ALL (EFA)

The World Conference on Education For All[11] was organized in Jomtein in Thailand during 5-9 March 1990 with the objective of making an attainable goal of basic education for all. During the discussion in the Conference, it was well realized that education was a fundamental right for all women and men of all ages, throughout the world. It can help ensure a safer, healthier, more prosperous and environmentally sound world, while simultaneously contributing to social, economic and cultural progress, tolerance and international cooperation. It is an indispensable key to social and personal improvement. It should be made more relevant and universally available. It is fundamental to the strengthening of higher level of scientific and technological literacy and capacity and thus to self-reliant development. The following action plan was adopted by the participating countries and agreed on the framework for action to meet basic learning needs to achieve goals set forth in the declaration.

Meeting Basic Learning Needs: Every person—child, youth and adult should be able to benefit from educational opportunities designed to meet basic learning needs which comprise both essential learning tools (such as literacy, oral expression, numeracy and problem solving) and basic learning content (such as knowledge, skills values and attitude) required by the human beings to be able to survive, to develop their full capacities to live and work in dignity, to participate fully in development, to improve quality of their lives, to make informed decisions and to continue learning.

Extended Vision and Renewed Commitment: To serve the basic learning needs requires more than a recommitment to basic education as it now exists. An expanded vision is needed for—

- Universalising access and promoting equality;
- Focusing on learning;
- Broadening the means and scope of basic education;
- Enhancing the environment for learning; and
- Strengthening partnerships.

Developing a Supportive Policy Context: Supportive policies in the social, cultural and economic sectors are required in order to realise the full provision and utilization of basic education for individual and societal improvement. It all depends upon the political commitment and political will backed by appropriate fiscal measures and reinforced by educational policy reforms and institutional strengthening.

Mobilising Resources: If the basic learning needs of all are to be met through a much broader scope of action than in the past, it will be essential to mobilize existing and new financial and human resources, public and private voluntary. Society has a contribution to make, recognizing that time, energy and funding directed to basic education are perhaps the most profound investment in people and in the future of a country which can be made.

Strengthening International Solidarity: Meeting basic learning needs constitutes a common universal and human responsibility. It requires international solidarity and equitable and fair economic relations in order to redress existing economic disparities. Further to review and assess the situation of achieved goals of EFA, the next Asia Pacific Conference was held during 17-20 Jan., 2000 at Bangkok, Thailand. The following gains were noticed.:

- Increase in primary school enrolment;
- Expansion of early childhood care and education programmes;
- Higher priority given to quality;
- Increase in functional and adult literacy;
- Improvement in educational MIS;
- Increase in a national budget for basic education;
- Effective use of existing resources;
- Increase in international assistance to basic education;
- Increase in number of legislative measures, campaigns, projects and reforms in basic education;
- More innovative and initiative in basic education; and
- More partnership between the private sectors and civil society.

Even after achieving partial goals set forth in the Conference, there were still major challenges ahead like gender gaps, rural- urban gaps, shortfall in budget and other resources, lack of participation of society, lack of reliable data pertaining to basic education, lack of infrastructure, limited testing and evaluation and assessment of the learning process and performances and disparities between developed and developing countries in terms of living standards, poverty and awareness, etc.

Keeping above points in view the Conference again set the following strategic objectives and goals:

Early Childhood Care and Education Programme: Children should be provided with quality, comprehensive, integrated care and education through synergistic partnership among families, communities, civil societies, NGOs and the government.

Universal Basic Education Programme: The individual must have the opportunity to receive good quality basic education focusing on health, nutrition and psycho-social development.

Basic Learning and Skills Development Programme: Basic literacy and numeracy skills must be developed in context of relevant life skills related to work or any kind of risk like AIDS/HIV, etc.

Learning Achievement: Improvement may be made in curriculum content and all processes which are learner centred and problem solving. In this regard, training of teachers and educational managers is required to support curriculum reforms.

Elimination of Gender Disparity: Essentially to eliminate systematic gender disparities among girls and boys through- out the education system in enrolment, achievement and completion in training and career development in learning practices and processes, etc.

Literacy and Continuing Education: Support of literacy campaigns to achieve universal literacy should be aspired to before the date and time set forth for the goal.

In both the conferences, emphasis was given to basic education through teaching learning process, resource mobilization and international participation but not a single participant made a point for achieving literacy and its sustainability without library or information centre. Though the programme is running successfully but without providing reading materials and its availability through a systematic way creates doubt about the continuing education and its long term sustainability of literate masses.

UNESCO has produced a series of the following nine short five-minutes films on EFA. These are quite relevant to India.

1. Education for disabled children.
2. Education for street and working children.

3. Peer education.
4. National Literacy Mission.
5. Status of teachers.
6. National Literacy Mission and HIV/AIDS education.
7. Political will in education.
8. Multigrade teaching.
9. Quality of education.

Each film, made in Hindi, deals with particular focus on EFA, poses problems, raises the issues, and enunciates, through interviews, what is being done to tackle it.

4.16 NON-FORMAL EDUCATION (NFE)

Due to various socio-economic constraints, a large number of children remain outside the stream of the formal education. Under the Article 45 of the Constitution, the NEP-1986 envisaged a large and systematic programme of non-formal education as an integral component of the strategy to achieve UEE. The scheme has been in operation since 1979-80. Scheme presently covers educationally backward states of Andhra Pradesh, Arunachal Pradesh, Assam, Bihar, Jammu & Kashmir, Madhya Pradesh, Orissa, Rajasthan, Uttar Pradesh and West Bengal. It also covers urban slums, hilly, desert and tribal areas. At present, there are 2.97 lakh NFE centres covering 74.20 lakh children in 24 states and UTs. Out of which 1.18 lakh centres are run exclusively for girls, 58,788 centres are run by the 816 VAs. The scheme of NFE has been revised and to be known as the Scheme of Alternative and Innovative Education (SAIE) with the following salient features:

- All habitations that do not have an elementary education centres within the radius of one km will have one at the earliest;
- The quality of NFE will be upgraded to a level matching the formal education system;
- The local community will be more active in the implementation of the scheme;
- It will provide instructions with enhanced honorarium;
- As a part of the scheme, an elaborate school mapping exercise will be undertaken; and
- It will be a part of the SSA programme.

4.17 OPERATION BLACKBOARD (OB)

In pursuance of the NEP-1986, the scheme of Operation Blackboard (OB) was launched in 1987-88 with the aim of improving the human and physical resources available in the primary schools of the country existing as on 30 September 1986 and to improve the retention and learning achievement of children in school. There are three main components of the OB:

- Provision of at least two class rooms in each primary school with toilet facilities for boys and girls;
- Provision of an additional teacher to single teacher primary schools; and
- Provision of essential teaching-learning equipments, including furniture for teachers.

The scheme is being implemented through the State Governments with cent-per-cent assistance from the Central Government towards salary of additional teachers and provision of teaching and learning equipments. Under the scheme from 1st April 1999 the financial assistance for the construction of the school buildings given by the Central and State Governments are in the ratio of 75:25. Due to lengthy and non-flexible operation of the scheme, it is not being fully implemented in many states.

This programme has successfully provided financial assistance to 523,000 primary schools with a minimum double rooms building, teaching materials, play-kits (in all about 22 items called the minimum items) necessary to run an educational institution. Almost all primary schools of the country have been covered by the programme. Teaching-learning equipments have been provided to 99.9 per cent primary schools of the country. Since 1993-94, the scope of the programme was extended to cover upper primary schools. Unfortunately, no attention was paid to set up libraries in these primary schools under this scheme. Table 4.8 gives a brief statement of funds released for OB during Eighth Five Year Plan.

4.18 SARVA SHIKSHA ABHIYAN (SSA)

A Committee was constituted under the chairmanship of Minister of Human Resource Development to develop the structure and outlines of implementing UEE in a mission mode. On the basis of suggestions made by the Committee, a scheme of Sarva Shiksha Abhiyan (SSA) was launched to incorporate all the existing schemes and programmes in elementary education. Its objective is to provide quality elementary education to all children coming under the age group of 6-14 years by 2010. To mobilize social support, a national programme of media publicity and advocacy for UEE was launched as a part of SSA. This programme was focused on the following groups for operationalising the elementary education as fundamental right:

Table 4.8: Funds Released Under Operation Blackboard During Eighth Five Year Plan (1992-97)

State	*Funds Released (Rs in crore)*	*Percentage*
Andhra Pradesh	105.67	9.54
Assam	69.37	1.44
Bihar	126.42	11.41
Gujarat	29.29	2.64
Jammu & Kashmir	26.79	2.41
Karnataka	107.78	9.73
Madhya Pradesh	25.27	2.28
Maharashtra	236.94	21.40
Orissa	135.54	12.23
Rajasthan	107.60	9.72
Tamil Nadu	6.46	0.58
Uttar Pradesh	21.32	1.92
West Bengal	32.41	2.93
Other	76.56	6.91

Source: Department of Education, Ministry of Human Resource Development.

- Teachers and all those involved in education of children;
- Students and parents of students, particularly non-literate parents;
- Community opinion leaders; and
- Policy makers and public representatives.

In particular, objectives of SSA are:

- All children in school, Education Guarantee Centre, Alternate School, *"Back-to-School"* by 2003;
- All children to complete five years of primary schooling by 2007;
- All children to complete eight years of schooling by 2010;
- Focus on quality elementary education with emphasis on education for life;
- To bridge all gender and social category gaps at primary stage by 2007 and at elementary education by 2010; and
- Universal retention by 2010.

4.19 JAN SHIKSHAN SANSTHAN (JSS)

The Jan Shikshan Sansthan (Institute of People's Education), previousely known as the Shramik Vidyapeeth, was first established in Mumbai in 1967. Its number was gradually increased to 17 in 1983. By the end of Eighth Five Year Plan, its number reached 58. There were 92 JSSs upto 2000 and 16 more have been sanctioned by the Government of India during 2001-2002. The JSS organizes vocational training and skill development programmes for neo-literates and other target groups of non-literates, less educated, SCs, STs, women, etc. under continuing education schemes. Besides literacy programmes, it offers technical and vocational skills development programmes like candle and agarbatti making, sewing and embroidery and computer courses. About 225 vocational training courses are being offered by the JSS to more than 5 lakh beneficiaries of which, 65 per cent are women. Most of the JSSs are set up under the aegis of NGOs and financially supported by the Government of India. Basic objectives of JSS are:

- To improve the occupational skills and technical knowledge of neo-literates and the trainees and also to raise their efficiency and to increase their productive ability;
- To provide academic and technical resource support to ZSS in taking up vocational and skills development programmes for neo-literates in both urban and rural areas;
- To serve as nodal CEC, coordinate, supervise and monitor 10-15 CECs/nodal CECs;
- To organize training and orientation courses for Key Resource Persons;
- To organize equivalency programmes through open learning system;
- To widen the range of knowledge and understanding of the social, economic and political system; and
- To promote national goals such as secularism, national integration, population control, gender equality, protection and conservation of environment.

4.20 SHIKSHA KARMI PROJECT (SKP)

One of the major obstacles in achieving the goal of UEE was absenteeism of non-resident teachers in the school. Under this project regular teachers are replaced by the local teachers, possessing training to teach elementary classes. The project is being implemented by the Government of Rajasthan through Rajasthan Shiksha Karmi Board (RSKB) with assistance from VAs. The Village Education Committees (VEC) have contributed to the improvement of school environment, augmentation of infrastructure and facilities, under the SKP. 4829 Prehar Pathshala (PPs) (school of convenient timings) provide educational programmes for out of the school children who cannot attend regular day-schools due to pre-occupation at home. At present, 22,359 girls who constitute 71 per cent of learners in PPs are benefiting from this project. The SKP has emerged as a unique instrument of human resource development. The project covers 2715 villages in 146 development Blocks of 32 districts in Rajasthan and 6285 Shiksha Karmis provide primary education to 21.6 lakh children in day schools and PPs.

During its first phase (1987-1994), Government of Rajasthan and SIDA spent Rs 21.12 crore on 10:90 basis. In the second phase of SKP (July 1994-June 1998) the money was raised to Rs 72.21 crore with equal share by both agencies. Later on, Department of International Development, UK joined hands with the Government of Rajasthan in the third phase (July 1998 - March 2003) with a total expenditure of Rs 240 crore and fifty-fifty share by each. Before the completion of the project, it has been proposed to cover 4100 villages/day schools, 7333 PPs, 121 upper primary schools covering all districts of Rajasthan with an expected enrolment of 324,345 students.

4.21 LOK JUMBISH

About a few years ago, fifteen year old Sapana was illiterate and spent her time grazing cattle at Jangroo village in Rajasthan's Bikaner district, where the nearest school was six kilometer away. In April 1998, she and other girls joined the Balika Shikshan Shivir organised under the government-backed project called Lok Jumbish. Within six months, she reached class V and was enrolled in a school. Now she is studying in senior secondary class along with her husband. In Ahalwara village in Bharatpur district where not a single girl has cleared class V since Independence, enrollment of boys and girls has increased and drop-out rate has fallen since Lok Jumbish project started.

Lok Jumbish[12] means people's movement for education for all. And that is what it has been in the real sense of the word. The Lok Jumbish programme started in 1992 in Rajasthan where adult illiteracy was widespread, affecting 45 per cent of men and 80 per cent of women; and over one-half population of the children of school-going age did not attend school, 70 per cent of them being girls.

The basic objective of the project was to achieve education for all by the year 2000 through people's mobilisation and their participation. Its first phase (1 June 1992 - 30 June 1994) was approved by the Government of India to cover 25 Blocks spread over several districts with an estimated cost of Rs 14.03 crore. Lok Jumbish started a people-centred movement for literacy, with a special focus on female education. The local community was made responsible for bringing children to school and retaining them there. The salient features of Lok Jumbish are the decentralization of education planning and management through the mechanism of VECs, the provision of educational facilities to all unreached children, especially girls, and an improvement in the quality of education.

The programme has a decentralized structure. The power to open schools, upgrade primary schools, create new posts for teachers are all vested in the Block Management Committee (BMC) which is composed of local individuals and organizations. Each Committee is responsible for 100-150 villages, which are further subdivided into clusters of 25 villages for the purposes of administration.

Lok Jumbish has emerged as an ideal mix between VAs, local community, local government and international donors. By February 1997, Lok Jumbish had established more than 1,500 NFE centres, with 20,000 girls and 9,200 boys enrolled in them, which were extended to a population of 10 million. Evaluation of the programme shows that the level of learning in these centres is as good as in government schools. After achieving satisfactory result from first phase, second phase (1 July 1994-30 June 1998) was approved by the Government of India with an outlay of Rs 96.92 crore which was shared by the Swedish International Development Authority (SIDA), the Government of India and the Government of Rajasthan in the ratio of 3:2:1.

Immediately after the Pokharan Nuclear Tests conducted by India in May 1998, SIDA stopped its part of funding to Lok Jumbish. It again started funding for the remaining period of the phase II after a great persuasion. Since the funding of SIDA was not certain, therefore, Department for International Development, UK was approached to provide support to phase III of the project 1999-2004. The Department for International Development has approved the assistance of Pound 31.43 million as local cost grant and Pound 3.0 million as technical cooperation. The project extended to 75 development Blocks belonging to 27 districts covering one-third of the state's rural population. About 6954 village core teams, with 80,000 active members and 6000 women groups of 55,000 active members are working in the villages as part of the project. Nearly 6 lakh children and their families, belonging to around 8675 villages, are direct beneficiaries of this project. Five hundred twenty nine new schools have been opened and 268 primary schools have been upgraded under the programme.

4.22 BAREFOOT COLLEGE PROJECT

In 1972, the Social Work and Research Centre (SWRC) started work in a small and neglected village of Tilonia in the Ajmer district of Rajasthan. It leased 45 acres of government land and an abandoned tuberculosis sanitarium at a nominal rent to provide educational services, safe drinking water, elementary healthcare and employment opportunities to the villages around. This was the modest start of what came to be known as the Barefoot College Project. By 1996, it had set up 150 night schools in 89 villages for children who work during the day, and 15,000 children had passed through these schools. Literacy and numeracy are not the primary objectives of this project. However, this project is contributing much in eradication of illiteracy in this district.

4.23 SAHAJ SHIKSHA PROGRAMME (SSP)

The Lok Jumbish Parishad, an autonomous registered society responsible for Lok Jumbish, has launched another programme known as Sahaj Shiksha Programme which has spread over 3000 centres in Rajasthan. This programme caters to drop-outs and out-of-the-school children, especially girls. This programme has resulted a tremendous increase in the learning ability of the students. Under the programme, many new schools and Sahaj Shiksha Centres have been opened, besides conducting regular training courses to teachers involved in literacy programme and universalisation of primary education.

4.24 JANA SHIKSHAN NILAYAM (JSN)

The scheme of Jan Shikshan Nilayam was launched by the Government of India in March 1988. Government decided to establish JSNs all over the country in a phased manner with basic objective to provide opportunities of continuing education to neo-literates to facilitate retention of their literacy skills. This enables the learners to continue their learning beyond elementary literacy and to create scope for application of their learning for improvement of their living conditions. JSNs institutionalised post-literacy and continuing education so that those who have achieved literacy do not lapse into illiteracy. JSNs organise programmes like farmers' training programmes, rural radio forums and *Charcha Mandals*, youth clubs, *Mahila Mandals*, mobile and village library systems, rural reading rooms, etc. JSNs are performing more or less the same functions as those of a modern rural public library. It is quite unfortunate that JSNs have no link with general public library systems and RRRLF, which is the funding body for public libraries in India.

4.25 MAHILA SAMAKHYA (MS)

Since independence, provision of educational opportunities for women has been an important part of the national endeavour in the field of education. The NEP realised that the education could bring about basic change in the status of women. In pursuance to the NEP, a programme called Mahila Samakhya was designed. Mahila Samakhya means women's equality through education, a Dutch-assisted project was launched in 1986 in 15 districts of four states as a women's empowerment project. Its basic objective was to empower women through education to bring about a change in women's own perception about themselves and their society. Under the project, women are organised at various levels to deliver services, to provide resource support and to supervise. Literacy camps are organised in which an environment is created to motivate women to acquire literacy. The MS workers take part with full spirit to meet the objective of the project. MS has established Mahila Siksha Kendras, which are residential schools where girls and women can stay away from home, for at least three months at a time, to study.

4.26 DISTRICT PRIMARY EDUCATION PROJECT (DPEP)

The District Primary Education Project (DPEP) in India is a classic example of utilizing external financial assistance for education by following a decentralized approach. The Project was implemented by the Government of India in 1994-95 in 42 districts in 7 low-literacy states. The programme has now been extended to cover 319 districts of 15 states — Assam, Haryana, Kerala, Maharashtra, Tamil Nadu, Madhya Pradesh, Gujarat, Himachal Pradesh, Orissa, West Bengal, Uttar Pradesh, Bihar, and Rajasthan. It will further be extended to 8 districts of Orissa, 6 districts of Gujarat and 9 districts of Rajasthan. The major emphasis of this project was on increasing enrollment, retention of students and quality in primary education. Around 88 per cent of the total estimated outlay for DPEP during the Eighth Five Year Plan was mobilized from external sources, including the United Kingdom's Overseas Development Agency, UNICEF, SIDA, the Government of Netherlands, the World Bank's International Development Agency (IDA) and the European Community. Under the various phases of the programme, financial assistance provided by the World Bank US $260.3 million, EC US $150 million, IDA US $425.2 million, Government of the Netherlands US $25.8 million, DIFD (UK) Pound 84.2 million, and UNICEF US $10 million to expand DPEP programme.

Although the DPEP finances for the construction of some new schools, the major emphasis is on investment in the quality of education, particularly in-service teacher training, improved teaching and learning materials and improved school facilities. The distinctive element of the programme is its policy of involving states and districts in making proposals. Funds are extended to states and districts on the basis of performance reviews and proposals for the next year. States are especially for innovative schemes; a special facility called the "fund for innovations" is managed by the project, which evaluates the innovative proposals through a national programme of research and evaluation. The DPEP programme has shown promising results according to the reports of various supervision missions. Access, retention and quality of education have been tremendously improved through innovative and practical interventions. So far, 8000 new formal schools have been set up and 15,000 are in pipeline, 38,000 alternative schooling centres have been set up and 75,000 are planned. In addition, about 16,000 summer schools are functioning annually. Under the scheme, a compound annual growth of 6.2 per cent was reported in enrolment in the country during 1995-1998.

4.27 FUNCTIONAL LITERACY FOR ADULT WOMEN (FLAW)

The scheme of Functional Literacy for Adult Women (FLAW) was started in 1975-76 in the experimental ICDS project areas. It was gradually expanded along with the expansion of ICDS up to the year 1981-82. Till then, 300 ICDS projects were approved. Sanctions were also given for FLAW scheme in these project areas. However, the Planning Commission decided to stop the expansion of FLAW scheme in ICDS project areas mainly due to constraint of resources.

The aim of the FLAW scheme was to enable illiterate adult women to acquire functional skills along with literacy, to promote better awareness of health, hygiene, childcare, practices and to bring about attitudinal changes. The target age group was 15-45, with greater attention to those in the 15-35 age group.

4.28 FARMERS' FUNCTIONAL LITERACY PROJECT (FFLP)

This project was initiated as a part of the Green Revolution with the objective of making farmers functionally literate. Started in 1967-68 as an inter-ministerial project for farmers' training and functional literacy, the project aimed at popularization of high-yielding varieties of seeds through the process of adult education. Although the long term objective was to establish one project in each of the 400 districts but the project was confined to 144 districts of the country by 1977 where nearly 8640 classes were organized for about 2.6 lakh adults. The project was discontinued due to lack of financial support and very limited coverage.

4.29 RURAL FUNCTIONAL LITERACY PROJECT (RFLP)

This was a major centrally sponsored scheme started in 1978 for rural areas. The erstwhile 144 Farmers' Functional Literacy Projects and 60 NFE projects were added and the number of projects throughout the country in 1987 were 513, each having up to a maximum number of 300 adult education centres and each centre having 25-30 learners.

4.30 EDUCATION COMMISSION (1964-66)

The appointment of the Education Commission (1964-66) was a significant event in the history of education in India. Among several measures, it recommended that high priority be accorded to ending illiteracy. It urged that adult education be promoted both through *"selective"* as well as *"mass approach"* and stressed on the active involvement of teachers and students and the wider use of the media for the literacy programme.

The Education Commission also stated that in the world of science and technology, the main objective should be to relate it to life, needs and aspirations of the people so as to make it an instrument of socio-economic and political change.

4.31 NATIONAL EDUCATION POLICY (NEP)

India has set itself an ambitious target of attaining complete literacy by the year 2005. This means enrolling and retaining all children within the age group of 6-14 years to class eighth level, and providing functional literacy to more than 100 million adults in the age group of 15-35 years. A Constitutional amendment has made elementary education an inalienable right of all children in order to attain the goal of Universal Primary

Education and eradicate illiteracy. The Government has adopted policies and initiated actions to attain this goal. The National Education Policy[13] (NEP-1986), which was revised in 1992, set out the guiding principles and strategies for basic education in India. In this policy, priority was given to eradicate illiteracy and to reduce the drop-out rate at the primary level.

The policy reflects an unqualified priority to UEE, total literacy and ending of gender differentials. It goes beyond ending of gender gaps in educational system, it seeks to alter the process and content of education so that it can change people's and societal mindsets. The Eighth Five Year Plan (1992-97) facilitated the implementation of the National Education Policy by allocating 40 per cent of the education budget to elementary education. To implement the NEP, Government of India started a series of programmes, i.e. NFE, OB, TLC, etc. Despite the steps taken by the Central and State Governments through various schemes and Five Year Plans, we have to go a long way as centuries of exploitations cannot be wiped out in a decade or two of corrective measures.

4.32 EXPENDITURE ON LITERACY PROGRAMMES

Table 4.9 gives scheme-wise actual expenditure on various literacy programmes during Ninth Five Year Plan.

Table 4.9: Scheme-wise Actual Expenditure During Ninth Five Year Plan (1997-98 to 2000-2001)

Scheme	*1997-98*	*1998-99*	*1999-2000*	*2000-2001*
		(Rs in crore)		
Special Project for Literacy	25.80	20.00	20.97	10.89
VAs	7.07	6.65	9.00	11.00
DAE	13.59	10.55	14.00	16.50
JSS	3.92	4.63	6.71	14.00
Administrative Structure	4.00	5.00	—	—
RFLP	0.40	1.00	—	—
CEP	23.94	23.32	35.00	54.38
Mass Programme for FL	0.21	—	—	—
Cultural Exchange Programme	0.02	0.03	0.03	0.01
NLM Authority	0.49	0.75	0.91	0.73
NIAE	0.30	0.30	0.45	0.64
TOTAL	79.74	72.23	87.07	108.15

Plan funds for basic education are being distributed among states/ UTs through several centrally sponsored schemes. This has led to overlapping of activities and rise in the cost per enrolment. The segmented approach and lack of integration and convergence in efforts of different agencies is one of the causes for the dismal performance. Schemes are operated not only by the Department of Education, but also other departments like Department of Women and Child Welfare, Ministry of Social Justice & Empowerment, Ministry of Tribal Affairs, Department of Poverty Alleviation & Rural Employment and Ministry of Labour.

4.33 GOVERNMENT SCHEMES AND BENEFICIARIES

On several occasions, resources and assets created in a particular area under particular scheme are not shared with others who are engaged in the same activity due to lack of awareness, lack of coordination, inflexible attitude of different government agencies etc. It is often quite possible that the same set of children are targeted by these agencies to convince the funding departments and organizations and justify their expenditure. The situation at ground level is very complex, since there is no single agency either at Taluk level or district level to monitor closely all the programmes focused at promoting literacy and elementary education. This has slowly led to creation of watertight compartments, making coordination a gigantic task both at macro and micro levels. Table 4.10 provides a bird' eye view of schemes being implemented by several departments of Central Government for the children of 0-14 years age group.

It is needed to ensure proper management of resources for elementary education seriously both at macro and micro levels to improve the efficiency of funds utilisation and to avoid the following pitfalls, which led to dismal performance:

- Multiplicity of schemes and agencies implementing the programmes;
- Loss in the transfer of funds from Central to State Governments and their further percolation to school level; and
- Liberal attitude of the states in the utilisation of funds provided by the Central Government and the external agencies like World Bank.

At district or Taluka level there is a need for an organisation or department to keep track of resources that are coming from Centrally sponsored schemes, Central schemes, State Governments schemes, schemes funded by the external agencies like World Bank, SIDA, EC, etc. Presently, District Collector is expected to undertake this kind of job. It is

Table 4.10: Educational Schemes and Beneficiaries

	Name of the Scheme	*Nature of the Assistance*	*Age Group (in years) of beneficiaries*
1.	Operation Blackboard	Provides assistance for appointing teachers and purchasing teaching-learning materials	6-14 All Children
2.	Non-Formal Education	Provides assistance for running non-formal education centre for out-of-school children	6-14 All Children
3.	Teacher Education	Setting up District Institutes of Education and Training and imparting training to teachers	6-14 All Children
4.	DPEP	Improving quality of primary education by providing package of services, school buildings, para-teachers, revision of textbooks, teacher training, non-formal education, etc	6-11 All Children
5.	Lok Jumbish and Shiksha Karmi Project in Rajasthan	Improving the quality of primary education on the same lines of DPEP	6-11 All Children
6.	Nutritional Support to Primary Education	Provides assistance to the states for Mid-day Meal programme in Primary schools	6-11 All Children
7.	Area Intensive Programme	Improving basic education infra-structure in primary and upper primary schools	6-14 All Children of Minorities
8.	Modernisation of Madarsa Education	Modernising the schools engaged in Madarsa Education	6-14 All Children of Minorities
Department of Women and Child Development			
9.	Integrated Child Development Schemes	Provides package of services to children including pre-school education	0-6 All Children
10.	Early Childhood Education	Provides assistance for running ECE Centres	3-6 All Children
11.	Creches/Day-Care Centres	Assistance is provided for running crèches/day care centres	0-5 All Children
12.	Adolescent Girls Scheme	Provides package of service including education	11-18 All Children
13.	Balika Samridhi Yojana	Provides one-time grant of Rs. 500 on birth and incentives for retention of girl child in schools	0-11 Girls belonging to below Poverty Line
Ministry of Social Justice and Empowerment			
14.	Ashram Schools in Tribal Areas	Establishing residential school in Tribal areas	6-14 ST Children

Table 4.10 (*Contd.*)

	Name of the Scheme	*Nature of the Assistance*	*Age Group (in years) of beneficiaries*
15.	Educational Complex for Girls in low literacy pockets	Provides assistance for setting up of Educational Complex	6-11 ST Girls
16.	Hostels for ST Boys and Girls	Provides assistance for construction of hostel buildings	11-21 ST Children
17.	Hostels for SC Boys and Girls	-do-	11-21 SC Children
18.	Special Educational Development Programme for SC Girls belonging to very low literacy level	Provides package of education inputs through residential schools	6-11 SC Girls
Department of Poverty Alleviation and Rural Employment			
19.	National Child Labour Projects	Provides assistance for setting up Non-Formal Education centres for working children	6-14 Working Children
20.	Jawahar Rojgar Yojana	Provides assistance for undertaking various works including construction of school buildings in rural areas under Operation Blackboard Scheme	6-14 All Children
21.	Employment Assurance	-do-	6-14 All Children

a known fact that the District Collectors are fully preoccupied with the law and order problems, protocols of political leaders and other day to day work of revenue collections.

It is not very easy to achieve UEE without resorting to convergence of all kinds of resources made available for basic education. There is a need for converging several schemes of the Department of Education and other departments of Central and State Governments into a single comprehensive scheme to reduce the cost of operation and to improve flow of funds for achieving optimum utilisation of resources of elementary education.

4.34 CONCLUSION

Literacy is not acquired once for all. Literates fall back into illiteracy if they cannot apply and widen their literacy skills. Literacy work is meaningless in a non-literate environment. Therefore, there is an utmost need to create literate environment in the country. Struggle for eradication of illiteracy is a struggle against poverty and hence simultaneously for social and economic development, justice, equality, respect for traditional cultures and recognition of the dignity of every human being.

Eradication of illiteracy requires many things such as good and stable learning environment, good infrastructure for production of well-visualised and well-illustrated teaching learning materials which are of direct interest and relevance to learners, etc.

In India, it is true that extermination of illiteracy has received priority in basic and elementary education programmes. To change the outlook of the people, to make people aware to become self-reliant, responsible citizens, capable and willing to participate effectively and with knowledge and understanding in the building of the nation and to upgrade their social status are some of the objectives of the these programmes. These programmes can become successful only with full participation of planners, public and agencies involved in implementation of these programmes. Once we move step forward, other national and international agencies will also provide full cooperation and support towards eradication of illiteracy.

Illiteracy is spreading like an epidemic and growing at an alarming speed. Due to high growth rate of population and illiteracy, all our economic developments are in dilution. Mere planning and policies on papers and heated discussions in Parliament and other fora will not make any fruitful result. Proper implimentation of policies and coordination among people, NGOs, States and Central Governments, academic and social institutions is the need of the hour. As Lenin said:

> "The liquidation of illiteracy is not a political problem; it is a condition, without which it is impossible to speak of politics. An illiterate man is outside of politics before he can be brought in he must be taught the alphabets. Without this there can be no politics - only rumours, gossip, tales, superstitions".

India has to set a goal and firm commitment to speed up literacy rate and slow down population growth rate. As we had celebrated the birth of billionth baby girl at Safdarjang Hospital on 11th May 2000, we should also celebrate billionth literate person very soon.

REFERENCES

1. National Literacy Mission: Towards a Literate India, Ministry of Human Resource Development, Department of Education, Government of India, New Delhi, 1996.
2. National Literacy Mission awarded top UNESCO prize. *The Asian Age*, 22 July 1999, p. 3.
3. RANJAN (KR), *Mass literacy: The Ernakulam experiment*, Ernakulam District Literacy Society, Ernakulam, 1991.
4. *INDIA: A reference annual*, New Delhi, Publications Division, 1999, p. 96.
5. AIYAR (Swaminathan S Anklesaria): Institutional change spurs literacy breakthrough, *The Times of India*, New Delhi, 23 May 1999.
6. http://www.infoindia.net/nlm/arun.htm
7. CHATTERJEE (Bhaskar): Strategies for post literacy in the next decade, *Indian Journal of Adult Education*, Jan-March 1996, p. 28.
8. ABRAHAM (V): Fading letters: Five lakh Keralites slip back to illiteracy, *The Week*, 6 June 1999, p. 30.
9. http://www.infoindia.net/nlm/voluntary.htm
10. http://www.ilpnet.org/projects.asp
11. WORLD DECLARATION on Education for All and framework for action to meet basic learning needs. Documents adopted at the World Conference on Education for All: Meeting basic learning needs, Thailand, 1990, UNESCO, p. 134
12. Lok Jumbish builds up pressure for survival, *The Times of India*, New Delhi.
13. JANAK RAJ: National Policy on Education - 1986 and libraries, *ILA Bulletin*, 24, 1; 1988; 4-13.

Chapter 5

Library and Literacy Movement in Delhi

There's only one thing money won't buy, and that's poverty

—*Joe E. Lewis*

5.1 HISTORICAL BACKGROUND OF DELHI

As per available historical records, Delhi was founded in 746 AD by the Tomar Rajputs. It was first constituted as a territory in 1803 when General Lake defeated the Marathas in a battle at Patparganj and captured Delhi. It was first constituted as district in 1819 with two Paraganas. Between 1848 and 1853, a considerable tract on the eastern Yamuna consisting of 160 villages and an area of approximately 500 sq km from the district of Meerut and Bulandshahar was added to Delhi. In 1861, the Sonipat Tehsil was transferred to Delhi and from 1862 onwards, Delhi consisted of three Tehsils — Sonipat, Ballabgarh and Delhi.

On 12 December 1911 when change of capital from Calcutta to Delhi was announced, Delhi Tehsil and Mehrauli Thana were separated from Punjab and organised into a separate 'Province of Delhi' headed by a Commissioner. With effect from October 1, 1912, Sonipat was transferred to Rohtak and Ballabgarh to Gurgaon in Punjab. In 1915, Shahdara with 55 villages of Ghaziabad was transferred to Delhi.

There was a minor jurisdictional change within the Territory of Delhi during the decade 1961-71. The only Tehsil of Delhi was bifurcated into two—Delhi and Mehrauli Tehsils with 258 villages. The urban area of Delhi comprised Delhi Municipal Committee and Delhi Cantonment Board. In 1981 the number of villages declined to 231 as 27 villages were classified as Census Towns. The number of villages came further down to 209 as per the Census Report 1991. Thus the urban areas of Delhi include the newly treated 27 Census Towns also. The rest of the area was treated as rural. The entire rural area of Union Territory of Delhi was comprised with 331 villages (of which 228 villages were populated, 10 villages were inhabited and remaining 93 villages were shown nil population) against 258 villages under 1971 Census. Till 1991, there were only two tehsils, namely, Delhi and Mehrauli. Due to exponential growth of population, increase in urbanisation and multi-dimensional development during the past decade, the Government of Delhi reorganized its administrative structure and created more number of districts. Now the number of districts has reached to 9 with 27 tehsils but the number of villages has gone down to 165 from 209 in 1991 census. Only 11 tehsils have urban population and remaining 16 tehsils are with rural population. A list of Districts, Census Towns and villages of Delhi is given at *Appendix D* whereas, present status of number of districts, tehsils and villages is given in Table 5.1 and variation in number of villages and their percentages are given in Table 5.2.

Table 5.1: Number of Districts, Tehsils and Villages of Delhi in 2001

Districts	*Tehsils*	*No of Villages*
North-West District	Narela	46
	Saraswati Vihar	19
	Model Town	1
North District	Civil Lines	6
	Sadar Bazar	—
	Kotwali	—
North-East District	Seelam Pur	12
	Shahdara	—
	Seema Puri	1
East District	Gandhi Nagar	1
	Vivek Vihar	—
	Preet Vihar	2
New Delhi District	Parliament Street	—
	Connaught Place	—
	Chanakya Puri	—
Central District	Karol Bagh	—
	Pahar Ganj	—
	Darya Ganj	—
West District	Patel Nagar	1
	Punjabi Bagh	8
	Rajauri Garden	—
South-West District	Najafgarh	49
	Delhi Cantonment	1
	Vasant Vihar	2
South District	Defence Colony	1
	Hauz Khas	12
	Kalkaji	3
TOTAL		165

Table 5.2: Variation in Number of Villages of Delhi from 1961 to 2001

Year	*Number of Villages*	*Percentage Decrease in Number of Villages*	*Cummulative Decrease in Number of Villages (in per cent)*
1961	300	—	—
1971	258	14	14
1981	231	10	24
1991	209	9	33
2001	165	20	53

It may be seen from Table 5.2 that there was a declined trend in number of villages of Delhi. During 1961 Census, the total number of villages were 300 which decreased to 165 (53%) in 2001 due to impact of urbanization in Delhi.

5.2 GEOGRAPHICAL LOCATION OF DELHI

With the change in its jurisdictions, geographical area of Delhi was also changed. It was 1536 sq km in 1921 and changed to 1484 sq km, 1487 sq km, 1497 sq km and 1484 sq km in 1931, 1941, 1951 and 1961 respectively. At present its area is 1484 sq km. It is situated between the Himalayas and the Aravali ranges. It is a narrow strip of Indo-Gangetic plain lying between 280 25′ and 280 50′ North latitude and 760 50′ and 770 22′ East longitude. It is surrounded by Haryana in the north, west and south and by Uttar Pradesh in the east separated by the Yamuna river flowing in the north-south direction. Its greatest length is 51.90 km and breadth is 48.48 km. Delhi's altitude ranges between 231 metre and 305 metre above the sea level. Geographical map of Delhi is given in Figure 5.1.

5.3 DEMOGRAPHIC PROFILE OF DELHI

Delhi has suffered ravage at the hands of invaders several times. The exodus and destruction of its population was the natural result. The invasion of Nadir Shah in 1739 and the massacre of people of Delhi ordered by him reduced the population to 500,000 against 2,500,000 during the period of Aurangzeb (1657-1707). The subsequent unsettled conditions further led to the exodus of the population. With the establishment of British rule, Delhi became a thriving commercial centre and with the improvement of civic amenities, there began a stable growth in its population. The city passed into the British hands in 1803 and at that time

Since independence, there was a growing trend in population of Delhi at a rate of about 50 per cent per decade. For the past two decades this trend has not only been arrested but reverted back and the same has been reflected in Table 5.5.

Table 5.5: Variation in Decadal Growth of Population of Delhi from 1951 to 2001

Year	*Decadal Growth of Population (%)*	*Variation in Decadal Growth of Population (%)*
1951-1961	52.4	—
1961-1971	52.9	+0.5
1971-1981	53.0	+0.1
1981-1991	51.5	–1.5
1991-2001	46.3	–5.2

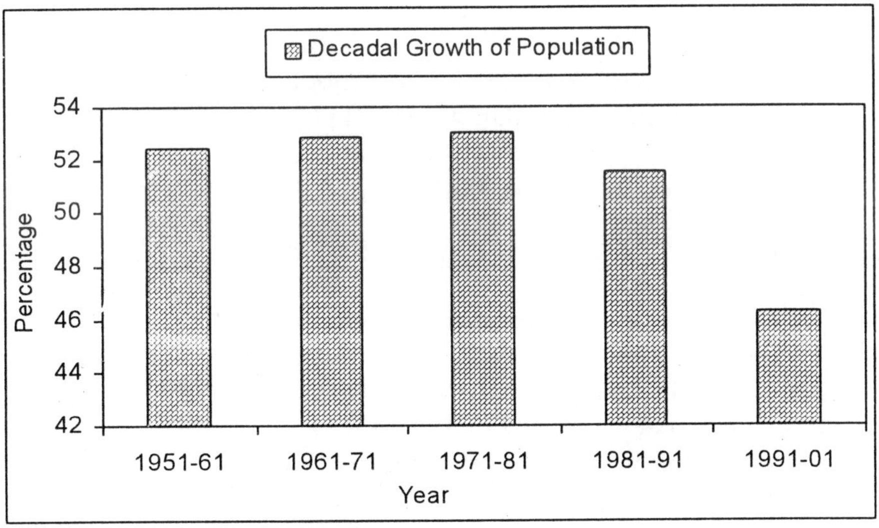

Fig. 5.4: Decadal Growth of Population of Delhi from 1951 to 2001

A summary of demographic profile of Delhi is given below:

Population (2001)

Total	: 13,782,976 (1.34% of the total population of India)
Male	: 7,570,890
Female	: 6,212,086

Rural population

Total	: 963,215
Male	: 533,219
Female	: 429,996

Urban population

Total	: 12,819,761
Male	: 7,037,671
Female	: 5,782,090

Absolute decadal growth of population during 1991-2001

Total	: 4,362,332
Rural	: 14,196 (0.32%)
Urban	: 4,348,136 (99.68%)

Percentage decadal growth of population during 1991-2001

Total	: +46.31
Rural	: +1.50
Urban	: +51.33

Percentage of rural population to total population	: 6.99
Percentage of urban population to total population	: 93.01
Rank among all States and UTs in India	: 16th
Population density (per sq. km.)	: 9294 persons (1st rank)

5.4 LITERACY STATUS OF DELHI IN 2001

Being National Capital, Delhi has made tremendous efforts to improve its literacy status. All efforts are diluted because every year a significant number of people from other parts of the country migrate in search of employment and settle in Delhi. They are mostly settled in JJ colonies. This migrated population neutralises not only the growth of literacy but arrests other developmental works. This also affects the planning and programmes already going on. Some times this extra population forced programme implementing agencies to review and revise the plans which causes delay and overrun cost. The situation of literacy projects is not different from this problem. Although the number of literates are increasing but the literacy rate is not increasing in the same proportion due to regular intake of illiterate population in Delhi. A brief status of current literacy of Delhi is given below:

Literacy rate (2001)

Total	: 81.82 per cent
Male	: 87.37 per cent

Female	: 75.00 per cent
Rural	: 78.75 per cent
Urban	: 82.04 per cent

Difference in rural-urban literacy rates (2001)

Total	: 3.29 per cent

Literacy rank among all States and UTs in India (2001)

Total	: 5th Rank
Male	: 7th Rank
Female	: 7th Rank
Computer literacy	: 1st Rank
Internet literacy	: 1st Rank

Decadal growth of literacy rate during 1991-2001

Total	: +6.5% (+3.35% during 1981-1991)
Male	: +5.4% (+2.73% during 1981-1991)
Female	: +8.0% (+4.39% during 1981-1991)

In terms of literacy, Delhi was ranked 4th in 1981 Census but slipped to 6th rank in 1991 Census. However, it improved to 5th place in 2001 Census. In terms of computer and internet literacy, it has top rank among all States and UTs.

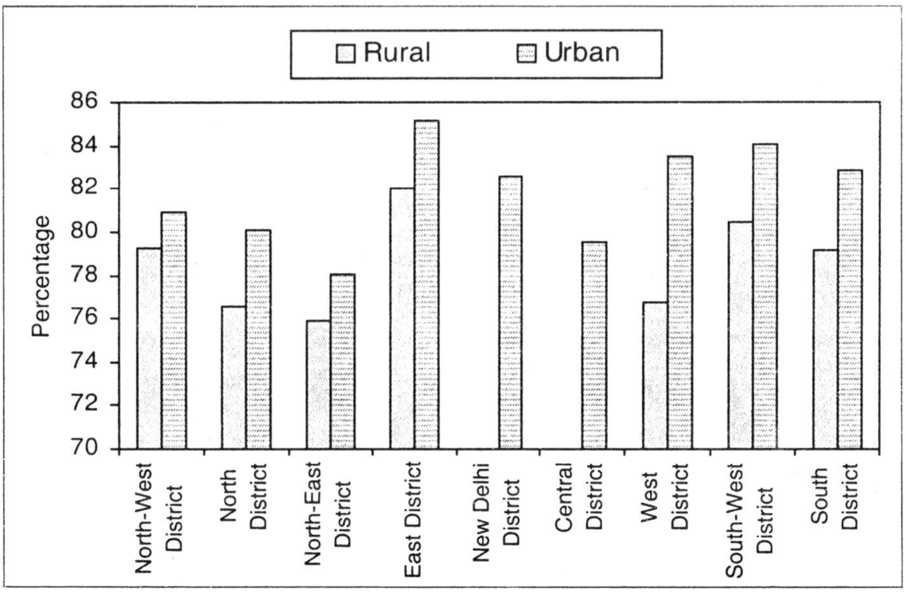

Fig. 5.5: District-wise Rural-Urban Distribution of Literacy of Delhi in 2001

It is important to analyse the literacy rate of each district of Delhi along with rural and urban distribution of literacy. This has been presented in Table 5.6.

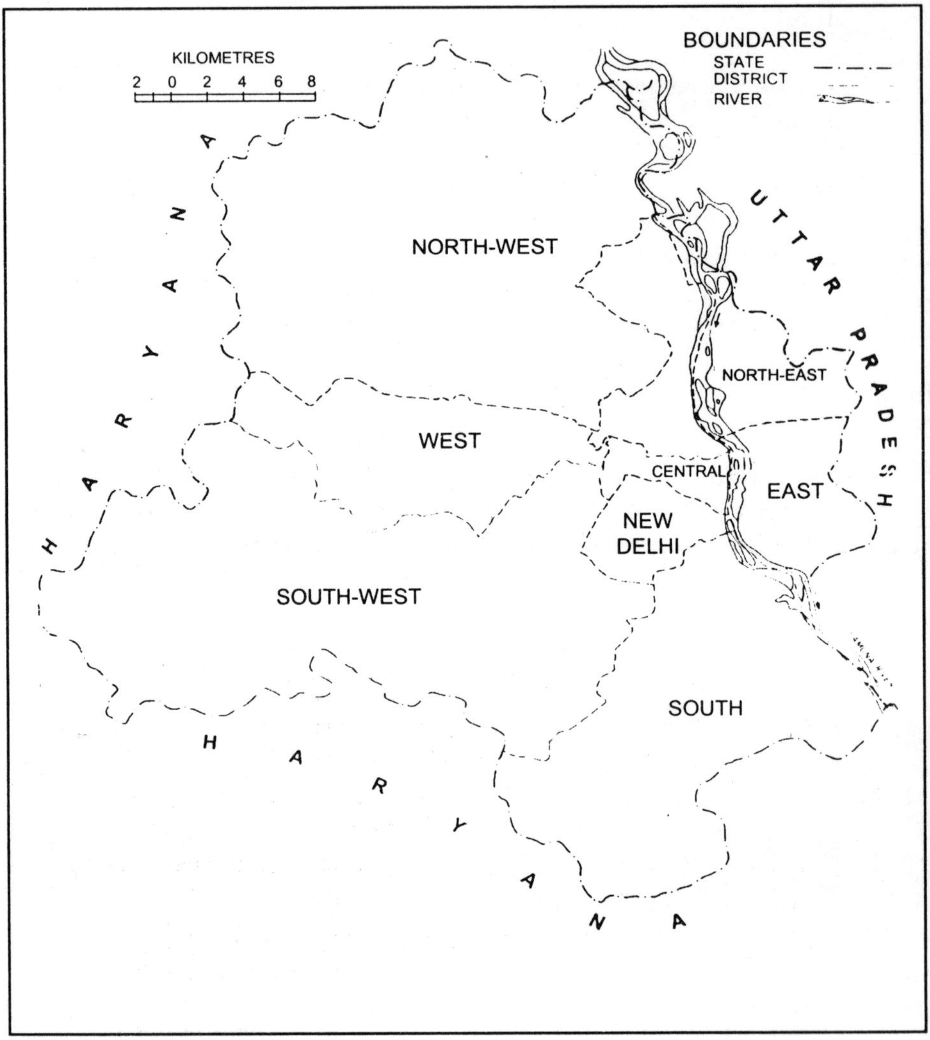

Fig. 5.6: District Map of Delhi

literacy rate of Delhi, whereas urban literacy rate was 0.22 per cent higher than the average literacy rate of Delhi. North-West District, North District, North-East District and Central District have recorded lower literacy rates than the total average, whereas East District, New Delhi District, West District, South-West District and South District have recorded more than the total average literacy of Delhi.

While looking at the male-female literacy rates of each tehsil of Delhi, Parliament Street, which is considered to be one of the most literate part of Delhi, has recorded maximum total literacy rate 88.34 per cent and male literacy rate 93.00 per cent whereas female literacy rate was found maximum in Karol Bagh District with 83.61 pre cent. Kotwali District was recorded minimum literacy in male and female categories.

Distribution of literacy in rural and urban areas are tabulated in Table 5.8 and Table 5.9 to find out the trends in gap between male and female literacy in each district and tehsil.

Table 5.8: Distribution of Literacy in Rural Areas of Delhi in 2001

	Literacy Rate (in %age)		
District/Tehsil	*Persons*	*Males*	*Females*
North-West District	**79.27**	**87.68**	**68.70**
1. Narela	78.80	86.75	68.60
2. Saraswati Vihar	79.88	88.96	68.83
3. Model Town	—	—	—
North District	**76.59**	**86.84**	**63.76**
1. Civil Lines	76.59	86.84	63.76
2. Sadar Bazar	—	—	—
3. Kotwali	—	—	—
North-East District	**75.90**	**85.28**	**64.74**
1. Seelampur	78.45	86.38	69.07
2. Shahdara	—	—	—
3. Seemapuri	74.94	84.88	63.12
East District	**82.03**	**83.58**	**80.08**
1. Gandhi Nagar	50.30	59.38	32.87
2. Vivek Vihar	—	—	—
3. Preet Vihar	97.94	99.24	96.59
New Delhi District	—	—	—
1. Parliament Street	—	—	—
2. Connaught Place	—	—	—
3. Chanakyapuri	—	—	—

Table 5.8 (*contd.*)

District/Tehsil	*Literacy Rate (in %age)* Persons	Males	Females
Central District	—	—	—
1. Karol Bagh	—	—	—
2. Pahar Ganj	—	—	—
3. Darya Ganj	—	—	—
West District	**76.72**	**84.93**	**65.67**
1. Punjabi Bagh	77.26	85.12	66.61
2. Patel Nagar	71.90	83.22	57.42
3. Rajauri Garden	—	—	—
South-West District	**80.48**	**88.69**	**70.54**
1. Najafgarh	81.60	90.38	70.95
2. Delhi Cantonment	86.50	90.44	81.97
3. Vasant Vihar	70.72	79.25	60.15
South District	**79.20**	**87.35**	**68.44**
1. Defence Colony	85.71	90.09	79.98
2. Hauz Khas	77.53	86.46	65.84
3. Kalkaji	78.10	87.27	65.74
TOTAL	78.75	87.15	68.23

There was no rural cluster in 12 tehsils, and among all tehsils, Preet Vihar in the East District has recorded maximum literacy rates of male and female categories. Gandhi Nagar in the same District has recorded minimum male and female literacy rates, which were less than the average national literacy rates in 2001.

As far as urban literacy rate is concerned, Parliament Street Tehsil has recorded 93 per cent literacy rate of male, whereas Gandhi Nagar Tehsil has recorded 84.22 per cent female literacy rate in 2001. Kotwali Tehsil has the minimum literacy rates among all categories.

Distribution of male, female and total literacy rates in Census Towns of Delhi is given in Table 5.10 to analyse the status of literacy in these Census Towns in 2001.

Table 5.9: Distribution of Literacy in Urban Areas of Delhi in 2001

District/Tehsil	*Literacy Rate (in %age)* Persons	Males	Females
North-West District	**80.94**	**86.81**	**73.75**
1. Narela	78.76	86.10	69.35
2. Saraswati Vihar	82.01	87.82	75.00
3. Model Town	79.03	84.23	72.54
North District	**80.07**	**84.40**	**74.81**
1. Civil Lines	83.61	88.81	77.39
2. Sadar Bazar	77.10	80.38	73.14
3. Kotwali	69.12	71.71	65.68
North-East District	**78.02**	**84.46**	**70.42**
1. Seelampur	77.26	83.83	69.40
2. Shahdara	80.60	85.94	74.45
3. Seemapuri	77.60	84.64	69.39
East District	**85.14**	**89.99**	**79.37**
1. Gandhi Nagar	87.56	90.41	84.22
2. Vivek Vihar	87.33	91.49	82.61
3. Preet Vihar	83.55	89.44	76.41
New Delhi District	**82.54**	**88.70**	**74.64**
1. Parliament Street	88.34	93.00	82.60
2. Connaught Place	79.93	85.34	72.53
3. Chanakyapuri	79.23	87.31	68.97
Central District	**79.52**	**82.55**	**75.90**
1. Karol Bagh	87.71	91.26	83.61
2. Pahar Ganj	79.04	82.60	74.60
3. Darya Ganj	75.97	78.45	73.02
West District	**83.50**	**87.79**	**78.32**
1. Punjabi Bagh	82.41	88.20	75.54
2. Patel Nagar	84.00	88.24	78.90
3. Rajauri Garden	83.53	86.35	80.06
South-West District	**84.09**	**89.65**	**76.83**
1. Najafgarh	83.11	89.05	75.68
2. Delhi Cantonment	83.41	88.81	75.23
3. Vasant Vihar	85.86	91.01	79.31
South District	**82.86**	**88.85**	**75.24**
1. Defence Colony	84.91	89.15	79.64
2. Hauz Khas	83.28	89.56	75.41
3. Kalkaji	79.78	87.31	69.65
TOTAL	82.04	87.38	75.49

Table 5.10: Distribution of Male and Female and Total Literacy in Census Towns of Delhi in 2001

District/Census Town	*Literacy Rates (in %)*		
	Persons	*Males*	*Females*
North-West District			
Bankner	75.70	84.73	64.78
Ghoga	80.16	89.52	69.52
Sanoth	85.69	94.07	76.59
Bawana	82.93	90.55	73.25
Nangal Thakran	83.94	94.22	72.21
Pooth Khurd	83.08	91.57	73.02
Khera Khurd	82.95	90.66	73.44
Alipur	80.43	86.13	72.29
Libaspur	76.96	85.13	66.15
Bhalswa Jahangirpuri	71.82	79.81	61.80
Siraspur	78.16	86.24	67.45
Sahabad Daulatpur	63.76	74.33	49.57
Pehladpur Bangar	82.72	90.46	72.70
Begampur	78.71	89.36	65.34
Pooth Kalan	77.00	85.53	66.70
Kanjhawala	79.02	88.36	68.11
Gheora	79.63	86.53	69.71
Kirari Suleman Nagar	73.67	84.51	59.94
Sultanpur Majra	72.72	82.45	61.26
North District			
Burari	81.63	89.52	72.03
Jharoda Majra Burari	78.97	85.20	70.61
North-East District			
Karawal Nagar	79.34	89.91	67.03
Dayalpur	85.20	93.87	75.06
Jiwanpur alias Johripur	82.08	91.16	71.19
Mustafabad	68.14	79.30	55.36
Khajoori Khas	66.38	75.15	55.93
Sadatpur Gujran	78.18	88.63	65.06
Mirpur Turk	76.51	85.30	66.07
Ziauddinpur	80.37	87.72	71.72
Gokalpur	65.82	71.53	59.08
Babarpur	77.86	83.93	70.65
Jaffarabad	73.92	79.54	67.44

Table 5.10 contd.

District/Census Town	Literacy Rates (in %)		
	Persons	*Males*	*Females*
East District			
Gharonda Neemka Bangar alias Patpar Ganj	81.73	86.50	75.74
Gharoli	84.40	89.79	77.51
Kondli	86.70	93.56	77.77
Dallopura	76.67	85.27	66.49
Chilla Saroda Bangar	82.66	89.33	74.01
West District			
Mundka	80.70	88.54	70.53
Nangloi Jat	75.67	85.65	63.54
Quammriddin Nagar	80.38	88.75	70.10
Hastastal	77.87	86.04	67.52
South-West District			
Roshanpura alias Dichaon Khurd	83.88	91.05	75.46
Chhawala	87.73	95.73	77.25
Nangal Dewat	74.52	82.54	63.71
Sambhalka	73.53	81.74	60.09
Kapas Hera	84.02	90.99	71.01
Rajokri	77.86	86.68	66.56
Ghitorni	81.16	93.51	64.63
South District			
Sultanpur	80.91	86.83	72.69
Saidul Ajaib	78.46	85.33	67.25
Tigri	73.74	83.88	61.42
Molar Band	83.92	92.61	72.60
Mithepur	82.80	91.89	70.98
Tajpur	83.60	92.50	72.15
Pul Pehlad	77.27	86.94	64.47
Deoli	79.09	88.43	67.00
Bhati	57.15	70.95	39.97
Jonapur	73.93	82.96	61.58
Asola	79.25	86.00	70.44

Census Town Chhawala in South-West District has recorded maximum male literacy rate of 95.73 per cent, whereas Kondli from East District has recorded maximum female literacy rate of 77.77 per cent. Census Town Bhati in South District has recorded minimum literacy in all categories.

5.5 ECONOMIC INDICATORS OF DELHI

Table 5.11: Variation in Human Development Index and Human Poverty Index of Delhi During 1981-1991

Area	*Year 1981*	*Rank*	*Year 1991*	*Rank*	*Decadal Increase/Decrease*
Human Development Index (per thousand)					
Rural	0.439	(3)	0.530	(4)	+0.091
Urban	0.531	(7)	0.635	(6)	+0.104
Total	0.495	(3)	0.624	(2)	+0.129
Human Poverty Index (per hundred)					
Rural	27.36	(1)	20.90	(3)	-6.46
Urban	18.66	(4)	16.60	(11)	-2.06
Total	19.27	(2)	17.01	(3)	-2.26

Source: National Human Development Report 2001

Table 5.12: Variation in Per Capita Consumption and Expenditure in Delhi During 1983-2000

Area	*Per Capita* *1983*	*Consumption -Expenditure* *1993-94*	*(Rs per month)* *1999-2000*
Rural	208.81	605.22	917.21
Urban	230.43	794.95	1383.46
Total	228.64	777.01	1316.30

Source: National Human Development Report 2001

Table 5.13: Poverty Status in Delhi

Year Area	*No of Persons Below Poverty Line (in lakh)*	*Population Below Poverty Line (in % age)*	*Poverty Line (Rs)*
1983			
Rural	00.44	07.66	88.57
Urban	17.95	27.89	123.29
Total	18.39	26.22	—
1993-94			
Rural	00.19	01.90	233.79
Urban	15.32	16.03	309.48
Total	15.51	14.69	—
1999-2000			
Rural	00.07	0.40	362.68
Urban	11.42	9.42	505.45
Total	11.49	8.23	—

Source: Planning Commission
Poverty Line is in Rupees per capita per month

Table 5.14: Employment Status in Delhi in 2001

Employer	*Employed Manpower (in thousand)*
Central Government	213.5
State Government	113.5
Quasi Central Government	169.0
Quasi State Government	35.1
Local Bodies	95.2
Total	626.3
Private Sectors	221.4
Grand Total	847.7

Source: Employment Review
DGE&T, Ministry of Labour, Government of India

5.6 LITERACY ACTIVITIES IN DELHI

Being the National Capital, Delhi has become the centre of social, political, cultural, economic and industrial activities offering enhanced and sometimes better employment opportunities. It has become a major centre for migration from neighbouring states. Besides growth of its population, the literacy rate of Delhi has always remained above the national average. In the area, where majority of the employees of Central Government and Government of NCT of Delhi, private and public sector undertakings, MNCs, foreign embassies, etc. are living and there is no further scope for migrated people to create housing facility, the status of literacy is found satisfactory. However, the basic constraint in raising Delhi's literacy rate lies in mobilising migrant people, mostly settled in slum pockets in the outer skirt of Delhi. These migrants come to Delhi almost at the stage when their personal needs are higher than the need of literacy. To literate them means to provide employment before enroll them in literacy programme and finally to provide back up support to sustain the literacy. Thus, the literacy programmes have to bear tripple burden.

Many government organisations and NGOs have taken the gigantic task of eradication of illiteracy from Delhi. In 90's the Delhi administration had set up 40,000 Adult Literacy Centres throughout Delhi. These centres were located in Jhuggi-Jhopri clusters and resettlement colonies. About thirty learners were enrolled in each centre. Classes were held at the residence of tutor or some other place in the community two hours daily for a period of two years. Delhi School's Literacy Project started in 1988 and made approximately 9,000 learners literate through 70 schools and 8,000 volunteers. In the late 80's and early 90's State Resource Centres at

Jamia Millia Islamia and University of Delhi also participated in this venture under the Mass Programme of Functional Literacy (MPFL). A volunteery ogranisation, Delhi Saksharta Samiti, has attempted to promote literacy through campaign mode in Ambedkar Colony area in Delhi. Other NGOs like Dr A V Baliga Memorial Trust, Mahila Chetna Kendras, Patel Education Society have also implementing TLC project in some selected pockets of Mangolpuri and rural areas of Mehrauli. The Directorate of Education, Government of NCT of Delhi initially launched TLC in six pockets of Delhi, through the Delhi Sarva Shiksha Abhiyan Samiti on a pilot basis in Nand Nagari, Jehangirpuri, Raghubir Nagar, Shakurpur, Jama Masjid and Kalkaji. The TLC was launched in the last decade in the entire Delhi, excluding NDMC area. In the NDMC area this programme was launched seperately by the New Delhi Nagar Palika Parishad Serva Shiksha Abhiyan Samiti for eradication of illiteracy. Education for all project has been successfully operated through schools of Delhi.

5.7 LIBRARY AND LITERACY PROGRAMMES FOR RURAL DELHI

As per the Census Report 2001, about 7 per cent of the Delhi's population live in rural areas. This constitutes a significant segment of Delhi. Unless over all development at the grassroots level in rural areas is made, further development may be quite difficult. Hence, all developmental programmes should give priority attention to rural areas. A good proportion of rural population is illiterate and susceptible to exploitations in several ways. Lack of opportunity is one of the basic causes of backwardness in rural areas. This factor has widened the economic and social gaps between rural and urban communities in Delhi. Rural communities need to be provided equal opportunity to access resources including information for their developmental work. Rural people have valuable information on food, medicine and medicinal plants, health, social and cultural value systems, music and arts, etc. So far, information is transmitted from one person to other by oral means. This information should be recorded, stored, processed and disseminated to the community for their use. These types of activities may not be possible for individual. Here, responsibility lies with the government and NGOs to establish rural libraries and information centres to act as information base for local communities.

It has been observed that there is a big economic and social gap between urban and rural population. Although the life styles in rural Delhi is quite different from rural areas of other states and UTs. This is due to large scale of urbanisation, migration of workers from different parts of the country, multi-culture and multi-traditions. The case of literacy is similar to other states and UTs. Here also literacy rate of urban areas is higher than the rural parts. Even libraries are regarded as urban utilities. There are very few libraries exist in rural areas and they have less impact on rural population. A big proportion of rural population is not aware of the use of library as they are not functionally literate. As a result, this reduces the effectiveness of efforts to modernise the rural areas. Rural people require better use of land, seeds, new and effective fertilisers and irrigation methods, equipment and other agricultural techniques. As we know, the increase in agricultural product is a result of application of latest knowledge in the field. For example, in a study conducted by the World Bank[4] in Asia, Africa and Latin America during 1978-79 regarding productivity in their agriculture. The result showed that the farmers having four years of primary education had achieved 7.6 per cent higher yield in their fields than the illiterate farmers. Libraries in rural areas have significant role in educating farmers by providing them relevant materials.

Keeping all the above points in view, a need was felt to initiate a library and literacy movement to establish library and literacy centres in each village of Delhi within a definite timeframe to provide the following services to rural community:

- Organising literacy classes for illiterates and neo-literates;
- Providing reading and borrowing service of books;
- Organising seminars/lectures/group discussions, talks on topics relevant to rural community;
- Television viewing and radio listening;
- Current awareness/alert service;
- Organising exhibition of books and other library materials;
- Personal guidance service;
- Documents supply service;
- Press clipping service;
- Reprographic and photographic service;
- Multimedia presentation;
- SDI service;
- E-mail service; and
- Internet search service.

5.8 GRAMIN SWABHIMAN

Gramin Swabhiman, a voluntary organization formed by eminent social workers, educationists and ex-service personnel to instill, create feelings of self-esteem and pride while working for development and upliftment of rural people of with the following prime objectives in view:

- To act as an agency for the overall societal development of people living in rural Delhi;
- To take a leading role and to coordinate with various educational and literacy agencies i.e. NLM, DAE, NAEA, etc., for eradication of illiteracy from the map of rural Delhi;
- To alleviate poverty, encourage self-employment, help widows, orphans, disadvantaged children, disabled and handicapped, war victims, etc., and to rehabilitate senior citizens and physically and economically challenged people;
- To take up varied and comprehensive programmes for women's empowerment and gender equity which may help women to acquire a better status within their families and communities, assist in bringing out equality between boys and girls;
- To assist National Population Commission in implementation of National Population Policy for population control and help achieve national socio-demographic goals for 2010;
- To encourage people for the spacing of children, to promote family planning practice, to follow minimum age at the marriage and to teach them to maintain higher levels of domestic sanitation;
- To assist National AIDS Control Organisation (NACO) to implement National AIDS Control Programme (NACP) through various awareness activities in rural Delhi;
- To impart complete knowledge of national values like, national integration, national welfare, patriotism, brotherhood, selflessness and benevolence, broad-minded approach and dissociation from narrow strives of language, religion, caste and creed, etc to the people so that they become alert and are able to conduct themselves accordingly to ensure their contribution to the national progress and upliftment;
- To organise conferences, seminars, symposia, workshops and other activities related to health, sports, consumers protection rights, environment protection, etc and to promote Indian arts, culture, value system through relevant events;
- To protect environment by making masses aware of the increasing levels of noise, water and air pollution;
- To eradicate social evils like alcoholism, smoking, dowry system, child marriage, untouchability, castism, etc from the society;
- To educate people before any natural calamities and to provide help to the affected people in case of natural calamities like flood,

fire, earthquake, etc and help them in rehabilitation work;
- To coordinate and assist State and Central government and other NGOs in implementation of government policies for the welfare of the rural people of Delhi; and
- To educate people about the policies and programmes launched by the Government of NCT of Delhi and Central Government for the welfare of the rural people of Delhi.

5.8.1 SWABHIMAN KENDRA

The programmes and activities undertaken by Gramin Swabhiman are implemented at grassroots level by various centres, known as Swabhiman Kendras (SKs). One Swabhiman Kendra has been established in each village of Delhi. Each Kendra is being looked after by a Local Committee and following types of facilities have been created in these Kendras:

- Library and Literacy Centre;
- Audio-visual Room;
- Conference/Seminar Room;
- Vocational Skills Development and Training Centre;
- Health and Family Welfare Centre;
- Discussion Forum;
- Sports Club; and
- Cultural and Recreation Centre.

5.8.1.1 Functions of Swabhiman Kendras

Swabhiman Kendras organize, monitor and manage the following activities and programmes:

Organising Lectures/Seminars/Talks/Group Discussions: A large segment of population is not aware of the programmes and policies of the Central Government or Government of NCT of Delhi. Libraries and Literacy Centres (LLCs) functioning under the aegis of SKs organise regular talks on general topics relevant to local people i.e. obtaining loan from banks and other financial institutions, welfare schemes launched by the governments, consumers right protection, comfort living, calculation of taxes on income, properties, etc. Eminent persons in their fields are invited for discussions and also to deliver talks on special topics from time to time.

Television Viewing and Radio Listening: Lectures, seminars, recorded in audio and video forms, are found very helpful in mass communication. Audio-visual aids such as televisions which communicate important messages in a very attractive and effective manner are of immense value. Television, a composite of audio and video presentation, is extremely helpful in bringing out changes in the mental development of people, particularly who cannot read and write. It possesses the capacity to reach viewers of unlimited size. It also possesses the capacity to transmit live programmes and immediately from its occurrence to reception. Being the National Capital, a number of educational and entertainment channels operated by the government and cable operators in rural areas are quite effective in dissemination of information. Connections of these channels are being provided in the Kendras.

Awareness Services: With the advancement of science and technology, the situation in the country has changed. As a result, many social, economic and cultural problems have emerged. Kendras have taken up responsibility to create awareness to those problems amongst masses and also provide them with solutions through right information in appropriate manner. Through LLCs, these Kendras help in execution of national plans and programmes by providing relevant reading materials to planners and policy makers. LLCs acquire books and other reference materials i.e. general and subject encyclopedias, dictionaries, geographical sources, directories, handbooks, etc. which may be used by the regular users. Annual reports, progress reports issued by various organisations, institutions, government departments/ ministries are found very useful for the users to make them aware of the government plans and policies. They also create awareness of national concerns such as national integration, conservation and improvement of environment, women's equality, observance of small family norms and sharing of common problems of the community. Regular legal literacy camps are being organised to create legal awareness among people, especially among women with respect to rights and laws pertaining to women. Advocates and judges, retired from District and High Courts, are invited to deliver talks on the relevant topics.

Service to Job-seekers: People living in rural areas lose employment opportunities due to non-availability of information pertaining to jobs. They do not have any other channel to seek job-related information except few newspapers, magazines and announcements in television. LLCs subscribe to national and international newspapers, magazines, employment news, provincial rojgar samachars, bulletins, syllabi, pamphlets of training programmes and also those advertised job opportunities as well as admission bulletins in various academic and training institutions regularly. A large size of unemployed youths are being benefitted from this service.

Organising Exhibition and Publicity: Organising exhibition of books and other newly acquired reading materials is a regular activity of the LLCs. It is an important event to attract people and to motivate them to develop reading habits. In addition to textual books, pictorial books, charts which are of use to villagers, book exhibitions related to village life and various agricultural tools and techniques helpful in day to day work in farming are also arranged. This has been found very successful for awakening public interest. Publicity is also made in the local fairs, daily newspapers, sandhya times, banners, signboards, etc regarding various kinds of activities organized by the LLCs. Vehicles are used as prime carriers of messages in the form of slogans and logos. Human chains are formed with the help of rural people in almost every village to spread message of library and literacy. More than one million people including students, farmers, academicians, social workers, public servants and volunteers participated in this progamme to make it complete success.

Mobile Library: Mobile library service is very important for people living far from the location of the LLCs. Sometimes people feel lethargic in going to the library. This is an important medium through which library materials are provided to the people living in distant areas to fulfill their requirements. Mobile libraries carry books from door to door and help keep literacy alive and induce literates to continue their interest in reading and knowing new skills and techniques in their vacation periods.

Personal Guidance Service: Very often, bright students loose admission because they do not have sufficient knowledge about admission schedules and courses offered by the colleges, universities and other professional institutions. Even their parents are also not aware of the benefits and scope of various professional courses. Students desire to seek information about admission in colleges and other institutions need to find out addresses and syllabus, etc. In this regard, LLCs play vital roles in guiding and counselling students and their parents. People desired of seeking employment in various trades are categorised on the basis of their qualifications, skills, etc. They are given orientation training relevant to their fields which could help them in facing interviews and trade tests. Besides these, some of the LLCs are providing following types of services and remaining may start soon to serve the rural cluster:

- Document Supply Service;
- E-mail Service;

- Internet Search Service;
- Press Clipping Service;
- Reference Service;
- Reprographic/Photographic Service; and
- Selective Dissemination of Information (SDI) Service.

Information Window: Illiteracy was found as one of the major barriers in the development of rural area of NCT of Delhi. Due to illiteracy people do not utilise services rendered by the libraries. Therefore, there was a need to open an information window which could supply relevant information to the local people on demand. Each Kendra has an Information Window for dissemination of information. They collect, select, store, process, retrieve and disseminate information on developmental programmes and widening and improving participation of traditionally depressed sections of the society and also provide information to masses about agricultural, social, economic, cultural and ethnic problems and suggest their proper solutions.

It is not quite easy for the people to get necessary technical and legal information to solve their problems. If the LLCs are well equipped with such kind of information and knowledge then these may become indispensable for the villagers. Simultaneousely, the heads of the LLCs are also required to update their knowledge by reading relevant literature or by meeting and discussing with relevant knowledgable persons e.g. officials and specialists from various departments of the government, academicians, tehsildars, lawyers, doctors, bank officials, industrialists, scientists, engineers, etc. Some of the problems which the rural people generally face are:

- How to apply for a new ration card, replacement of a lost one, or, entry of names of new family members;
- How to get one's name entered in the voters list or get his name transferred from one location to the other.
- Benefits given by the government to senior citizens, war widows, national award winners, sports persons, social service providers, freedom fighters and other beneficiaries in railways, airlines, etc.;
- What are the further educational chances for boys and girls;
- What are the procedures for admissions and scholarships in the academic institutions;
- What to do if the police refuses to register an FIR;
- What are the rules for land transfer and use;
- What are the rules for getting maintenance for the wife and children;

- How to get old age pension;
- When to give next dose of immunisation vaccine to his child;
- What are the contact numbers of the important services in health, water, sanitation, etc in rural areas;
- What are the fundamental rights of a person according to the Constitution and his duties towards service of the nation;
- How to get loan from a bank and other financial institutions; and
- How to form a Cooperative Society or Trust and so on.

Continuing Education Programme: Continuing education helps life long learning. It provides an opportunity to all citizens to integrate learning, working and living. These three aspects of personal development must grow together so that overall quality of life improves and society as a whole becomes a learning society in true sense. The basic objective of continuing education is to promote and foster informal learning so that adults are empowered to pursue any educational endeavour that they wish to undertake without being dependent on formal courses. It provides an opportunity to unleash hidden potential of the people and brings out the best in them. It is an extended part of literacy and primary education to promote human resource development. The main focus of continuing education is on neo-literates, semi-literates, non-literates, school dropouts and specially on women, SCs/STs and minorities and other unreached population. In case these groups become involved in continuing education and improve their level of knowledge and general understanding, they may become more involved in decision-making process, particularly in development of societal issues. This programme has been divided into the following three sub-programmes:

1. Enhancement of literacy

This sub-programme is related to transformation of non-literates into functionally literates; to help the literates to retain and enhance their literacy skills; and to make provision for them to use their literacy for information and reading for pleasure and finally for health, wealth and knowledge.

2. Improvement in living standards

This sub-programme is directly related to the improvement of living standards of rural people. It refers to the level of well beings of the society and the degree of satisfaction of a number of human needs. Its basic aim is to equip learners and the community with the essential knowledge, attitudes, values and skills, which enable them to improve the quality of life of individuals and as member of the community. During the implementation of this sub-programme the following indicators have been taken into consideration for the improvement of quality of life of the rural people of Delhi:

- Availability of balanced food, clean water and air;
- Freedom from illness;
- Good sanitation quality of housing;
- Quality of family life (parenting);
- Socialisation process and participation in social affairs;
- Freedom of choice and decision-making;
- Opportunity to work and generate adequate income;
- Level of achieving self-actualisation through financial security;
- Level of happiness;
- Degree of inner harmony;
- Level of spiritual fulfillment;
- Loyalty, ethics and tolerance;
- Preservation and conservation of natural environmental and natural resources; and
- Population control.

It was not possible to translate the above concept into action without a permanent base in rural areas. Therefore, LLCs were established in each village of Delhi to fulfill the following needs:

- To make provision of facilities for retention of literacy skills and continuing education to enable the learners to continue their learning beyond basic literacy i.e. to help literates to retain and enhance their literacy skills and to make provision for them to use their literacy for information and reading for pleasure and also to create scope for application of functional literacy for improvement of living condition and quality of life;
- To make provision of facilities for library and reading rooms for creating conducive environment for literacy efforts and learning society, and also to inculcate the habit of reading among the community; and
- To provide basic literacy to the non-literates, left over, neo-literates, semi-literates and school dropouts and specially women, SCs and STs and other unreached population.

3. Improvement in financial conditions

This sub-programme enables learners to acquire skills for economic self-reliance. Each Kendra identifies the different occupations under which local people can generate income and improve their financial conditions. Handicrafts sewing project has been launched with the aim to train rural women to use sewing machine to prepare saleable items such as handkerchiefs, etc. The project has taken off very well. A large number of women have taken part and developed trading links for sale of items in local market. Rural males are trained in some other activities like:

- Agriculture and organic compost production;
- Animal husbandry, fish farming, dairy farming, poultry farming;
- Floriculture, terrace gardening and green house gardening;
- Social forestry and nursery plantation;
- Cup and plate making from leaf and paper;
- Rope making from coir and sutali;
- Handicraft work like *mudha* making from *sarkandas;*
- Carpentry;
- Television and radio repairing;
- Repairing of bicycles and scooters;
- Carpets and durries weaving;
- Tailoring, cutting, stitching, kasheedakari;
- Food processing like badi, achar and murabba making;
- Lathe machining;
- Preparation of herbal medicine;
- Motor driving; and
- Book binding, typing, shorthand, computer data processing and secretarial practice, etc.

Help from local ITIs is being obtained to train new literates. They are provided orientation programmes, taken to the industries for a visit. Sometimes local industrialists are invited for selection of job seekers. This activity motivates other learners to come forward and become part of the literacy campaign.

Health and Family Welfare Programme: It was found that health is in more than one way related to the economical status of the society. It is difficult to bring a permanent improvement in health of those who do not have the means to sustain themselves and their family. Free diagnostic and treatment camps for general health check-up are regularly organised at various Kendras. A good number of patients availed of consultations for cataract, night blindness, pterigium, partial loss of vision, glaucoma, trachoma, conjuctivities, etc. Many camps were organised to eliminate the occurrence of preventable blindness, specifically due to cataract. It included free screening of patients, free transport and stay for identified cases, free surgery and medical help in post-operative cases. Several drug de-addiction camps were organised and a large number of addicted people felt relieved to have rid themselves of an expensive, socially disturbing and counter-productive habit. Similarly, blood donation camps were also organised at various occasions i.e. Kargil operation, Gujarat earthquake tragedy, etc.

Kendras also undertake health improvement activities in cooperation and coordination with the local dispensaries and hospitals of the Government of Delhi and Central Government Health Scheme (CGHS), Employees State Insurance Corporation (ESI), etc. Assistance is also taken from Delhi Medical Association (DMA), Indian Medical Association (IMA), Lok Kalyan Samiti, private hospitals, Rotary Club, Lions Club and other agencies involved in healthcare activities.

It is well established fact that education can reduce infant mortality rate, increase life expectancy, reduce birth and death rates, improve maternal and child health. Therefore, basic objective of this programme was to spread knowledge in the rural Delhi through appropriate mode about the healthcare and nutrition, benefit of small family norms and family planning and other policies adopted by the Central and State Governments or WHO. Under this programme the following activities are being undertaken regularly:

- Health and hygiene camps not only in these Kendras but at the remote locations in the rural villages;
- Dental, eye, blood, TB, cancer, thyroid checkup camps and general check up and treatment of common ailments;
- Cataract operation camp;
- AIDS awareness camp;
- Immunisation programmes like pulse polio vaccination, etc.;
- Promotion of breast feeding;
- Vaccination of pregnant women;
- Legal psychological and family counselling;
- Small family norms and family planning campaigns; and
- Preventive healthcare and sanitation and hygiene programme.

In future, permanent allopathic, homeopathic and Ayurvedic treatment centres would be opened in each Kendra and local people would be provided free treatment in these Kendras. Various charitable hospitals and dispensaries have given good response to provide help in establishing these centres.

Sports Programme: Swabhiman Kendras organise indoor and outdoor games, sports competition at village level, zonal level, state level and national level. These activities are organised in cooperation with the Sports Authority of India (SAI) and various sports clubs. These Kendras acquire sports materials for this purpose. Winners are awarded trophies and prizes on the Foundation Day of Gramin Swabhiman. Emphasis is given to organise local sports. Some of the events organised every year are: hockey, badminton, cricket, volley ball, foot ball, table tennis, lawn tennis, kabaddi, swimming, kho-kho, boating, athletics, etc. Besides these events, community people are encouraged to participate in adventurous sports like rock climbing, rafting, cross-country race, gliding, parachuting, etc.

Promotion and Dissemination of Arts and Culture: The social and economic conditions of rural Delhi are quite different from other rural parts of the country. Being the national capital, there is easy access of information through printed as well as audio-visual media. As a result, people are much aware of their rights. They are much concerned about their rights rather than their duties. The society is of complex nature and people from many states belonging to various castes and religions come and live. In such a progressive and heterogeneous society the original identity of Delhi seems to be lost. Adopting the tradition and culture from all parts of the country, almost every week there is a festival whether Chhath Puja from Bihar, Ganesh Chaturdashi from Maharashtra, Nag Panchami from Uttar Pradesh, Baishakhi from Punjab, Teej from Rajasthan, Pongal from Andhra Pradesh, Durga Puja from West Bengal and so on. Each festival is celebrated with full participation.

These are the occasions when LLCs record cultural events to enrich our cultural heritage. To sustain and carry forward the rich cultural tradition of rural Delhi, each event is properly recorded in printed or audio-visual form, well documented and preserved in the library for future reference and use. Due attention is being paid to the specialised disciplines of fine arts, musicology, folklore, etc. Local artists, musicians, dancers are identified and they are provided opportunity to display their creative activities and performance on local, state and national levels. Activities of artistic interest are organised such as sculpture, designing and simple skills like *Rangoli* and *Mehndi* application.

To revitalize the learning system by creating and understanding and awareness among rural people about the plurality of the regional folk and arts and culture of India and integrating this knowledge with the learning system, all LLCs act as cultural centres for creative development of Indian culture of various regions. The basic functions of these centres are to create a cultural awareness among people and to identify, nurture and promote the vanishing folk art traditional in the rural area of Delhi. They also document the vanishing and dying arts and preserve them in the library. Since a large population from various parts of the country have been migrated and living in the rural areas of Delhi. Therefore, these centres organise local cultural events on the festival days. LLCs prepare and preserve audio and vedio cassettes and CD ROMs on regional songs, freedom movement songs and speeches of freedom fighters. These centres also prepare and distribute charts, posters, booklets etc. on topics relating to the aspects of Indian art and culture. They also organized culture competitions, fancy dress shows among children of various communities and give away prizes to outstanding artists participated in the programming. Quiz contest, painting competition, drawing competition on the themes of natiional integration, tolerance, healthcare, library and literacy, education, environment, etc were organised by the LLCs. Every year on the occasion of Holi, Dushehra and Diwali Kavi Sammelans are organised to highlight the burning topics and current problems faced by the society like corruption, terrorism, food adulteration, pollution, etc.

Development and Selection of Literacy Materials: Developing literacy materials is an innovative and creative process. There is a consistent need for careful selection of materials already available in the market. Both for development and selection of literacy materials, a systematic and strategic approach was followed so that materials could be relevant to the local needs and could be used effectively. These materials are developed and selected on the base of curriculum contents of literacy programmes. After identifying the specific needs of the target population, existing materials were also adapted according to the needs of the learners. In order to develop effective materials relevant to the needs of the women, understanding of their social, cultural and economic situations and tremendous workloads and responsibilities in the family undertaken by the women were also considered. Participation of local community members during the process of development of literacy was crucial, particularly in conducting need assessment and in selection of themes. Community members provided vital information and ideas, which could not be found anywhere else. Due consideration was given to the literacy materials reflecting states and national policies related to skill improvement and income generation programmes. The following are some of the important aspects, which were covered during these processes:

- Information regarding health, nutrition, sanitation and personal hygiene;
- Proper housing, better living and family;
- Environment and pollution;
- Maternal and child healthcare;
- Sewing, knitting and embroidery;
- Agriculture, horticulture, dairy farming, social forestry and food processing;
- Financial saving and its proper utilisation;
- Consumer awareness;
- Organising and leadership skills;
- Scientific knowledge and logical understanding of the issues;
- Development and welfare schemes;
- Awareness regarding social, economic and political issues;
- Legal matters particularly related to girls, women and weaker sections of the society; and
- Information regarding further educational and professional avenues.

A dedicated team of intellectuals from academics and social services has developed a variety of materials for the literacy programmes which were produced in the following formats and distributed to these LLCs:

- Printed books
  - Booklets
  - Primers
  - Comics
- Printed non-book materials
  - Posters
  - Flip charts
  - Wall newspapers
  - Cards
  - Calendars
  - Newsletters
  - Stickers
- Games and plays
  - Card games
  - Jigsaw puzzles
  - Snakes and ladders
  - Audio-visual materials
  - Cassette tapes

- Radio programmes
- Television programmes
- Films/movies/video tapes
- Slides
- Multimedia

- Other media
  - Street plays
  - Puppet shows
  - Stories
  - Songs
  - Dramas

Carrying out Surveys: This was one among the core activities of the SKs. To implement the Target Specific Programmes (TSPs), it was necessary to have essential relevant information about the people and area to be served by them. This was done through a comprehensive survey in each village by a survey team. Initially, it was done in a formal manner, using a proforma. Later on, formal discussions with the people belonging to the local community were also done to gather relevant desired information. The following information was gathered through these formal and informal surveys:

- Population of male, female, age-wise and SCs/STs, OBCs and minorities;
- Level of literacy — neo-literates, semi-literates, illiterates, school passouts/dropouts, NFE passouts/dropouts;
- Existing facilities like schools, libraries, clinics, industrial establishments and other relevant public/government institutions, if any;
- Other local support available like VAs, functionaries from other developmental departments, teachers, social workers, a suitable place to establish SK and LLC;
- Duration of time they can spare for participation in relevant activities organised by the LLC;
- Existing source of income;
- Liabilities towards family members;
- Whether born in Delhi or migrated from other state or UT;
- Mode in which he can be associated with the SK i.e. as worker, volunteer, learner, etc.; and
- Type of input he can provide to the SK i.e. intellectual, financial, manpower, infrastructure, etc.

The heads of the LLCs are made responsible for the following activities:

Organising Local Meetings: Community participation is the foundation of LLC. Community involvement may not be strong enough if only a few individuals take interest in the activities. The strength of the LLC becomes more effective if the community participates in a group. The head of the LLC, being convener of the Local Committee organises the meetings. In consultation with the President of the Committee, he prepares the agenda, calls the meeting and keeps all records of decisions arrived at.

Conducting Classes: As one of the prime responsibilities, the head of the LLC and his deputy teach neo-literates, semi-literates in the classes for upgrading their literacy and numeracy skills atleast 24 hours in a week.

Maintaining LLC: One of the most important functions assigned to the head and his team is to maintain a good library. As a librarian he should know the accessioning of books, classifying them and making them available to the users. For accessioning books, an Accession Register is maintained in the LLC. Similarly, the newspapers and magazines received in the library are recorded in a separate register, simply showing their titles, periodicity and date of receipt.

The head of the LLC reads as many books as possible, so that he becomes familiar with the content and recommends relevant books to different readers. The LLCs have become more useful by acquiring map of the district, tourist attractions, information about development programmes, telephone numbers and addresses of local offices, addresses of higher schools and different types of forms etc. that may be useful to the people. The LLCs also conduct books collection campaigns from the community. Old newspapers and magazines of no archival values are being sold and new books and other reading and learning materials are purchased from the return on regular basis. Reading sessions are organized to create interest in book reading. Reading rooms are the part of the LLCs, where people come and read newspapers, periodicals, reference books, magazines etc. Newspapers and reference books are not being issued for home use. Timings of the LLCs are fixed as per the convenience of the local community/people. Opening and closing time of the library/reading room have been prominently displayed at the entrance of the LLCs. Short-duration training programmes/ courses with the help of local resource persons/agencies are also organized from time to time.

Organising Meetings of Discussion Forum: Organising discussions with and among the beneficiaries of the literacy programme is one of the important roles of the LLCs. The head of the LLC makes all efforts to cover the following points:

- What are the topics/issues that can be taken for discussion;
- How to continue it for large coverage and duration;
- How to conclude, and if possible, help people to arrive at a decision; and
- The decision of the group is written and displayed at a prominent place in the LLC.

The following are some of the important topics usually taken up for the discussion:

- Safe drinking water for villagers and how do the participants plan to get it, what decisions are needed, which agency has to be contacted to get the water i.e. Delhi Jal Board, Municipal Corporation of Delhi, New Delhi Municipal Committee, etc and who will share what kind of responsibilities?
- Whether road transport facility exists in the village., how to plan to get it, whom to meet, who will take the initiative?
- Sometimes crops are attacked by some unknown or uncontrollable disease. To seek the help of Department of Agriculture is a must. How to go about it? Who will contact officers and persuade them to visit the village?
- People in a village want to celebrate a festival or days of national importance. What arrangements will have to be made?
- What should be the basis of voting;
- What are the problems in girls' education and how to overcome them, etc.;
- Policy of the government on disinvestment; and
- Other topics discussed in various LLCs during the past couple of years were terrorism, infrastructure development, rural development, Five Year Plans, population control and National Population Policy 2000, employment opportunities for unemployed youth in rural areas, proper utilisation of developmental funds allocated to legislators, energy savings, etc.

Resource Mobilisation: Looking at the various activities and programmes, it is obvious that the LLCs alone with the limited budget find it extremely difficult to run the centres effectively. Therefore, they try to mobilize as much additional resources as possible with the help of Local Committees. These resources have been categorized into three types – human resources, physical resources and financial resources.

1. *Human Resources:* These resources comprise volunteers, cultural artists, members of Mahila Mandals, voluntary organisations/ workers, members of Youth Clubs, crafts- men, officials of government departments, donors, people's representatives, etc. Other persons who have interest in the activities and programme of LLCs and are willing to offer their services free of cost and without any conditions, whenever necessary. They render services in drafting the action plan, environment building activities and helping in implementation of programmes.
2. *Physical Resources:* These resources are tables, almirah, chairs, books, toys, games, sport materials, cycles, audio-visual equipments, mats, newspapers, magazines and other resources available in physical form, etc. Some of these resources are purchased from the funds allocated to the LLCs, but for additional materials the community people are approached for donation and contribution.
3. *Financial Resources:* These consist of corpus fund, membership fee, donations from various agencies, government grants to LLCs.

Maintenance of Records and Registers: The following types of registers are being maintained in LLCs:

Stock Register: A permanent register kept in the LLC. All stock received for the LLC are entered in it.

Cash Book: This register is maintained regularly and all financial transactions are mentioned in this register. As and when any financial transaction occurs, it is entered in the Cash Book.

Accession Register: All library books procured or received on donation are entered in this register. Books are classified into different categories/ subjects and class numbers are assigned accordingly.

Library Issue Register: It is used for lending books to LLC members for a specific period as decided by the Apex Committee from time to time.

Register for Periodicals, Newspapers and Magazines: A register is maintained for registration of periodicals, newspapers and magazines received in the LLC periodically.

Membership Register: It contains the personal profile of the persons registered as members of the LLC.

Visitor Register: Visitor registers are maintained in all LLCs. All visitor excluding regular learners, are requested to express their views and suggestions in this register.

Outward/Dispatch Register: All the outgoing letters and reports are entered in this register.

Donation Register: All donations received in cash or in other kind are registered in this register.

Daily Diary: Head of the LLCs maintain daily diary in which they can record details of activities, major suggestions, problems faced, number of persons attended, resource persons/experts invited for special lectures, etc.

Minutes Book: Proceedings of the meetings convened by Local Committee and other committees are recorded in this book.

Information/Document Supply Register: Information and documents supplied by the LLC to the users are recorded in this register.

Voucher Files: A voucher file is maintained in which all the vouchers regarding purchase, etc are filed.

Guard File: A guard file is maintained in which all the important letters, circulars, etc received from any source are filed.

Rubber Stamp: All LLCs keep rubber stamps which may be used for all correspondence and issue of receipt for receiving donations, etc.

Preparation of Action Plan: To carry out programmes in a systematic manner, it is necessary for the heads of LLCs to think and plan for future activities. This gives time to do advance preparation to carry them out and not to miss some of the essential ones. An example of such common action plan for a period of three months being carried out in LLCs is given in Table 5.15.

Table 5.15: Action Plan for Library and Literacy Centres

Duration	*Activity Conducted*
1st Week	Training in specified vocational courses.
2nd Week	Health issues, common diseases i.e. viral fever, water born diseases, diabetes, hypertension, etc.
3rd Week	Training in agricultural aspects i.e. high yield variety of hybrid seeds and plants.
4th Week	Explanations of scientific phenomenon, earth quake, solar and lunar eclipse, day and night formation, etc.
5th Week	Population control measures and NPP 2000.
6th Week	Women empowerment and social justice.
7th Week	Moral values, ethics, brotherhood, national integration, communal harmony and tolerance.
8th Week	Live-stock management.
9th Week	Parenting and upbringing of children.
10th Week	Banking procedures, investment and savings.
11th Week	Human rights and constitutional rights.
12th Week	Consumer awareness and other legal aspects.

5.8.2 NETAJI SUBHASH LITERACY MISSION (NSLM)

We have tendency to advise others. We believe that advice is for giving others only not acting upon it. Advice becomes more effective if we act upon before giving to others. Today we have a good number of examples wherein people emerged as leaders in their areas. Before advising or guiding others they had acted upon and convinced people to follow the route. Acharya Vinoba Bhave started Bhudan Andolan, Shri VJ Kurien started White Revolution, Dr M S Swaminathan started Green Revolution and another great leader Shri Bindeswari Pathak started Sulabh International for sanitation and environmental control. Similarly, there are other leaders in other areas who have contributed significantly in national development. Following the examples set by our great leaders, an effort has been made to act on the setting and achieving goal of absolute literacy for NCT of Delhi. In this regard, a mission, known as Netaji Subhash Literacy Mission (NSLM), was set up to fulfil the goal for eradication of illiteracy from the map of Delhi. With the limited human and financial resources it may not be possible to take big step but we believe that several small and strong steps taken by various groups or individuals can produce fruitful result in making Delhi a literate state. Therefore, under the aegis of Gramin Swabhiman, many such events have made to fulfil dream of literate Delhi through NSLM within a timeframe.

The NSLM is functioning under the aegis of Gramin Swabhiman, which is a registered institution and actively involved in various educational and social welfare activities. The Mission was launched by Shri Atal Bihari Vajpayee, Prime Minister of India, on 25 December 2000. The main objectives of the Mission and the activities aimed under it include the following:

Objectives:

- To make Delhi as an absolute literate state by making all persons (age 7+) in Delhi functionally literate;
- To make neo-literates and semi-literates more aware of the national concerns such as national integration, conservation and improvement of environment, observance of small family norms, equality of sex, communal harmony, brotherhood, ill effects of traditional social customs and beliefs and also to make them aware of the other social evils like dowry, purdah, alcoholism, child marriage and to promote primary health and education;
- To improve economic conditions and general well-being of the

people by organising various income generating programmes;
- To provide information and knowledge of the developmental programmes;
- To provide social and cultural platform for community development;
- To provide facilities of post literacy and continuing education to neo-literates by establishing Libraries and Literacy Centres (LLCs) in each village of Delhi for creation of a learning society;
- To create symbiosis between library movement and literacy movement in Delhi;
- To develop a network of LLCs in all the villages of Delhi; and
- To encourage neo-literates in the age group of 9-14 years to join National Open School or any other educational institutions to upgrade their education.

5.8.2.1 Organisational Setup

Apex Committee (AC): The Apex Committee consists of one chairman, one secretary and minimum three members. The working period of the Committee is initially for five years which may be extended for another five years. This Committee has the following authority, responsibilities and functions:

- To take all policy decisions, and decisions on all matters of vital interest of the Mission and in consonance with the objectives of the Gramin Swabhiman;
- To overall manage and implement all occupations and activities of the NSLM;
- To exercise control over the functionaries of the Mission and instill discipline in them;
- To prepare and implement detailed action plan for establishment, development, management and administration of the Mission;
- To obtain grants-in-aid, other grants, gifts, cash assistance, aid-in kind, securities or remuneration from Government of India, Government of NCT of Delhi, NLM, any other funding agency or individual;
- To purchase the essential materials or obtain the services for the Mission;
- To prepare the annual report, financial details and financial grants of the Mission for approval of the parent organisation, Gramin Swabhiman;

- To maintain the proper records pertaining to income-expenditure accounts;
- To implement all programmes required for activities of the Mission;
- To prepare necessary regulations for management of activities of the Mission;
- To constitute all the committees, sub-committees and adhoc committees to assist and advise the Apex Committee and can entrust them with appropriate authority and responsibilities for execution of action plan or part thereof;
- To take any decision in the interest of the Mission, Gramin Swabhiman, state as well as in the interest of the nation;
- To engage volunteers at all levels for motivating illiterates to make them literate and organise literacy programmes;
- To take all steps, actions and perform all activities to transform the community of illiterates/neo-literates into a learning society;
- To undertake periodical monitoring and evaluation of the literacy and related programmes;
- To establish rapport among government, non-government and voluntary organisations; and
- To organise post-literacy and continuing education programmes even after the completion of the literacy programme.

Executive Committee (EC): Apex Committee appoints one Executive Committee (EC) for a period of three years, consisting of one chairman, one secretary and minimum three members. The Executive Committee performs the following functions:

- Selection of heads, deputy heads and other staff of the LLCs;
- Selection of manpower;
- Arranging suitable accommodation for the LLCs;
- Collection and management of corpus funds under the authority of Apex Committee;
- Procurement and distribution of library and literacy materials, furniture, stationery, etc to all LLCs and any other items required by them;
- Designing of continuing education programmes;
- Overseeing the proper utilisation of funds allotted for the purpose; and
- Frequent supervision and review of activities of LLCs.

The EC performs other duties and responsibilities as assigned by the

Apex Committee from time to time.

Local Committee (LC): Each LLC has one Local Committee in each village to advise Executive Committee for the development of collection in LLC and any other requirements. This Committee is appointed by the Executive Committee. The working period of the Committee is normally for two years. The Committee consists of one chairman from the local area, one secretary (head LLC) and minimum five members from the village. The Committee also performs duties and responsibilities as assigned by the Executive Committee from time to time.

5.8.2.2 Literate Rural Delhi Project

To meet the challenge of making Delhi as a functionally literate state, a seminar was organised on 18 November 2000 at India International Centre (IIC), New Delhi. A group of about 250 intellectuals, retired public servants, businessmen, bureaucrats, technocrats and social workers was addressed by Smt Sumitra Mahajan, Hon'ble Minister of State for Human Resource Development and Smt Mridula Sinha, Chairperson, Mahila Kalyan Board and other renowned personalities in various fields. After a day long discussion, in the conclusion of the seminar, it was recommended that all efforts must be made to make Delhi as an absolute literate state within a definite timeframe. In the first phase "Literate Rural Delhi" project was undertaken by the NSLM with the following objectives:

- To eradicate illiteracy from rural Delhi by 25 December 2005;
- To transform all illiterates, neo-literates, semi-literates of rural Delhi into functionally literate;
- To establish Swabhiman Kendras in each village of Delhi;
- To establish one LLC in each village of Delhi; and
- To create symbiosis between library and literacy movement in rural Delhi to create a learning society in true sense.

A brief summary of the project is given below:

Area of work	: Rural Delhi
Date of launch of project	: 25 December 2000
Date of completion of project	: 25 December 2005
Total population of Delhi (as on 01 March 2001)	: 13,782,976
Urban population	: 12,819,761
Rural population	: 963,215
Decadal growth rate of rural population (1991-2001)	: 1.50%

Estimated total rural population (in 2005)	: 970,439
Rural literacy rate	: 78.75%
Estimated total literate population (in 2005)	: 764,220
Estimated total illiterate population of rural Delhi (in 2005)	: 206,219 (say 206,000)
Total number of villages	: 165
Illiterate population per village (To be made literate)	: 1248

Estimation of financial requirements

Total number of illiterates	: 206,000
Cost of forms, registers, bags, reading, writing and other learning materials, audio-visual aids for distribution in literacy classes including incentives to the participants (@ Rs 200 per kit per illiterate)	: Rs 41,200,000
Cost of reporting of literacy events in the form of newsletters, magazines and progress reports	: Rs 5,00,000
Cost of movement of personnel and transportation of materials	: Rs 5,00,000
Cost of evaluation of literacy including preparation, printing and distribution of evaluation sheets, preparation of performance reports for each participant (@Rs 10 per illiterate)	: Rs 2,060,000
Cost of preparation of final report	: Rs 200,000
Miscellaneous expenditure	: Rs 100,000
Total expenditure	: Rs 44,560,000

Estimated financial requirements for HQrs expenditure

Cost of conference tables, office tables, chairs, almirah and other furniture	: Rs 1,000,000
Cost of computers (4Nos @ Rs 50,000 per computer)	: Rs 200,000
Cost of photocopiers (2Nos @ Rs 150,000 per copier)	: Rs 300,000
Cost of laser printers (2Nos @ Rs 25,000 per printer)	: Rs 50,000
Cost of scanner (1No @ Rs 25,000 per scanner)	: Rs 25,000
Cost of fax machine (1No @ Rs 25,000 per machine)	: Rs 25,000

Cost of computer accessories	: Rs 100,000
Miscellaneous expenditure i.e. stationery, publicity materials, exhibitions, rallies, workshops, conferences, seminars, etc. and publicity through media, etc.)	: Rs 500,000
Building rent including water, electricity charges (@ Rs 50,000 per month for 5 years)	: Rs 3,000,000
Total expenditure	: Rs 5,200,000

Estimated financial requirements for Library and Literacy Centres (LLCs)

Number of LLCs	: 165
Expenditure on procurement of books (@ Rs 25 per book for 1000 books per LLC)	: Rs 4,125,000
Expenditure on subscription to newspapers (@ Rs 2.00 per newspaper for 5 newspapers per LLC for a period of 5 years)	: Rs 3,011,250
Expenditure on subscription to magazines (@ Rs 200 per magazine per year for 25 magazines per LLC for a period of 5 years)	: Rs 4,125,000
Expenditure on registers, writing pads, ink, pens, pencils, maps/atlases, charts/roller boards, magnetic boards, pictorial books, chalks/dusters, etc. (@ Rs 2000 per LLC per year for a period of 5 years)	: Rs 1,650,000
Expenditure on CD players, audio/video cassettes, CD-ROMs, multimedia kits, overhead projector, etc. (@ Rs 100,000 per LLC)	: Rs 16,500,000
Cost of television (@ Rs 15,000 per set)	: Rs 2,475,000
Expenditure on installation of telephones (Installation charges @ Rs 1,000 per telephone per LLC)	: Rs 165,000
Expenditure of telephone calls (Call charges @ Rs 6,000 per year per LLC for 5 years)	: Rs 4,950,000
Cost of computers (@ Rs 50,000 per computer)	: Rs 8,250,000
Cost of printers (@ Rs 5,000 per printer)	: Rs 825,000
Expenditure on Internet connection (@ Rs 1,000 per year per LLC for a period of 5 years)	: Rs 825,000

Estimated financial requirements for sports activities

Expenditure on procurement of recreational materials (@ Rs 1,000 per LLC)	: Rs 165,000
Expenditure on procurement of sports materials (@ Rs 25,000 per LLC)	: Rs 4,125,000

Estimated financial requirements for infrastructure development

Expenditure on book almirah (@ Rs 5,000 per almirah for 2 Nos per LLC)	: Rs 1,650,000
Expenditure on book shelves (@ Rs 2,500 per book shelve for 2 Nos per LLC)	: Rs 825,000
Expenditure on books stands (@ Rs 30 per books stand for 40 Nos per LLC)	: Rs 198,000
Expenditure on readers' tables (@ Rs 2,000 per table for 10 Nos per LLC)	: Rs 3,300,000
Expenditure on readers chairs (@ Rs 300 per chair for 50 Nos per LLC)	: Rs 2,475,000
Expenditure on office tables (@ Rs 2,000 per table for 2 Nos per LLC)	: Rs 660,000
Expenditure on office chairs (@ Rs 300 per chair for 5 Nos per LLC)	: Rs 247,500
Expenditure on TV trolley (@ Rs 1,000 per trolley one for each LLC)	: Rs 165,000
Expenditure on computer tables (@ Rs 1,500 per table one for each LLC)	: Rs 247,500
Expenditure on computer chairs (@ Rs 1,000 per chair one for each LLC)	: Rs 165,000
Expenditure on UPS (@ Rs 15,000 per UPS one for each LLC)	: Rs 2,475,000
Miscellaneous expenditure (@ Rs 2,000 per LLC per year for a period of 5 years)	: Rs1,650,000

Estimated financial requirements on rent, maintenance, etc.

Annual expenditure on rent of building, electricity, water charges, conservancy, security, etc. (@ Rs 5,000 per month per LLC for a period of 5 years)	: Rs 49,500,000

Estimated financial requirements for human resources

Honorarium to Heads of LLCs (@ Rs 4,500 per month for a period of 5 years)	: Rs 44,550,000

Honorarium to Dy Heads of LLC (@ Rs 4,000 per month for a period of 5 years)	: Rs 39,600,000
Honorarium to part-time helpers (@ Rs 1,500 per month for a period of 5 years)	: Rs 14,850,000
Total expenditure (in all heads)	: Rs 263,509,250
Number of illiterates (target population)	: 206,000
Expenditure on each illiterate (to make literate)	: Rs 1280

Some of the activities recently being carried out by the LLCs are discussed below:

A mass movement among villagers of rural Delhi was launched for blood donation in aid to soldiers wounded in Kargil operation. Nearly 20,000 people came forward and donated blood to save the lives of soldiers.

About 3,500 non-school going children were identified in a massive survey conducted by the Gramin Swabhiman. A special awareness programme for childrens' education was organised for motivating children and their parents. Personal contact method was found very successful, besides group meetings, discussions, etc. School headmasters, principals and teachers were very cooperative in this regard.

A function was organised on 16 September 2001 to honour best teachers, students and state level players who had shown good results during last year.

- Book exhibition was organised in Tikri Kalan village in October 2001 to promote reading habits among children and villagers. This has now become a regular practice in every LLC.
- Cutting and tailoring classes were started in 47 LLCs in first phase and these are now well-equipped with sewing machines and other items needed for learners. From 1 July 2001 to 30 June 2002 about 2650 rural women were trained in tailoring and cutting. Centre-wise break-up is given in ***Appendix E***. At present 68 centres are being functional in rural areas.
- To promote computer literacy, eight LLCs have started computer classes. The scheme has been found very useful and the same would be started in other centres soon.
- A significant achievement was made by transforming 3472 number of illiterates into literates.
- Old age pension was provided to 178 people aged 60 years and above through these LLCs.
- Bhagya Shree Bima Yojana, Jan Shree Bima Yojana and Rajeswari Bima Yojana are being implemented in rural areas of Delhi. Besides,

loan of Rs 50,000 was sanctioned to needy SCs, STs and OBCs learners to provide financial support after attaining literacy and to start small scale industries under the income generating scheme.

- Organised health check-up camps in various villages. Recently, a large scale medical camp was organised in Mundka village on 14 July 2002 in which 4,500 people were treated free. The camp was inaugurated by the Union Health Minister Shri Shatrughna Sinha.
- In the field of ecological conservation, about four lakh trees were planted from 1 August to 15 August 2002.
- With the help of Indian Agriculture Research Institute (IARI) about 1,350 farmers were provided training in agriculture area.

Besides above activities, a number of programmes are being organised for the betterment of the rural people. Infrastructure facilities are also being enhanced in these LLCs. Some of the items have been added recently:

About 170,220 award winning books from Government, National Book Trust, Children Book Trust, Jnan Peeth Prakashan, etc, 330 steel almirah, 660 benches (four seater), 330 tables (eight seater), 495 chairs, 900 charts, with sufficient quantity of stationery have been provided to LLCs.

5.9 CONCLUSION

One day morning a migrated worker, Mangat Ram, from Koraput District, presently living in a village in outer Delhi and a member of LLC being operated by the Gramin Swabhiman, was asked to explain the advantage of being literate. He said:

> "Now I am able to read the letters sent by my son from my native place and my married daughter from Ranchi... Even I write letters to both of them quite frequently. Now I need not to go on begging from door to door to ask some one to read or write letters. I shall also be able to read the DTC bus numbers and the destination boards, which saves me from embarrassment of getting into the wrong bus. Now my contractor and supervisor cannot cheat me in case of attendance and payment of wages. I can operate bank account independently without any hesitation and fear. Now I feel more confident than the earlier."

There are more people, like Mangat Ram, who have been benefitted from literacy programme organised by the Gramin Swabhiman through various LLCs in rural Delhi.

In the seminar organised at India International Centre, New Delhi, there was disbelief amongst participants that such a large project can be completed by an NGO to literate people of various kinds i.e. migrants, farmers, unemployed youths, minorities etc. They had reasons because a number of NGOs are being run in the country and results are yet to be seen in the field of literacy. Besides their disbelief, they assured all kinds of support to the project. About a couple of months later, when some outputs were shown to them, they realised that their disbelief was not correct. Only elite section of the society sat watching and all other sections came forward in overwhelming numbers to make the project their own. Training programmes were organised at SRC, Jamia Millia Islamia, New Delhi. In the first eight batches, 236 people were trained. Survey was conducted by these trained people and problems of illiteracy and number of illiterates, neo-literates were identified. Literates and others were motivated to join hands for this noble cause. A large number of students had shown enthusiasm in this regard. Aspiration of the people was seen who were not enough fortunate to access the information and gain knowledge. Contractors, builders, restaurant owners, factory owners in the rural Delhi, who employed a large number of illiterate workers, supported the programme by sparing them for literacy classes at the timings suitable to these learners. These learners were offered some extra financial benefits by their employers after completing the course and those have acquired more skills. Roadside dhabawala, barber and rikshawala have also helped volunteers by offering free services to them and even now this practice is continue.

During the implementation of the project, it was observed that the volunteerism was the only way to make the project successful. The monetary incentives can also enhance and accelerate the efficiency of the programme. Villagers of each village made it a prestige issue of eradication of illiteracy and backwardness while living in the national capital. They felt it a black mark on the map of Delhi and took it as their personal insult. This further motivated them and created competitive environment among various neighbouring villages. Participants of the literacy classes, those had hundred per cent attendance and good score in evaluation sheets, were awarded special continued in both the ends — first to literate the illiterates and second to provide help in sustaining their literacy skills through reading and learning materials. Therefore, libraries are the best source for the retention of literacy and seeking co-operation from every one has to be obtained for achieving ultimate goal.

Chapter 6

Library, Literacy and Prosperity

Poverty anywhere is a danger to prosperity everywhere.

—*Pt. Jawahar Lal Nehru* in Delhi on 27th October, 1947

6.1 ROLE OF LIBRARIES AND LITERACY CENTRES IN NATIONAL DEVELOPMENT

Poor and illiterate people are susceptible to social, political, economic and technological exploitations. Illiteracy causes ignorance, which leads to poverty. These two are inter-linked and are the prime factors, which have widened the economic gap between rural and urban communities. There are numerous examples and case studies available establishing fact that literacy is the prerequisite to initiate developmental process in any country. Illiteracy is one of the biggest barriers to make use of libraries and information resources, which are helpful in nation development. Since one-third of population of our country is illiterate, therefore, the illiterates may not be able to use libraries effectively due to illiteracy. Now the information and communication technologies have broken up the barriers to use libraries by illiterates up to some extent. Access to information through modern information technology has opened up a variety of new channels of information exchange that are not restricted by time, languages and cultures. It has offered tools to overcome these barriers.

There is no doubt that our country has made tremendous progress in eradication of illiteracy since independence. However, even today, on the world's illiteracy map, every third illiterate person in the world is an Indian. Thus, there is an urgent need to accelerate ongoing literacy programmes organised by Central and State Governments and NGOs. LLCs need to play active part by participating in these programmes and some of the roles are discussed in the following sections.

6.1.1 Implementation of Government's Plans and Policies

About seventy per cent of India's population lives in the rural areas. Therefore, all round socio-economic transformation of rural India is a must for securing the position of a developed nation. After independence, Government of India has launched various schemes for the welfare of the society and infrastructure development, particularly in rural areas. These schemes were implemented through various Five Year Plans and financial resources were made available to these schemes from time to time. Due to lack of information and awareness, benefits of these schemes did not reach the final destinations. There was no agency, which could disseminate information in appropriate manner. Only radio, television and some printed sources were used for this purpose. Government has accorded high priority to rural development through implementation of various programmes and schemes and some of them are:

- Accelerated Rural Water Supply Programme (ARWSP)
- Annapurna Yojana
- Antyodaya Yojana
- Balika Samridhi Yojana (BSY)
- Central Rural Sanitation Programme (CRSP)
- Desert Development Programme (DDP)
- Drought Prone Area Programme (DPAP)
- Employment Assurance Scheme (EAS)
- Indira Awas Yojana (IAY)
- Indira Mahila Yojana (IMY)
- Integrated Child Development Scheme (ICDS)
- Integrated Wastelands Development Programme (IWDP)
- Jawahar Gramin Samridhi Yojana (JGSY)
- National Family Benefit Scheme (NFBS)
- National Maternity Benefit Scheme (NMBS)
- National Old Age Pension Scheme (NOAPS)
- National Rural Employment Programme (NREP)
- National Social Assistance Programme (NSAP)
- Pradhan Mantri Gram Sadak Yojana (PMGSY)
- Pradhan Mantri Gramodaya Yojana (PMGY)
- Rastriya Mahila Kosh (RMK)
- Rural Landless Employment Guarantee Programme (RLEGP)
- Rural School Sanitation Programme (RSSP)

- Samagra Awas Yojana (SAY)
- Swarnjayanti Gram Swarojgar Yojana (SGSY)
- Total Sanitation Campaign (TSC)

There are several other programmes and schemes launched by the State and Central Governments for the development of nation and societal welfare. To deliver the benefits of these schemes, various implementation modes were exercised and even some of them were found partially successful. In one of its modes, sustained efforts were made to strengthen local governance, institutionalising people's participation and empowering women through the Panchayati Raj Institutions (PRIs). To improve the quality of life of people, five elements of social and economic infrastructure have been identified knowing fully well that these five elements lead to development of the country. These are health and hygiene, literacy and education, drinking water, housing and roads.

These programmes and schemes are also meant for providing employment opportunities to people to improve their financial conditions. Once their financial conditions are improved, they can think of literacy and education. Here the role of LLCs is to inform people about various welfare programmes and schemes launched by the government. While launching of the new programmes and schemes, the government can use LLCs as information windows to disseminate information about the scope of the programmes and their beneficiaries. Monitoring and evaluating of on going programmes can be done by conducting surveys and collecting data through these LLCs.

Since the Government of India, Ministry of Rural Development is very much concerned about reach of benefits of rural development schemes to the target groups. Therefore, maximum benefits of the programmes can be ensured to reach the people in the villages through the following strategies:

- Creating awareness about the ongoing programmes;
- Ensuring transparency in the implementation of the programmes at all levels;
- Encouraging participation of the people in development process; and
- Promoting the concept of social audit for accountability.

Although some actions are being taken by the government to ensure that the people should be made aware of the schemes and programmes, the allocation and the works taken up along with the estimates. These are being done through wall paintings and sign boards on road sides, bus stations, etc in towns and villages. This awareness programme can be made through LLCs in more effective manners using multimedia presentations, slides shows, etc besides all conventional modes of publicity.

6.1.2 Agricultural Prosperity

The single largest mass of India's population consists of farmers, therefore, future of the farmers and farmers of the future determine the destiny of our country. We have not been able to exploit the opportunities available in the untapped potential in agriculture sector. In this sector, productivity is very low, infrastructure of storage and distribution of food grain is fragile, marketing strategies are not so developed, quality of seeds and high yield variety of crops are not so good, irrigation techniques and balanced fertilizer are not proper. The cause for this is the agricultural illiteracy in our farmers. Taking an example of groundnut farming in our country. We, being the largest producer of groundnut in the world, in aggregate terms, have very poor yield. Our average yield is 1,500 kg per hectare as compared to Chinese average yield of 12,000 kg per hectare. Recently, one of our literate farmers in Kolhapur district of Maharastra has produced 10,000 kg per hectare groundnut through Gamma Radiation technique with the help of scientists from Bhabha Atomic Research Centre (BARC), Mumbai and ICRISAT, Hyderabad. He has set an example for others to become agricultural literate and apply knowledge in agriculture for better yield. Thus, the farmers should be agricultural as well as *biotech literates* which deal with making a person literate of many aspects of basic inputs to agriculture and biotechnology such as plants, soil treatment, seeds, pesticides, insecticides, fertilizers, etc.

During the 20th century, technology has been the prime mover driving agricultural productivity. Now majority of improvements in crop yield has come through utilisation of more irrigation, fertilizers and pesticides. In the forthcoming years, farmers will face more challenges because sophisticated biotechnology will enter into their fields. Biological test kits will be available to the farmers for identifying viruses and other diseases. Pest resistant genetically modified seeds and terminator seeds will be available to them. Post-harvest technology, like preservation of agricultural products i.e. potatoes, onions with irradiation will also be available. Success of a farmer will depend upon his knowledge-based decisions, particularly in the field of biotechnology. Coordination with the Field Stations of ICAR, Agriculture Universities and Krishi Vigyan Kendras (KVKs) can be established to literate farmers and provide information relevant to their areas. At present only one-third of the technology generated by the country's vast agricultural research laboratories networks is estimated to have been utilised at the field level. If this level could be raised to say about double the present position, the food grains output could undergo a substantial jump. Therefore, LLCs need to function as link between agriculture scientists and farmers for technology transfer. Thus, the technology can be transferred from laboratories to farms through these centres.

6.1.3 Food Security

The concept of food security is no longer confined to availability of adequate food. Now it has been linked with other aspects like nutrition, health, education, economic access to nutritious food, safe drinking water and livelihood security. Dr M S Swaminathan, a famous agriculture scientist, has redefined the food security keeping in view of the following parameters:

- Food security should be considered at the level of individual, rather than of household, since women and children tend to suffer more from poverty-induced under-nutrition;
- Non-food factors like income, environmental hygiene, primary healthcare and literacy are equally important; and
- Poverty is the primary cause of under-and malnutrition.

To meet the growing demand of food grains, vegetables, fruits, milk, poultry and cash crops, we have to adopt modern technology for storage, processing, preservation and supply. The increase in our present agricultural products is due to transformation of forest land into agricultural land, better irrigation system and use of high-yielding variety of crops. Farmers and consumers are not integrated through dynamic market. They need to be literate about the market trends, consumption, food processing, preservation and storage technologies, climatic conditions, high-yielding variety of crops, etc. Just modernising storage and processing techniques can reduce at least 10 per cent loss of cereals, milk, vegetables, and fruits. Through awareness and literacy, one can increase production of these items by reducing the substantial loss. Therefore, today's task is to literate farmers in many areas and not only to sustain their literacy but also to improve by providing current and latest information. With a view to promote marketing of agricultural products, LLCs can provide space for display of products. These centres can help in providing trade inquiry, participation in trade fairs and can employ trade representatives to promote marketing and sales, which an individual may not be able to do. Thus, the literacy through these centres can be used as a tool to help in agricultural prosperity, self-reliance in food grains and finally to eliminate the rural poverty.

6.1.4 Land Record Management

Maintaining, consolidating *(Chakbandi)* and updating of land records is vital for increasing productivity of land, implementing various rural development programmes and also for effective enforcement of land reforms. Each day several thousand villagers visit government offices from remote places just to seek information regarding their land records. Cultivators also need record of land *(Khasra)* for loans from banks. Getting a copy of the updated record of land is very difficult task. One has to run from pillar to post and waste valuable time to collect a copy of his land records. This travel represents a significant hardship and usually involve's loss of the hard-earned income, cost of transportation, uncertainty regarding availability of the relevant official records or even dealing clerks and officers on that particular day of visit, repeated visits for expediting of picking up the required information and harassment at the hands of corrupt officials, who hold monopoly. To make it transparent and easily retrievable, a centrally sponsored scheme for computerisation of land records is already being implemented in 544 districts of the country. The same records can be kept in LLCs in printed form or can be accessible through computer installed in these centres. Financial institutions should accept duly issued print outs of land records given by the LLCs for the purpose of loan transactions, etc. This system may not only help people to save time, money and energy but also to motivate them to utilise resources of LLCs, break monopoly and reduce corruption in land record offices.

6.1.5 Village and Cottage Industries

During the Constituent Assembly debate in 1949 Dr B R Ambedkar expressed his views about the Indian villages at that time:

> "What is a village – a sink of localism, a den of ignorance, narrow mindedness and communalism".

Now more than five decades have passed but the situation of majority of villages remained more or less unchanged. The conditions of remotely located villages are not much satisfactory. Since independence, the government has made special concern and commitment for the well being of the rural population particular to SCs, STs, minorities and weaker sections of the society, and also who suffered as a group due to their social and economic backwardness and relative isolation. Village and cottage industries were considered as one of the important sectors for providing employment opportunities to this segment of the society. The basic objectives were to provide training to artisans in various trades with a view to improve their technical and entrepreneurial skills; help in marketing of products and financial assistance from appropriate agencies; techno-economic surveys and feasibility reports based on available raw materials, etc. Now LLCs, as their charter of duties, need to provide help in preparation of project reports for new literates or others who are interested in establishing village and cottage industries or their upgradation. These can be: forest-based small industries like bee-keeping and honey extraction; collection of leaves and cups and plates making; collection of grass, bamboo and making of cane crafts and various decorative articles; carpentry and wood-crafts; extraction of fibres from different sources and making of ropes; manufacturing of hand-made card board and paper; oil extraction from oil seeds; manufacturing of soaps and detergents; collection of lac, processing and manufacturing of lacquered goods, etc. Mineral-based cottage and village industries like diamond cutting and polishing; lime stone burning and lime making; pottery and blacksmith work; stone polishing and stone utensils and idols. Weaving sericulture like handloom weaving – carpets and blankets; spinning and weaving of wool items and embroidery work; weaving of polyester fibre; canning and food preservation, etc. The arrangement of marketing can be done through India Trade Promotion Organisation (ITPO), Khadi and Village Industries Commission (KVIC), Gramodyog societies, etc. Participation can be made in regular trade fairs organised at Pragati Maidan, New Delhi. This should be the part of literacy programme for income generation to improve the financial conditions of the new literates.

6.1.6 Public Grievances

Complaints regarding common public grievances like water, hand pumps disorder, absence of teachers from the schools, mid-day meals distribution, doctors of PHCs not attending patients, scholarships to SCs, STs and poor students, pensions to freedom fighters and war widows, poor quality and non-availability of seeds and fertilizer in cooperative stores, harassment from apathetic government officials, non-supply of electricity or its frequent cut off, water and air pollution caused by the polluting industrial units, poor conditions of the roads, danger of spread of epidemics in the area, etc. can be registered at the LLCs. The LLCs should transmit it to the concerned authorities in appropriate manner and ensure that necessary action is taken within a reasonable time and also provide feed-back information to the concerned person. Thus, the LLCs can act as problem solving centres i.e. *Samadhan Kendras* to solve various problems.

6.1.7 Protection of Community's Intellectual Property Rights

India has been very rich in herbal and medicinal plants since ancient times. Even now, these are available throughout the country. As on today, about 2000 drugs have been used extensively in India for treatment of various kinds of diseases. Out of which about 200 are originated from animals and mineral and the remaining are extracted from plants. The processes of extractions and applications of some of these medicines have been documented and published in literature. There are other herbal medicines and medicinal plants used by the rural people for treatment of various diseases but their extraction processes and treatment procedures are not available to the masses. Even these are not properly documented. The intellectual property or knowledge about the usage of medicinal plants, acquired by an individual or by the community as a whole in the rural area, is transmitted from one generation to other through oral means. Rural communities have not only created several thousand races of medicinal plants but also have identified genes in the plants and maintained them over generations through highly sophisticated system of crossing and selection. A large volume of bio-resources in the country is owned by the local communities and it is they who possess knowledge of their properties and uses. In other words, we can say that they possess the technology about the bio-resources. Rural people carry knowledge of application of these medicinal plants. The indigenous knowledge of the local communities confers on them certain rights including the right to share the benefits derived from the commercial exploitation of the medicinal plants.

In present environment of capitalisation of knowledge, people are demanding more equitable share of the fruits of modern knowledge, skills and experiences. We have to protect rights of the people who have preserved knowledge from ancient time. Traditional system of medicine, the use of herbs, neem, tamrind, or turmeric, we have to literate people and help them to protect their rights, which in turn can create sustainable wealth.

Recognising and rewarding the traditional contributions of the rural communities to the conservation of bio-diversity and in particular raising of medicinal plants and to their use in human welfare have become very important in the context of the current globalisation in intellectual property rights (IPRs). These knowledge carriers should be paid for their intellectual contribution. Even the issue of the economics of the community's intellectual property is very complex, but the objectives should be to reward the contributions of the rural communities in the field of traditional plants, medicines and their use in human welfare and to create the protection of rights of the communities and also to defend them against any challenge to their rights that may surface from within and outside country as was the case of *Basmati rice*.

We do not bother to patent our century old intellectual properties. We do not act but react when others file patent of our products, processes or inventions. The burning examples of *Basmati rice, Haldi, Neem,* etc. have evoked reactions in Indian inventors. *An ounce of prevention is worth a pound of cure* is truly applicable in intellectual property protection. Sometimes, we take corrective action which means implementation of effective action to eliminate problems identified in infringement of intellectual property right. Preventive action may also be taken for a long term solution. We should take proactive action which means anticipating infringement of intellectual property right and to take action for its permanent and non-occurring solution.

Indian *Basmati rice* is an example of Indian agro-based product which was produced by India after prolonged efforts. The same was got patented by a Texas-based firm, *Rice Tec Inc.*, in the name of *Texmati*. Similarly, there are so many other products *like Haldi, Neem, Kala Jeera,* etc, which are produced and used in Indian medical system for centuries, are also being claimed by other countries to be their products. Had their been such system to prevent our intellectual property, these would have been patented at that time. In case of *Basmati rice* we have taken preventive action whereas we would have taken proactive action. Similar to *Basmati rice,* there are so many examples of agro-based products which were required proactive action to protect intellectual property right. A list of some of the commonly used Indian agro-based products is given in Table 6.1.

Most of the herbal plants are located in tribal and hilly areas where literacy is very low and people are not aware of the commercial value of these plants. LLCs should provide help them in documentation of location of medicinal plants, knowledge on the usage of these plants, patenting the claim of individual or community for property rights and payment of royalties for technology transfer, defend the rights of individual or community against rights that might have been or might be taken in other countries. A database of patents can be created for reference and use by the people. Patents should be filed at the Patent Office by the LLCs on their behalf, royalties should be paid to them and copies of patent document, in regional language, should be made available to the readers of LLCs, because this is the only place in the rural area, where knowledge can be recorded and kept for societal use. A part of the royalty should also be given to the LLCs to support them financially.

Table 6.1: Commonly Used Indian Agro-based Products

Popular Name	*Scientific Name*
Neem	Azadirachta Indica
Brahmi	Centella asiatica
Bhu Amla	Phyllanthus niruri
Jangli Erand	Jatropha cureas
Karela	Momordica charantia
Kali Mirch	Piper nigrum
Sharifa	Annona squamosa
Arand	Ricinus communis
Haldi	Curcuma ionga
Choulai	Amaranthus spinosus
Angoor	Vitis vinifera
Harad	Terminalia chebula
Indian Mustard	Brassica campestris
Ber	Zizphus jujuba
Kathal	Artocarpus integrifolia
Isabgol	Plantago ovata
Adarak	Zingiber officinale
Kala Jeera	Cuminum cyminum
Kumari	Alae barbadensis
Amaltas	Cassia fistula

6.1.8 Health and Hygiene

Health of people leads to better economy and social progress of the nation. Health conditions of rural people are not so good as compared to urban people due to various reasons. Providing medical facilities to all the patients is not an easy task for the government. The only way is to apply *"prevention is better than cure"* technique. People should be made aware of the causes of diseases, sanitation and hygiene, how to prevent them and what to do in case of illness. Primary Health Centres (PHCs), hospitals and dispensaries provide medicines to the sick people. But there is a need to literate people about observance of small family norms, birth control,

AIDS and other dreaded diseases and also the advantages of yoga, meditation and other exercises to prevent diseases.

Preventive healthcare system should be made available to all citizens of the country. Most of the communicable diseases can be prevented by suitable sanitation systems, immunization programme, dietary supplements i.e. iodised salt for thyroid, vitamin 'A' for blindness, etc. Even some diseases like hypertension, obesity, mental stress, etc can be cured or minimized through yoga, meditation and by simple living. Affordable and literate people can access information about health related matters from literature, medical professionals, etc. But the case for the illiterates and poor people are quite different. Only a small number of PHCs and dispensaries provide healthcare information to the people. LLCs can make general health awareness activities through health literacy programme.

It is a well-known fact that infectious diseases in the western countries have considerably declined due to implementation of sanitation and safe drinking water. Waterborne diseases such as diarrhea, viral hepatitis, polio and gastroenteritis are better controlled through safe drinking water and hygiene. Tuberculosis, which is the top most killer disease in India, is related directly to socio-economic conditions of the people. Since the financial conditions of the rural people are not so satisfactory and a large segment of rural population is living below the poverty line, they are more susceptible to these kinds of diseases. Only funding by the government to various healthcare and family welfare programmes may not produce desired results in prevention of diseases. Creating awareness among public and spreading health literacy through effective mode can be a proper solution to this problem. This can effectively be implemented by the LLCs, and not only by the PHCs. However, proper coordination and help can be taken from PHCs, local medical institutions, NGOs, NACO, NBT, CBT and other literary agencies which have produced reading and learning materials in variety of forms for the causes of diseases and their prevention. These need to be presented in a very simple manner so that any literate person can read and follow. As on today, not only in rural areas, even in the urban areas, majority of people do not know the National Population Policy (NPP) 2000 and its objectives. Then how can one expect to achieve its set goals for TFR of 2.1, IMR below 30 per 1000, MMR below 100 per 100,000 within stipulated time period. Information about all these can be disseminated through LLCs.

6.1.9 Ecological Preservation

Degradation of environment is seriously threatening the sustainability of the ecosystem in our country. Government has incorporated several plans and policies to prevent top soil, depletion of underground water, pollution of lakes and rivers, air pollution, deforestation, conversion of forest into agricultural land, safe disposal and recycling of garbage, sewage disposal and human wastes disposal, etc. Awareness about these degradations is spread by the school children through formal education. But a large segment of the society, not attending formal education, is deprived of this awareness programme. Awareness about the necessity of preservation of ecosystem needs to be spread in a large scale among masses, otherwise severe consequences like floods, drought, landslides, famine, hunger, diseases, etc., may occur.

There are certain environmental components, which are essentially required for our life such as clean air and water, temperature, humidity, light, etc. One must be aware of the necessity of these components and prevention of air, water and sound pollution, global warming, depletion of ozone layer, hazardous chemicals like pesticides, industrial chemicals and insecticides. By their characteristics, most of these compounds are harmful to human beings, animals and the environment because these are made to kill or otherwise adversely affect living organisms. At the same time, pesticides are useful to the society because of their ability to kill insects, weeds and other pests. Toxic chemicals used in insecticides and pesticides enter into our bodies through intake of grains, vegetables, fruits, edible oils, dairy products and meat. Some of these compounds are considered to be highly toxic and affect body systems of human beings and wild life. Therefore, there should be some mechanism to make people aware of the effect of these compounds. Here also, none other than the LLCs can be the appropriate agency for making people aware of the consequences of environmental pollution and ecological degradation.

6.1.10 Women Empowerment

Women constitute almost half of the country's population. They are bound in a network of social limitations affecting their whole lives. Which are further complicated by their own vulnerability and poverty. The Indian Constitution has granted equality to women in all spheres. Even the gain of economic development becomes null and void if the rate of reduction in fertility is not as per the desired speed. Realising the necessity, government has launched various schemes and programmes for the empowerment of women. No improvement in the standard of living would be possible if the status of women is low. Hence, there is an urgent need to empower them, especially in rural areas. The literacy attainment of women means enhancing their working capabilities and independent thinking on the issues in which they can play a significant role and augmenting their families' income. It also has the significant effect on the reproductive career of women i.e. an important bearing on fertility, observance of small family norms and contraceptive behaviour.

Women empowerment can positively influence the lives not only of women themselves but also of men and those of children. Literacy and access to education are the first steps to equality for women. It is the starting point for women to acquire new skills, self-confidence and greater independence. The gains from literacy for women extend beyond family to community. The success of their work in community development through introduction of new ideas largely depend upon the literacy and education they have acquired. The provision of literacy for women should be given priority, if the development process is to gain momentum in India. Illiteracy among women is a great handicap in the promotion of basic education and family planning. Access to the information on healthcare, nutrition and family planning can only be ensured through literacy. It is a well-established fact that literacy among women leads to a rise in their age at marriage, reduction in infant mortality, prenatal death rates and stronger desire for family planning. A literate woman can perform better in the society and can supplement her family income. She not only enriches herself but also enables her to make an enhanced contribution to the welfare of her family.

Social advocacy for prevention of atrocities on women and providing legal literacy to them can play vital role in empowerment of women. Empowering is a catalytic factor in achieving the goals of population control programmes and alleviation of poverty. Since women's poverty is directly related to the absence of economic opportunities and independence, lack of access to economic resources including credit, land ownership, inheritance and their minimal participation in decision-making process. A substantial change in their economic condition, through literacy, can be brought out by increasing the productive capacity of women. There is a need to broaden the range of agricultural literacy, through LLCs, to support their role in activities of agricultural production, processing, marketing, animal care, etc. so that they can improve their income, send their children to school and educate other family members.

6.1.11 Preservation of Cultural Heritage

Educational institutions and individuals take their children to fairs, circus, shows and exhibitions for entertainment and education. Sometimes children are taken to visit important places and buildings located nearby. They are hardly taken to the libraries and information centres as these are not attractive places. These can be made attractive by preserving our cultural heritage, ancient paintings, music records and literary collections in printed, electronic as well as in optical media. Thus the LLCs need to act as centres for comprehensive repository of literary, historical and cultural heritage by documenting and preserving rural traditions, arts, local culture, folk, ethics and values. These can play major roles by educating people and disseminating information, which could eradicate their superstitions, blind faiths and beliefs and also bring improvement regarding social evils like early marriage, dowry system, inequality of sexes. Lectures, group discussions, debates, quiz programmes, exhibitions, film shows and other appropriate modes of publicity involving neo-literates, young children and adults can be arranged to shape the psyche and mindset of the rural people. Many libraries, being run by the Department of Culture, are performing these activities but these are located in urban areas, especially in metropolitan cities. There is an urgent need to extend a chain of such types of libraries in other parts of the country. This function can be performed effectively by the LLCs at the village level.

6.1.12 Human Resource Development

Human resource development is the most important input for promoting economic growth and development of any country. Poverty also persists under the conditions where the human resource is under-valued and land and other material resources are over-valued. Thus, the development of any nation depends mostly upon the human resource than any other physical resource. Since it is the core competency of our country, therefore, its development is directly related to our progress and prosperity. According to Human Development Report 1999 of UNDP, India was ranked 132 among the list of 174 nations in Human Development Index (HDI). Our aim should be to put India within the category of ten top developed nations by 2020. During the past half century, we have made considerable progress in the areas concerning well-beings of people. In terms of higher education, we have reached the international standard. Our educational capabilities are well appreciated world over. But in certain areas like literacy and basic education, this is not so satisfactory. We have to work hard for improvement in quality education, literacy and many more areas related to development. LLCs need to act as the main sources for mass education and development of human resource.

6.1.13 Self Management and Personality Development

The quality of education and moral values that we are getting in our educational systems and families, is reflected in our personality and the quality of our national life. This is degrading day by day. Now time has come to examine the reasons for this degradation. Some of the values, qualities and abilities to be inculcated or enhanced in order to develop personality of individual are: good manners; cleanliness; clarity of mind; sense of responsibility; sense of belonging to the nation; clear vision; strong will power; concentration of mind; self confidence; sincerity; tolerance; patience; politeness and respectfulness; non-violence and not hurting any one's feelings intentionally; proper attitudes towards wealth of different kinds; goodwill towards all; cooperation; forgiving and forgetting a person's small mistake; broadmindedness; appreciating others' good habits; team spirit; loyalty; innovativeness; ability to recognise opportunities; ability to win confidence; mental stability; observance of proper protocol; economy of time, money and energy; habit of sharing of good things of life; honesty; integrity and high character.

Since these values are declining day by day, there is a strong need to provide training of self-consciousness for personality development. These should be the part of the curriculum of the LLCs and each new literate should be motivated to inculcate these moral values in them.

6.1.14 Sense of Societal Responsibility

Library and Literacy Centres have to play vital roles in programmes of social reconstruction and nation building. Due to accelerated developments taking place in science and technology, the face of the country is changing very fast in terms of political, economic, social and cultural fields. Modern technologies are influencing all aspects of our life and ways of living, particularly communication and information technology. There is growing awareness of human rights, consumer rights, exposure of social and economic crimes, etc. There should be a healthy mechanism of making people aware of their rights along with their duties and responsibilities towards their families, society and nation. LLCs can play a very vital role in this regard. Heads of the LLCs can act as public relation officers, interacting with different social groups, institutions and organisations, religious and political leaders, teachers, medical professionals, agricultural scientists and employment providers to discuss various problems and their solutions. They should closely cooperate with specialist groups in upholding human rights; healthcare, nutrition and sanitation; preservation of environmental and ecological balance; leveling down regional imbalances; and reconciling ethnic and cultural differences.

6.1.15 Sense of Belonging to the Nation

In a speech delivered by Dr B R Ambedkar in 1954, he said:

> "The most vital need of the day is to create among the masses of the people a sense of common nationality – the feeling not that they are Indian first and Hindus, Mohammadans and Sindhi afterwards, but that they are Indian first and Indian last".

This statement has much relevance in today's context as people display their identities on the basis of their castes, religions, languages and regions. There is a strong need to create sense of affiliation to the nation and patriotism. LLCs have to play their roles in this regard.

6.1.16 Help in Internal Security and Judicial Systems

We spend a large portion of our budget in maintaining internal security. Our jails are overcrowded with criminals and anti-social elements. This crowd is increasing day by day. Unless this exponential growth is arrested, we may face problem as a large quantity of human resources will remain out of the main stream, non-productive and burden to our judicial system. We have to take proactive action rather than reactive action. Root causes of this growth has to be examined. One of the reasons may be that they are not being properly guided, moulded towards better living, provided job opportunities and taught moral values, etc. At present, only formal education is the prime mode of these activities. Other modes have to be created which can be helpful in this regard. LLCs can be made instrumental in helping the internal security and reducing the burden on judicial system. As once, Dr Nagendra from International Court of Justice, while delivering a lecture in Arts Faculy at University of Delhi, said that a portion of budget allocated to internal security of the country should be diverted to institution imparting literacy and education. These institutions should include peace education in their curriculum. This may help in moulding the nascent minds towards communal harmony, peace and other good causes. Since LLCs are to be operational at village level, they can share this responsibility in more effective manner.

6.1.17 Everyone's Participation

Western countries have not achieved the status of developed nation in a year or two. These countries formed strategies, chalked out programmes and implemented in phased manner with full dedication and honesty. We should also act on the similar line and each one of us should participate with full spirit to achieve the goal of a functionally literate country. Unless our emerging population is made functionally literate and suitably developed and skilled to be useful and productive to the economy, the country can be trapped in the vicious circle of the poorer nation and we shall become poor day-by-day. Each state should prepare a vision document for development as prepared by the Andhra Pradesh. LLCs can help to implement their vision.

> "Each one enroll one – an appeal primarily to college students/akshara senas/NGOs. Each one teach one – an appeal to all educated citizens (including students, teachers, retired persons, educated youth, women, elder citizens, etc. Each one adopt one – an appeal to philanthropists, industries, volunteer agencies, educational institutions, etc. to adopt either a student for funding his/her education or a school or a village for its over all development. Each parent of – "out of school children" a special appeal enroll your child/children. As a citizen of the State let us share these concerns, rise, unite and mobilize all resources and meet this challenge of achieving 85 per cent literacy before 2005 and realise for ourselves "A Swarnandhra Pradesh."
>
> — From the Vision Document prepared by the Government of Andhra Pradesh

6.1.18 Developing Human Potentiality and Creativity

All are created equal by the Master Creator. Yet the world is full of a variety of people. What makes them so different from each other. Some of the basic factors may be parenting, imparting education, providing living environment, life style, way of thinking and acting, time management, etc. Creativity is an important skill which some people get as a natural gift and others have to develop. Creative people are more open and responsive to the world around them, positive self-image and open to criticism and ability to tolerate dissent. On the other hand, a non-creative person seldom takes responsibility for his own mistakes. He is one among the first to hold responsible for every thing that had gone wrong. His capacity for self-deception allows him to condemn all those who are weaker than him and worship all those who have power. These non-creative characteristics lies mostly among illiterates because of their limited access to information and little exposure to the outside world. LLCs can help in providing opportunities and rich information resources and learning environment to develop creativity and potentiality.

6.1.19 Value Addition

Persons having knowledge and skills enjoy better standard of living and are able to work more. The same is true for Indian farmers. Just producing agricultural products and selling them into market may not be able to enhance their economic conditions. Doing something more to raise the satisfaction level of consumers and enhancing the value of the product is known as value addition. It may be better presentation, good taste, durability in storage and preservation of products. Indian farmers can add value to their products and capitalize their products like cereals, milk, fruits and vegetables for generation of domestic wealth and employment. Emphasis can be given to add values to the products and services rendered by the farmers and further to generate wealth and make them prosperous. LLCs can play significant role in this regard.

6.2 LLCs OF THE FUTURE

Unless we transform our huge human resource base into knowledge resource, we may not be able to fulfill the desired goal. Now the time has come and each one of us need to contribute in some way or the other in this transformation process. Proposed LLCs can be instrumental and play significant role in eradication of illiteracy and alleviation of poverty for nation's development.

It is a well-known fact that the development of libraries have not taken place in relation to need of the society, particularly in making India a cent per cent literate nation. After performing these activities, LLCs would no longer remain warehouses for books, but the sources of all round development. They would act as social service agencies offering information, advice, recreation, guidance to children, adolescents and adults who do not come under the influence of formal education - regardless of social conditions, race, creed, language or profession. They would act at the service of the interest of the community to awaken the social conscience of the individual and of the group and also to contribute to the development of creative activities for the people. They would provide newspapers, magazines, books, audio-visual materials, films, cassettes, CD-ROMs, gramophone records, etc. for healthy recreation, which is an essential requirement of the society. They would organise various forms of performing arts, music events for recreation of masses. They would contribute towards cultural enrichment of the community by organising extension activities like lectures, seminars, symposia, book exhibitions and other cultural gatherings. They would also serve as information centres to provide information about the socio-economic needs of the society, i.e., employment opportunity, facilities provided by the government or other social welfare agencies, etc. People would come to these centres and collect information as per their requirements.

Besides several other functions, the LLCs should have:

- An attractive ornamental building, long opening hours, comfortable seats, aesthetic and peaceful environment for comfort reading and learning;
- A friendly and informal atmosphere where readers can seek help from staff who are academically, professionally and technically knowledgeable;
- A place where reader can study, relax, refresh and exchange ideas with others without any interference or barrier;
- An easy-to-use arrangement of reading and learning materials;
- A wide-range of current, archival, bibliographical, pictorial and classic materials for browsing and serious reading;
- Simple and speedy procedures for borrowing and returning of documents instead of standing in a long queue and waiting to borrow or return documents. Barcoding may be very useful in documents circulation system;
- Easy-to-use cataloguing, classification and indexing schemes;
- Speedy and easy access to information resources;
- Easy and free access of documents reproduction facility i.e. reprographic service;
- Access to information without paying any cost of services or products;
- A place where one can suggest ways to improve the services without hesitation and head of LLC has to accept criticism and suggestions to act on them appropriately and to respond whether or not action is taken; and
- Easy to access resources from any corner of the LLC or from home. This may be possible if the resources are made available on Internet or any other network connected to the information resource base.

LLCs need to fulfil as many of the above perceptions as they possibly can. They need to listen and learn, to find out what the users want, how to supply and how to satisfy them. Since the need of the users are not static, it has to be assessed periodically; otherwise LLC can go on serving the needs of yesterday or the day before rather than those of today.

Dynamic users are more and more demanding. When their one demand is met, they may expect more from LLCs. They may ask for better and faster service, personalized service and tailor-made response against a specific query. In case, users need would not fulfilled, they may drop their needs or take elsewhere. LLCs need to measure their performances regularly. These should listen, learn, adapt and constantly improve their performances in terms of quantity and quality. Therefore, there is need to design LLCs around people than to redesign people to fit in these centres.

Different people have different views about the role of a library. Some of them think that the role of a library is to store and issue books, a place where one can read newspapers, magazines, etc. About half of the users think that library is also an information centre where one can go and seek information relevant to his/her need. Most of the libraries are traditional and needed updation in terms of their collections and services. Materials acquired by them do not match with the basic needs of the users. These materials may be acquired in the local languages and in variety of forms i.e. audio, video, CD-ROMs etc. Information technology may be implemented in the library activities, services and dissemination of information to the society as well for archival storage.

Libraries largely concentrate on the materials acquired by them and type of services needed for the community. Libraries must be increasingly aware of their social, economic, cultural and political objectives. They must involve some effective mechanisms for better utilisation of their holdings by the users. Concurrent with the changes in the society, the concept of library has changed. Therefore, libraries must change their roles from delivery of books to an advance information resource and learning centre for literates as well as non-literates. People do not understand the proper role of libraries and they may require awareness programmes and these may be organised by the libraries from time to time. Libraries of Kerala have set example to the libraries of other states to follow the same path of progress towards achievement of perfect literacy.

Formal education only prepares us for the future, but one has to keep abreast of the current development taking place worldwide or in his area of interest. Libraries, well equipped with up-to-date information resources, can play an effective role in this regard. Each LLC should possess the following information resources:

Basic Reference Sources:

- Concise general and subject encyclopedias;
- Dictionaries, Glossaries;
- Directories;
- Biographical sources;
- Gazetteers;
- Maps, Atlases, Globes;
- Yearbooks;
- Local and national newspapers; and
- Popular and educational magazines.

Annual Reports of:

- Ministries and Departments of State and Central Governments;
- Universities, Academic Institutions, Professional Institutions;
- Autonomous Bodies, NGOs; and
- Public Sector Undertakings.
- International Organisations i.e. UNO, UNESCO, ILO, UNICEF,

Prospectus of:

- Universities, Colleges, Schools; and
- Government publications on plans and policies.

Books of:

- High literary standards;
- Award winning books from Jnanpeeth, NBT, CBT, NCERT, NLM, etc.

Audio, Video and CD-ROMs:

- Recorded events of various activities; Educational materials from IGNOU, Department of Science and Technology, UNESCO, ILO, WHO, NLM, etc.

Besides regular publications, like newsletters, bulletins and annual reports, LLCs should prepare wall calendars for the next year with each sheet depicting major schemes and projects run by them and distribute one copy to each family free of cost. Similarly, desk calendars and year diaries with addresses and phone numbers of important persons related to library and literacy programme should also be brought out every year and distributed in the rural areas. The basic objectives are to disseminate information at the grassroots level for promoting and strengthening the PRIs. Prasar Bharati may be approached for creating awareness about the activities being undertaken by the LLCs for nation development. A weekly one hour programme, like Krishi Darshan, may be telecast on services rendered by the libraries and on eradication of illiteracy. Contribution of NGOs and prominent personalities may be acknowledged through these media to motivate others to join this noble act of nation building. Like other pavilions, a permanent pavilion may be allotted to display the activities in trade fairs at Pragati Maidan, New Delhi. These LLCs may also participate collectively in Republic Day Parade with tableau on the theme of library, literacy and prosperity to sensitise people about the new initiatives taken by the LLCs.

Libraries need to have telekiosk with objectives to provide the basic information service to the rural communities and also provide means of communication with rest of the world. It consists of a personal computer, printer, modem, telephone and an assistant. This may increase communication between government agencies, non-governmental organisations, private sector and educational institutions. Enormous benefits could be drawn by sharing information in the areas of cultivation, forestry, health, nutrition, education, etc.

Libraries should be provided basic infrastructure including building, electricity, water, modern information and communication technology, trained professional manpower, adequate budget, etc. Unfortunately, over 90 per cent population, particularly in rural areas, do not have the minimum facility of either a reading room or access to even a newspaper.

Participation of libraries in literacy movement has not been given much importance by government or by any agency oriented to literacy or adult education programmes. Amalgamation of literacy and adult education programmes with libraries needs to be given a great thought. Literacy programmes are based on participation, therefore, all agencies involve in literacy programmes should coordinate each other to achieve the ultimate goal of hundred per cent literacy within a definite time frame.

School libraries may be integrated with LLCs for serving the population residing in that locality where school exists. These school libraries can serve as libraries after school hours and during vacation periods and holidays. School libraries can acquire materials useful for school going children as well for neo-literates.

As per the Constitution of India, the subject libraries form part of the State List, whereas education is part of Concurrent List (No 25). So it is obligatory on the part of the State Government to formulate a policy for library services and pass laws for implementation of the policy so framed. It should contain the essential components like library, education, provision for information and culture. To support these components there is a need to enact library legislation or restructure the existing Library Act. Because finance is the major constraint which hinders the development of libraries and programmes organised by them, provision of public funds can be assured by library legislation. Library Act should be enacted in all the states for proper development of libraries in the country. Keeping the above points in view, each state should have Policy for Library and Information Services to emphasis upon:

- Providing free access to information to all people;
- Preserving our rich cultural heritage and providing access to all forms of cultural expression;
- Making library resources available at the doorsteps and providing soft reading materials to the society for proper utilisation of leisure for change and recreation;
- Stimulating imagination and creativity in all sections of the society and arranging various activities like group meetings, discussions, prayers, etc.;
- Developing socio-economic needs of the citizens;
- Identifying target groups i.e. illiterates and neo-literates through personal contacts and implementing literacy programme;
- Identifying specific educational and vocational training needs and interest of the target groups;
- Preparing literacy learning and vocational training materials for them and printing and distributing these materials to the target groups;
- Helping learners to enhance their level of reading and intellectual level;
- Developing reading and writing skills and stimulating interest in learning so that reading habit can be formed and self-learning ability acquired;
- Creating learning environment by arranging small reading cells at various places; and
- Integrating literacy class activities with community development efforts.

Majority of existing libraries are not organising literacy programmes. Even in few cases where libraries are organising such programmes, users are not aware of such programmes. Libraries are not associated with education and literacy programmes i.e. NLM, NFEP, DPEP, UEE, TLC, PLP, AEP, CEP, EFA, Mass Education Programme, Operation Blackboard, Zilla Saksharata Nivaran Programme, Barefoot College Project, etc. A small number of libraries in Rajasthan are associated with literacy programmes as Jan Shikshan Nilayam, Lok Jumbish, Mahila Samakhya, Barefoot College Project, Shiksha Karmi Yojana and DPEP. ILP being a USA-based new project, therefore, no library is associated with it. Unfortunately, role of libraries not much recognised in these programmes/projects, whereas these can play vital role in eradication of illiteracy during literacy as well as post-literacy programmes.

The following are some of the major factors found responsible in implementation of literacy programmes:

- As far as human rights are concerned, every citizen, whether literate or illiterate, has equal right. There is no distinction between literate and illiterate. So long this non-distinction remains, no illiterate person would bother to become literate. Just by propagating literacy programmes through televisions, radios and other media would not help in eradication of illiteracy;
- Society is divided into various segments and groups on the basis of religion, culture, profession, ethics, caste, etc. Each one has different thinking about the advantage of being a literate person;
- Non-availability of suitable literature for common readers is also another factor;
- Non-availability of literature in regional language;
- Poor economic conditions of the people, particularly in rural and tribal areas;
- People are not aware of the advantage of literacy;
- Inability of the neo-literates to read and lack of confidence and hesitation to take up the books and read them;
- Lack of well-maintained libraries and lack of favourable borrowing facilities;
- Lack of trained professionals to serve the people; and
- Literacy programmes are not integrated with the library programmes.

LLCs are basic pre-requisite for the development of a culture-based reading, which is, of course, the base for education. These make provision of local, national and international newspapers and magazines. They allow an increased number of people, some of them with social and economic difficulties, to have access to common information about the state, country and the world. Audio-visual system, i.e. radio and television, has played significant role in this direction by providing access to so many local, national and international channels.

Now people can create their own discussion groups and web sites to communicate their problems and progresses to seek guidance and assistance from national and international agencies through Internet. Internet facility needs to be made available to LLCs and it needs to be accessible to the users free of cost. The exposure to Internet and the delivery of information, particularly in rural areas, would create several opportunities and also check labour migration from rural areas. To provide efficient services to the readers, these centres may automate their in-house activities and reader's services, establish E-mail and Internet connections and put their holdings on their web sites.

Resource sharing and networking of LLCs, at local, regional and national levels, can solve the problems of providing materials to readers up to some extent. Resources can be made available in machine-readable form and can be put on Internet for wider use by other LLCs all over the country. After installation of computers and communication facilities, including Internet connection, implementation of this concept may be quite easier.

It has been observed that there is heavy rush in opening of public schools, engineering, medical, professional colleges and other higher learning institutions by the government, NGOs, SSOs and individuals. These institutions are being granted heavy amount to run them. But hardly there is anybody or institution that come forward to open library for the benefit of the society. The fact is that the grant given by RRRLF to libraries is not sufficient to open and run a library.

Every village of a sizable population should have one LLC with proper infrastructure, equipment, reading and learning materials and professionally trained manpower. Management of this centre may be looked after by the Village Panchayat. It should be given as much importance as Primary Health Centre (PHC). As doctors are provided in PHCs, similarly, one professionally trained librarian and subordinate staff may be appointed in each LLC for its proper functioning. This may also generate employment in this area. Librarians working in LLCs can step out into the society, getting mixed-up with the people, talk to them at their doorsteps, apprise them about the ongoing and forthcoming activities of the centre. This may help in inspiring and attracting readers to the library. Librarian should also compile state-of-the-art reports in regional language, which are directly relevant to the users.

LLCs should conduct census operation every year, which is being conducted at the interval of ten years. The census data can be made available to the appropriate authority regularly through NICNET established by the NIC. Thus, the LLCs would help nation in updating information pertaining to development in the society.

Databases can be developed for literates, neo-literates and illiterates at local, regional and state levels for analysis of data. Databases can also be developed for holdings of library materials, which may be useful for the society. Multimedia libraries can be created by using available resources.

Realising the importance of connectivity of rural roads for rural development, Hon'ble President of India, while addressing the joint sitting of Parliament on 25 October 1999, emphasized all-weather roads in rural areas. As a result, Pradhan Mantri Gram Sadak Yojana (PMGSY) was launched, in which Parliament enacted legislation imposing diesel cess and earmarked 50 per cent of the cess to the development of rural roads. In a historic speech addressed to the nation on 15th August 2000, Prime Minister said:

> "For the first time since independence, the Central Government has devised a well conceived and time-bound programme for rural roads. This hundred per cent Centrally Sponsored Scheme, which is called the Prime Minister's Rural Roads Scheme" aims to connect within the next three years, every village that has a population of more than one thousand, through good all-weather roads. By 2007, every village with a population more than five hundred will be similarly connected".

Accordingly, a budget for Rs 60,000 crore was allocated to achieve the objective. The scheme is going exceedingly well and as per schedule. If such a large scheme can be implemented in our country to connect each village by roads, why not each village should have one LLC. Opening LLCs in all 640,000 villages of the country may provide job opportunity to about 2 million people immediately, besides other beneficial social factors. Taking a statistics of expenditure of Rs 1 lakh per LLC, the total initial cost may not be more than Rs 6,400 crore. It is also suggested that at least 10 per cent of the funds allocated to MPs, MLAs, MLCs, Councillors, etc. for development of constituencies should be spent on LLCs located in their constituencies which will be the prime resource for development of intellectual faculty of the residents.

Since 7 per cent population of our country is more than 60 years old, therefore, they may find suitable place for sharing their valuable and rich experiences and knowledge with the younger generation. These centres will work as nodal points for dissemination of information. Information generated at the grassroots level can flow to the highest level. Similarly, instructions of information can flow downwards without any barrier. This flow of information will become very fast after implementing communication technology. Knowledge industry may have boost in creating a learning society in true sense. As Dr. R. A. Mashelkar said:

> "Tomorrow's societies will be knowledge societies, tomorrow's markets will be knowledge markets and tomorrow's war will be fought not with the conventional weapons, guns, missiles and so on, but they will be fought in the knowledge markets with the new thermonuclear called information and knowledge".

This may also end the corruption in the system if well aware and literate society is created through the LLCs. Linkage of PHCs, LLCs, KVKs, public libraries and NGOs may be very effective for coordination of activities and to avoid overlapping of activities and resources. Professional associations and learned societies can help in providing intellectual inputs in fulfilling the set objectives. Networking of LLCs may be quite useful in sharing of available resources.

This can raise the heads of millions of people who can proudly say that now we are not illiterate and poor.

Glossary of Terms

The terms used in the text have specified connotations and are commonly found in the literature. Wherever possible, terms have been explained before they are used in the text. However, some of the terms are defined below:

Absolute Poverty: The degree of poverty below which the minimal requirements for survival are not being met. This is a fixed measure in terms of a minimum calorific requirement plus essential non-food components. While absolute poverty is often used inter-changeably with extreme poverty, the meaning of the latter varies depending on local interpretations or calculations.

Adult Education: The efforts put forth by a matured person to improve himself by acquiring new skills, information, understanding and attitudes of appreciation through learning process. It is a kind of schooling and learning programmes in which adults participate.

Adult Illiteracy Rate: The percentage of persons aged 15 years and above who cannot, with understanding, read and write, a short and simple statement about their everyday life.

Alliterate: A person who is able to read but do not read.

Computer Literacy: Knowledge and an understanding of computers combined with the ability to use them effectively.

Document Literacy: Knowledge and skills required in locating and using information in various forms like job application, etc.

Fertility Rate: Number of live births given in a year per thousand women in the age group of 15-49 years.

Functional Literacy: A term sometimes used to distinguish the ability to use literacy skills for particular purposes in the home, community or workplace. However, it is now generally considered that true literacy must be functional and relevant to the individual needs.

Functionally Literate: A person is called functionally literate who has ability to use literacy at a level high enough to deal independently with the demands of the economy, society and politics.

Human Development Index (HDI): United Nations Development Programme (UNDP) defines it as a composition of three factors (i) life expectancy at birth; (ii) adult literacy; and (iii) income per capita (adjusted for purchasing power parity).

Human Poverty: The lack of essential human capabilities, notably literacy and nutrition.

Human Poverty Index (HPI): UNDP measure of deprivation in basic human development. The variables used to determine the index are (i) the percentage of people expected to die before the age of forty years; (ii) the percentage of adults who are illiterate; and (iii) overall economic provisioning in terms of the percentage of people without access to health services and safe water and the percentage of underweight children below the age of five years.

Illiteracy Rate: Number of illiterate adults expressed as a percentage of the total population.

Illiterate: A person is deemed as illiterate if he or she cannot read and write any language with understanding.

Income Poverty: The lack of sufficient income to meet minimum consumption needs.

Infant Mortality Rate: The probability of death between birth and exactly one year of age expressed per 1000 live births.

Information Literacy: Ability to recognise when information is needed and individual has the ability to locate, evaluate and use information effectively.

Information Literate: An information literate person has ability to acquire information necessary for any task and he can use it effectively.

Library Manpower: Library manpower refers to those people who work in the library for the common goal and objectives of the library. Here in this text, library manpower has been restricted to only trained library professionals.

Library Professional: Library professionals are those having minimum professional qualification i.e. Bachelor of Library and Information Science from any recognised university or Associateship from DRTC or INSDOC.

Library User: It is defined as a person who visits the library and gets benefitted from its resources and services.

Life Expectancy at Birth: The average number of years a new born infant is expected to live if prevailing patterns of mortality in the country at the time of birth were to stay the same throughout his or her life.

Literacy: It has been defined in many ways, but here it has been used in the same sense, which was used for census purpose. It is the ability of a person to read and write.

Literate Person: A person who has ability to read, write and use numeracy skills is deemed as literate. In other words, he or she has sufficient reading, writing and numeracy skills to continue to learn alone in any language without the continuous guidance of a teacher.

Longevity: The ability to live long and healthy life.

Maternal Maternity Ratio (MMR): Reported annual number of deaths of women from pregnancy-related causes per 100,000 live births.

Media Literacy: Ability to effectively and efficiently comprehend and utilize media content.

National Poverty Rate: The percentage of the total population living below the National Poverty Line.

Neo-literate: A person who has just entered in the universe of knowledge i.e. who has completed a basic literacy training programme and is ready to continue to learn on his or her own without direct guidance of a literacy teacher.

Net Enrolment Ratio (NER): The number of pupils in the official school-age group expressed as a percentage of the total population in that age group.

Non-Formal Education (NFE): Educational activities for children, youth or adults that are organized outside the formal school system, sometimes referred to as out-of-school education.

Population: It is based on de facto definition, which counts all residents, regardless of legal status or citizenship, except for refugees not permanently settled in the country of asylum, who are generally considered part of the population of the country of origin.

Prose Literacy: Knowledge and skills needed to understand and use information.

Post-literacy: The term post-literacy has been used in different educational systems in different contexts. In this text, post-literacy has been used to include all forms of education, which follows after the achievement of basic literacy.

Public Library: A number of definitions of public library are given by individuals, societies/associations, organisations, etc. These have been discussed in chapter III in detail. Here in the text, the word public library has been used to denote any library which:

- is wholly maintained by public funds;
- charges no fees from readers and yet is open for full use by the public without any distinction of caste, creed or sex, i.e. the records of man's thoughts, ideas and expressions of his creative imaginations are made freely available to all;
- is intended as an auxiliary educational institution providing a means of self-education which is endless; and
- houses learning materials giving reliable information freely and without partiality or prejudice on variety of subjects which will satisfy the interest of the readers.

Quantitative Literacy: Knowledge and skills required to apply arithmetic operations.

Relative Poverty: Normally defined in relation to some ratio of the absolute poverty line or as in developed countries, as a proportion of average income per capita. As a relative measure it can differ across countries or over time.

Rural Poverty Rate: It is the percentage of rural population living below Rural Poverty Line.

Scientific Literacy: Understanding of mathematics and the various scientific disciplines.

Semi-literate: A person who has some literacy skills but he or she cannot use fully in his daily life. He or she is blocked or inhibited in learning further. For example, a semi-literate can-not effectively read a newspaper article and explain its content, write a simple letter, fill out a simple form, etc.

Technical Literacy: Ability to apply mathematics and science to the solution of problems.

Technological Literacy: Ability to understand, utilize and make decisions about the applications of science and mathematics.

Total Fertility Rate (TFR): Average number of children a women would bear if age-specific fertility rates remained unchanged during her lifetime.

Under-five Mortality Rate: The probability that a child born in the indicated year will die before reaching five years of age, if the child is subject to current age specific mortality rates. The probability is expected as a rate per 1000.

Urban Poverty Rate: The percentage of urban population living below the Urban Poverty Line.

Value-added: It is a net output after adding up all outputs and subtracting intermediate outputs.

Visual Literacy: Knowledge and skills required in dealing with visual information.

Appendix A

Delhi Public Library and its Branches

Central Library

1. Central Zone, SP Mukherjee Marg

Zonal Libraries

1. North Zone, Karol Bagh
2. South Zone, Sarojini Nagar
3. West Zones, Patel Nagar
4. East Zone, Shahdara

Branch Libraries

1. Patel Nagar
2. Laxmi Bai Nagar
3. Karol Bagh
4. Shahdara

Sub-branch Libraries

1. Andrews Ganj
2. Bawana
3. FG Sports Library
4. New Police Lines
5. Jai Rani Bagh
6. Jor Bagh
7. Mukhmelpur
8. Narela
9. KG Marg
10. Netaji Nagar
11. New Rothak Road
12. Nehru Sports Library
13. Old Secretariat
14. RK Puram (Sector VIII)
15. Sri Niwaspuri
16. Peshwa Road
17. Tri Nagar
18. Jagriti Enclave
19. Tihar Central Jail
20. IG Sports Library
21. Katewara
22. Mundka
23. Vigyan Vihar
24. Yojana Vihar
25. Gole Market DIZ Area

Full-time Community Libraries

1. Kalyan Vas.
2. Nanak Pura
3. RK Puram (Sector-I)
4. Lodi Colony
5. Pragati Vihar
6. Sarojini Nagar (BC Park)
7. Sarojini Nagar (X-Y Block)

Part-time Community Libraries

1. Azadpur

2. Ramesh Nagar
3. TilakNagar

RC Lending Libraries

1. Aruna Nagar
2. Dakshinpuri
3. Hastsal
4. Jahangir Puri
5. Jwalapuri
6. Kalyanpuri
7. Khanpur
8. Khayala
9. Khichripur
10. Inderpuri
11. Nand Nagri
12. Mangolpuri (S-Block)
13. Nangloi (A-Block)
14. Old Seemapuri
15. Sangam Park
16. Satya Niketan
17. Seelampur
18. Shakarpur
19. Sultanpuri (C-4)
20. Sultanpuri (E-7)
21. Trilokpuri (22-Block)
22. Madipur
23. Sawan Park
24. Tigri

RC Reading Rooms

1. Chaukhandi
2. Gokulpuri
3. Mangolpuri (K-Block)
4. New Seemapuri
5. Raghubir Nagar
6. Nangloi (Y-Block)
7. Kamla Market
8. Trilokpuri (13-Block
9. Sultanpuri(A4-Block)

Deposite Stations

1. Badli
2. Dhaka
3. Jharoda Kala
4. Kheda Khurd
5. Malviya Nagar
6. Model Town
7. New Police Line
8. Nimari Colony
9. NTPC
10. Pitam Pura
11. Shakti Nagar
12. VinayMarg
13. Love and Care
14. Durgawati Sewa Sansthan
15. Paschim Vihar
16. Nathu Colony

Areas Served by Mobile Libraries

1. AGCR Enclave
2. Amar Colony
3. Ashok Vihar Phase - I
4. Ashok Vihar Phase - II
5. Bhaktawar Pur
6. Burari
7. Chattar Pur Village
8. Darya Pur
9. Dilshad Garden
10. Fateh Pur Beri
11. Gandhi Nagar
12. Gautam Nagar
13. Ghitorni
14. Gujranwala Town
15. Gulmohar Park
16. GTB Enclave
17. Him Vihar
18. Indian Air Lines Colony
19. Janak Puri B-I
20. Janak Puri C-2-B

21. Janak Puri C-3
22. Janak Puri D-I
23. Janak Puri D-2-A
24. Jang Pura
25. Jawahar Nagar
26. Jia Sarai
27. Kalka Ji
28. Kalka Ji Extension
29. Kamla Nagar
30. Karala
31. Karkar Duma
32. Khera Kalan
33. Kingsway Camp
34. Krishna Nagar
35. Kutub Garh
36. Lajpat Nagar - I
37. Lajpat Nagar - II
38. Lajpat Nagar - IV
39. Laxmi Nagar
40. Libas Pur
41. Mahipal Pur
42. Malviya Nagar
43. Mayur Vihar
44. Model Town
45. Narayana Vihar
46. Narayana Village
47. OCS Chhattar Pur
48. OCS Greater Kailash
49. Palam Vihar
50. Pandara Road
51. Pooth Kalan
52. Pushpa Vihar
53. RK Puram - III
54. RK Puram - IV
55. Ram Pura
56. Rana Pratap Bagh
57. Rohini Sector - V
58. Roop Nagar
59. Sadar Bazar
60. Saraswati Kunj
61. Sewa Nagar
62. Sakar Pur
63. Shakti Nagar
64. Sakur Basti
65. Subhash Nagar
66. Sultan Pur
67. Tagore Garden
68. Timar Pur
69. Vishakha Enclave
70. Wazir Pur JJ Colony
71. Yamuna Vihar
72. Harevali

Appendix B

Matter Listed in the Schedule XI of the Constitution

Item No.	*Activities*
1.	Agriculture, including agricultural extension.
2.	Land improvement, implementation of land reforms, land consolidation and soil conservation.
3.	Minor irrigation, water management and watershed development.
4.	Animal husbandry, dairy farming and poultry.
5.	Fisheries.
6.	Social forestry and farm forestry.
7.	Minor forest produce.
8.	Small scale industries, including food processing industries.
9.	Khadi, village and cottage industries.
10.	Rural housing.
11.	Drinking water.
12.	Fuel and fodder.
13.	Road, culverts, bridges, ferries, waterways and other means of communication.
14.	Rural electrification, including distribution of electricity.
15.	Non conventional energy sources.
16.	Poverty alleviation programmes.
17.	Education, including primary and secondary schools.
18.	Technical training and vocational education.
19.	Adult and non-formal education.
20.	Libraries.
21.	Cultural activities.
22.	Markets and fairs.
23.	Health and sanitation, including hospitals, primary health centres and dispensaries.

24. Family welfare.
25. Women and child development.
26. Social welfare, including welfare of the handicapped and mentally retarded.
27. Welfare of the weaker sections, and in particular, of the Scheduled Castes and Scheduled Tribes.
28. Public distribution system.
29. Maintenance of community assets.

Appendix C

List of Regional/State Resource Centres in India

1. State Resource Centre, Asian Development Research Institute, BSIDC Colony, Off Boring Road, Patna, Bihar.
2. State Resource Centre, Rajasthan Adult Education Association, 7-A, Jhalana Dhoongri Educational Area, Jaipur, Rajasthan.
3. Regional Resource Centre, Punjab University, Chandigarh.
4. State Resource Centre, Tamil Nadu Board of Continuing Education, No. 1, West Street, Venkatrathnan Nagar, Adayar, Chennai, Tamil Nadu.
5. State Resource Center, Bengal Social Service League, 1/6 Raja Dinendra Street, Calcutta, West Bengal.
6. State Resource Centre, Bharatiya Grameen Mahila Sangh, Scheme No. 71, Sector-D, Indore City, Madhya Pradesh.
7. State Resource Centre, Literacy House, Andhra Mahila Sabha, MS College Campus, University Road, Hyderabad, Andhra Pradesh.
8. State Resource Centre, Karnataka State Adult Education Council, 501 Chitrabhanu Road, A and B Blocks, Kuvempunagar, Mysore, Karnataka.
9. State Resource Centre, Kashmir University, 1/17 Nasim Bagh Campus, Hazratbal, Srinagar, Jammu and Kashmir.
10. State Resource Centre for Adult Education, Gujarat Vidyapeeth, Ashram Road, Ahmedabad, Gujarat.
11. State Resource Centre, Deepayatan, Buddha Colony, Patna, Bihar.
12. State Resource Centre, Jamia Millia Islamia, Jamia Nagar, New Delhi.
13. State Resource Centre, Maharastra State Institute of Adult Education, Aurangabad, Maharastra.
14. State Resource Centre, For Non-Formal and Adult Education, Indian Institute of Education, J.P. Naik Road, Kothrud, Pune, Maharastra.
15. State Resource Centre, Jajashikhya Bhavan, Unit-V, Bhubneshwar, Orissa.

16. State Resource Centre, TC No 15/1531 Minchin Road, Thycaud, Thiruvananthapuram, Kerala.
17. State Resource Centre, India Literacy Board, PO-Alambagh, Lucknow, Uttar Pradesh.
18. State Resource Centre, Abhivyakti, E-III/22, Nupur Kunj, Arera Colony, Bhopal, Madhya Pradesh.
19. State Resource Centre, Rajya Gyan Vigyan Samiti, Sewa Shakti Bhavan, Sanjauli, Shimla, Himachal Pradesh.
20. State Resource Centre, Gyan Vigyan Samiti Assam, Naojan Road, Uzan Bazar, Guwahati, Assam.
21. State Resource Centre, Bharat Gyan Vigyan Samiti, Mahin Sadan, 17 HO, Basak Road, Agartala, Tripura.
22. Regional Resource Centre, Shiksha Prasar Vibhag, 41-Mahatma Gandhi Marg, Allahabad, Uttar Pradesh.
23. State Resource Centre, North Eastern Hill University, Bijni Complex, Laltumkaran, Shillong.
24. State Resource Centre, Bharat Gyan Vigyan Samiti, 74/22, Kishan Pura, Sonipat Road, Rohtak, Haryana.

Appendix D

List of Village of Delhi – Census 2001

District	*Census Town*	*Village*
1. **North-West District**	1. Narela	1. Lampur
		2. Mamoorpur
		3. Singhu
		4. Singhola
		5. Hamidpur
		6. Tajpur Kalan
		7. Akbarpur Majra
		8. Palla
		9. Qullakpur
		10. Jhangola
		11. Sungarpur Sahadara
		12. Sungarpur Delhi
		13. Tigipur
		14. Fatehpur Jat
		15. Bakhtawarpur
		16. Bankauli
		17. Khampur
		18. Shahpur Garhi
		19. Tikri Khurd
		20. Kureni
		21. Bhor Garh
		22. Rajapur Kalan
		23. Daryapur Kalan
		24. Hareoli
		25. Ochandi
		26. Mungeshpur
		27. Katewara
		28. Bazidpur Thakaran

District	Census Town	Village
		29. Sultanpur Dabas
		30. Iradat Nagar (Naya Bans)
		31. Holambi Khurd
		32. Holambi Kalan
		33. Zindpur
		34. Hiranki
		35. Mohdpur Ramzanpur
		36. Tehri Daulatpur
		37. Ibrahimpur
		38. Garhi Khasru
		39. Mukhmelpur
		40. Qadipur
		41. Nangli Poona
		42. Bodhpur Bijapur
		43. Khera Kalan
		44. Kankar Khera
		45. Pansali
		46. Barwala
	2. Saraswati Vihar	47. Qutab Garh
		48. Punjab Khor
		49. Jat Khor
		50. Salahpur Majra
		51. Budhanpur
		52. Chandpur
		53. Karala
		54. Mohammadpur Majra
		55. Nithari
		56. Mubarakpur Dabas
		57. Madanpur Dabas
		58. Rani Khera
		59. Rasoolpur
		60. Saoda
		61. Ladpur
		62. Chatesar
		63. Jonti
		64. Garhi Rindhala
		65. Nizampur Rashidpur
	3. Model Town	66. Shanjarpur

District	*Census Town*	*Village*
2. North District	4. Civil Lines	67. Salempur Majra Burari
		68. Badarpur Majra Burari
		69. Jagatpur ilaqa Shahdara
		70. Jagatpur ilaqa Delhi
		71. Kamalpur Majra Burari
		72. Mukandpur
	5. Sadar Bazar	Nil
	6. Kotwali	Nil
3. North-East District	7. Seelampur	73. Badarpur Khadar
		74. Pur Delhi
		75. Pur Shahdara
		76. Sabapur Delhi
		77. Sabapur Shahdara
		78. Baqiabad
		79. Sadatpur Musalmanan
		80. Biharipur
		81. Sherpur
		82. Garhi Mendu
		83. Tukhmirpur
		84. Khanpur Dhani
	8. Shahdara	Nil
	9. Seemapuri	85. Mandoli
4. East District	10. Gandhi Nagar	86. Shakarpur Baramand
	11. Vivek Vihar	Nil
	12. Preet Vihar	87. Shamaspur
		88. Chilla Saroda Khadar
5. New Delhi District	13. Parliament Street	Nil
	14. Connaught Place	Nil
	15. Chanakyapuri	Nil
6. Central District	16. Karol Bagh	Nil
	17. Pahar Ganj	Nil
	18. Darya Ganj	Nil
7. West District	19. Punjabi Bagh	89. Tikri Kalan
		90. Neel Wal
		91. Jaffarpur alias Hiran Kudna
		92. Bakkar Wal
		93. Bapraula
		94. Tilangpur Kotal
		95. Shafipur Ranhola

District	Census Town		Village	
			96.	Nilothi
	20.	Patel Nagar	97.	Rajapur Khurd
	21.	Rajauri Garden		Nil
8. South-West District	22.	Najaf Garh	98.	Jharoda Kalan
			99.	Dichaon Kalan
			100.	Nangli Sakrawati
			101.	Dindarpur
			102.	Khera
			103.	Mitraon
			104.	Surakhpur
			105.	Kair
			106.	Mundhela Khurd
			107.	Mundhela Kalan
			108.	Jaffarpur Kalan
			109.	Surera
			110.	Kharkhari Nahar
			111.	Paprawat
			112.	Goela Khurd
			113.	Qutabpur
			114.	Tajpur Khurd
			115.	Rewla Khampur
			116.	Pindwala Kalan
			117.	Kharkhari Jatmal
			118.	Khera Dabar
			119.	Ujwa
			120.	Samaspur Khalsa
			121.	Baqar Garh
			122.	Isapur
			123.	Qazipur
			124.	Malikpur zer-Najafgarh
			125.	Daryapur Khurd
			126.	Sherpur Deri
			127.	Kharkhari Mord
			128.	Hasanpur
			129.	Daulatpur
			130.	Pindwala Khurd
			131.	Kangan Heri
			132.	Salahpur
			133.	Raghupur

District	Census Town	Village
		134. Badhosra
		135. Nanak Heri
		136. Jhatikra
		137. Asalatpur Khawad
		138. Shikarpur
		139. Jainpur
		140. Goman Hera
		141. Jhuljhuli
		142. Sarangpur
		143. Dhansa
		144. Galibpur
		145. Raota
		146. Deorala
	23. Delhi Cantonment	147. Moradabad Pahari
	24. Vasant Vihar	148. Kusumpur
		149. Malikpur Kohi (Rangpuri)
9. South District	25. Defence Colony	150. Saidabad
	26. Hauz Khas	151. Aya Nagar
		152. Gadaipur
		153. Chhatarpur
		154. Maidan Garhi
		155. Neb Sarai
		156. Rajpur Khurd
		157. Satberi
		158. Shahurpur
		159. Chandan Hola
		160. Fatehpur Beri
		161. Dera
		162. Mandi
	27. Kalkaji	163. Kotla Mahigiran
		164. Aali
		165. Jaitpur

Appendix E

List of Cutting and Tailoring Centres in Rural Delhi

Village Name	*Number of Trainees During*	
	1 July -31 Dec 01	*1 Jan-30 June02*
Bakauli	32	30
Alipur	35	30
Mukhmailpur	40	42
Tikri Khurd	35	36
Sindhu	35	34
Hamidpur	40	41
Paprawat	40	42
Kakraula	35	38
Daulatpur	28	28
Nanak Hedi	20	26
Kheda Dabar	22	24
Kharkhari Jatmal	23	22
Ghuman Heda	20	28
Rawta	23	22
Ghalibpur	21	20
Dariyapur Khurd	39	45
Tikri Kalan	56	48
Kajipur	20	28
Mitrau	22	26
Dhansa	33	38
Daryapur Kalan	22	24
Harevali	20	24
Auchandi	18	22
Mungeshpur	24	22

Village Name	*Number of Trainees During*	
	1 July -31 Dec 01	*1 Jan-30 June 02*
Kutub Garh	32	34
Punjab Khond	30	32
Majra Dabas	28	30
Chandpur	32	30
Sultanpur Dabas	24	32
Nangal Thakran	22	22
Katewada	20	22
Mangolpur Kalan	30	32
Bangampur	24	28
Kheda Kalan	22	22
Sawada	25	24
Jaunti	25	24
Kanjhawala	20	24
Karala	20	23
Majri	20	21
Madanpur Dabas	20	22
Rani Kheda	40	32
Rasulpur	22	34
Mubarakpur	35	38
Kusam No 1	20	26
Kadipur	20	24
Hasanpur	20	25
Nangal Dewat	20	24
TOTAL	1274	1367

Bibliography

Advisory Committee for Libraries Report; 2nd ed; Delhi, Manager of Publication, 1958.

AGGRAWAL (Damodar); When education takes a backseat; *The Statesman;* New Delhi, 21 May, 1999.

AGGRAWAL (DS); Public library and the new literates in India: A survey of development; *Library Herald,* 12, 1; 1970; 43-56.

AIYAR (Swaminathan S Anklesaria); Institutional change spurs literacy breakthrough, *The Times of India,* New Delhi, 23 May, 1999.

ALSTON (Ruth); Delhi Public Library: A success story; *Public Library Journal,* 4, 1; Jan-Feb 1989; 1-4.

ALVI (Wajih Ahmad); Contemporary society and the public library. *In* Public library development perspectives and staffing pattern in libraries and information centres; Thirty First All India Library Conference; 1985, Baroda, pp. 220-24.

ALVI (Wajih Ahmad); Public libraries and adult education; *In* Twenty Eight All India Library Conference, Lucknow, 1982. pp. 104-109.

AMRIK SINGH; There is no evidence whatsoever of vision and leadership: Punjab, Himachal Pradesh and Haryana must ensure total literacy; *The Tribune,* Chandigarh, 22 May, 1998.

ANSARI (NA); *Adult education in India;* Delhi; 1984; Delhi, S. Chand and Co, p.164.

BALIAR SINGH (RK) and MAHAPATRA (M); Literacy and library consciousness; *ILA Bulletin,* 23, 4; 1988; 199-205.

BANERJEE (Shubhanker); National Literacy Movement; *Social Welfare,* 43, 6; 1996; 17-21.

BARODIA (Anil); Learning after the first reading; *The Telegraph,* Calcutta, 8 September, 1993.

BARUA (BP); Model Public Libraries Bills – A critical review; *Granthana,* 1-2, 1990, 15-23.

BARUA (BP); Perspectives on public library service in India; *In Handbook of Libraries, Archives and Information Centres in India;* Edited by BM Gupta *et al.* Vol. 2; 1984-85; 617-28.

BARUA (BP); Raja Rammohun Roy Library Foundation and library movement in India; *In* Thirty Ninth All India Library Conference Souvenir; Indian Library Association; Delhi, 1994, pp.63-73.

BASAK (Nanda Dulal) and DAS (Binod Bihari); Public library and adult education; *In* Twenty Eighth All India Library Conference, Lucknow, 1982, pp.64-73.

BHAGI (ML); Role of the public library in adult education of tomorrow; *Indian Librarian*, 11; Sept, 1966.

BHATTACHARJEE (R); Role of Raja Rammohun Roy Library Foundation in the promotion of public library movement in India; *Herald of Library Science*, 38, 1-2; Jan-April, 1999; 14-20.

BHOLA (HS); A policy analysis of adult literacy education in India: Across the two National Policy Reviews of 1968 and 1986; *In Adult Education in India: selected papers*; 2000; *Ed* by CJ Daswani and SY Shah; New Delhi, pp47-65.

BINWAL (JC); The role of library in learning; *Library Herald*, 25, 1; 1986; 1-8.

BOPEGAMAGE (A); *Delhi: a study in urban sociology*; Bombay, University of Bombay, 1957. 235p.

BURAGOHAIN (Alka); Public library scenario in India: Problem and prospects; *Herald of Library Science*, 38, 1-2; Jan-April, 1999; 5-14.

CAMPBELL (HC), Developing public library systems and services, 1983, UNESCO, Paris.

CHAKRABARTI (BN) and ROY (PK); Library associations and library legislation in India; *In* Ninth IASLIC Seminar, Nagpur, October 23-26, 1980.

CHAKRABARTY (NC); Problems and prospectus of library associations in India; *In* IASLIC Special Publication, 1966, pp. 74-80.

CHAKRABARTY (NC); Library association in India; *Cultural Forum*, 9, 2-3; 1967; 92-104.

CHATTERJEE (Bhaskar); Strategies for post literacy in the next decade; *Indian Journal of Adult Education*, Jan-Mar, 1996; pp.27-45.

CHOUDHARY (KC) and SACHDEVA (JL); *Ed;* Total literacy in the context of Education for All by 2000; Indian Adult Education Association, New Delhi, 1995.

CHOUDHARY (NB); Public libraries and adult education. *In* Twenty Eighth All India Library Conference, Lucknow, 1982, pp.90-95.

DASGUPTA (Kalpana); New role of libraries in developing society with particular reference to India; *ILA Bulletin*, 16, 1-2; 1980; 37-42.

DASGUPTA (RK); New Education Policy and libraries; *Herald of Library Science*, 25, 1-2; 1986; 36-46.

DAVIDSON (Judish); Adolescent illiteracy, what libraries can do to solve the problem - A report on the research of the project on adolescent literacy; *Journal of Youth Services in Libraries*, 1, Winter, 1988; p. 215

DESHPANDE (VW); Library legislations in India: A critical review, *ILA Bulletin*, 17, 1; 1981; 66-71.

DEV (AK); Role of public libraries in socio-economic development: Promotion of literacy; *In Public library development perspectives and staffing pattern in libraries and information centres*; Thirty First All India Library Conference, 1985, Baroda, pp.128-37.

DEV ANAND; Politics needs the literate, honest and dedicated: Only knowledge can take us out of the present mess; *The Tribune*, Chandigarh, 22 May, 1998.

DIMATTIA (EA); Libraries and literacy: A global to local perspective; *CLIS Observer*, 9, 1-2; 1992; 3-15.

EKBOTE (Gopal Rao); *Public Libraries System*; 1988; Ekbote Brothers, Hyderbad.

ESPERANZA (M); Role of public libraries in socio-economic development : Promotion of literacy and adult education; *In Public library development perspectives and staffing pattern in libraries and information centres*; Thirty First All India Library Conference, Baroda, 1985, pp.121-27.

ESWARA REDDY (DB); Access to information in rural areas, *The Hindu*, 15 Feb, 2000; p.22

GANGULY (SM); Library associations on national and state level: A critique; *In Ninth IASLIC Seminar*; Nagpur, Oct 23-26, 1980.

GANGULY (SM); Library movement and library associations. *In Library scene in India*: Seminar proceedings; Edited by S.K. Kapoor; IASLIC, 1977, Calcutta, p.55-58.

GOPALAKRISHANAN (R) and SHARMA (Amita), Literacy as social process, *Frontline*, 30 July, 1999; 93-96.

GOPINATH (MA); Community Information services for public library system, *Library Science with a Slant to Documentation and Information Studies* 29; 1, 1992; 26-31.

GOPINATH (MA); History of library legislation in India. *In* RANGANATHAN (SR) and NEELAMEGHAN (A), *Eds., Public library system*, Sarada Ranganathan Endowment in Library Science, Bangalore, 1972.

GOSWAMI (Omkar); Only trickle-down would not do, *Outlook*, 2 October, 1998; 50.

GOUR (PN); Public library services in India and National Adult Education Programme: A plea for their integration; *ILA Bulletin*, 16, 1-2; 1980; 3-9.

GUPTA (Anuradha); User's survey of the Laxmi Bai Nagar branch of Delhi Public Library, *Library Herald*, 15, 1-2; 1973; 47-64.

GUPTA (OP); Delhi Public Library System and its services, International Association of Metropolitan City Libraries Study Meeting, 1973, *International Library Review*, 6, 1; 1974; 35-41.

GUPTA (OP); Public libraries in Delhi, *ILA Bulletin*, 11, 3-4; 1975; 22-24.

GUPTA (Shameer) and GUPTA (Rashmi); Public libraries in India: A development perspective, *In Public library development perspectives and staffing pattern in libraries and information centres*, Thirty First All India Library Conference, 1985, Baroda, pp.138-52.

GURUSWAMY NAIDU (N); Financing public libraries; *ILA Bulletin*, 20(1-2), 1984, 7-13).

HASHMI (Syed Ali); Library legislation: Its future in India; *In Fifty years of Librarianship in India: past, present and future*: Seminar papers, ed by P B Mangla, et al. 1983, ILA, Delhi, pp. 343-60.

INAMDAR (NB) and RAMAIAH (LS); Role of libraries in adult education; *In* Twenty Eight All India Library Conference, Lucknow, 1982. pp.189-93

INDIA (Government of-); Planning Commission, Sixth Five Year Plan, 1980-85.

INDIA, Directorate of Adult Education; Books for post-literacy: Guidelines, Directorate of Adult Education, New Delhi.

INDIA, Education (Ministry of-); Model Public Libraries Bill, 1963, Ministry of Education, Government of India, Delhi.

INDIA, Education (Ministry of-); Report of the Advisory Committee for Libraries, Department of Education, Government of India, New Delhi, 1961.

INDIA, Education (Ministry of-); Report of the Committee for libraries, 2nd ed. 1962, Manager of Publications, Delhi,

INDIA, Human Resource Development (Ministry of-); National Literacy Mission on Jan Shiksha Nilayam, Department of Education, Government of India, New Delhi, 1988.

INDIA, Human Resource Development (Ministry of-); Scheme of continuing education for new-literates, Department of Education, Government of India, New Delhi, 1995.

INDIA, Human Resource Development (Ministry of-); National Literacy Mission, Department of Education, Government of India, New Delhi, 1987, pp.4-44.

INDIA, Human Resource Development (Ministry of-); Towards a literate India, National Literacy Mission, Department of Education, Government of India, New Delhi, 1996.

INDIA, Information and Broadcasting (Ministry of-); *India: A reference annual*, 1999, Research and Reference Division, Government of India, New Delhi, 1999.

INDIA, Planning Commission, Report of the Working Group on Libraries, 1966, Planning Commission, New Delhi.

INDIA, Planning Commission; Working Group, Report of the working group of the planning commission on modernisation of library services and information for the Seventh Five Year Plan 1985-90, Planning Commission, New Delhi, 1984.

INDIA, (Government of-); Planning Commission, Eighth Five Year Plan, 1992-97.

INDIA, (Government of-); Planning Commission, Fifth Five Year Plan, 1974-79.

INDIA, (Government of-); Planning Commission, First Five Year Plan, 1952.

INDIA, (Government of-); Planning Commission, Fourth Five Year Plan, 1969-73.

INDIA, (Government of-); Planning Commission, Second Five Year Plan, 1956.

INDIA, (Government of-); Planning Commission, Seventh Five Year Plan, 1985-90.

INDIA, (Government of-); Planning Commission, Third Five Year Plan.

INDIA, Education (Ministry of-), Challenges of education: A policy perspective, 1985. Government of India, New Delhi.

INDIA, Education (Ministry of-), Report of Education Commission (1964-66): Education and national development, Government of India, New Delhi, 1966.

INDIA, Human Resource Development (Ministry of-); District Primary Education

Programme, 1995. Department of Education, Government of India, New Delhi.

INDIA, Human Resource Development (Ministry of-); National Policy on Education–1986, Department of Education, Government of India, New Delhi.

INDIA, Planning Commission; National Human Development Report 2001, Government of India, New Delhi, 2002, p. 297.

INDIA, Planning Commission; Report of the National Development Council on Literacy, 1992, Government of India, New Delhi.

INDIA, Planning Commission; Report of the Special Group on targeting ten million employment opportunities per year over Tenth Plan Period, 2002, Government of India, New Delhi, (Chairman: SP Gupta).

INDIA, Planning Commission, Report of the Steering Committee on labour and employment of the Tenth Five Year Plan (2002-2007), 2002, Government of India, New Delhi, (Chairman: SP Gupta).

INDIA, Planning Commission; Report of the Task Force on employment opportunities, 2002. Government of India, New Delhi, (Chairman: MS Ahluwalia).

INDIA, Planning Commission, Report on labour and employment, 2002, Government of India, New Delhi, p. 532

INDIA, Rural Development (Ministry of-); Report of the Task Force on Devolution of Powers & Functions upon Panchayati Raj Institutions, 2001, Government of India, New Delhi, p. 129.

International Federation of Library Associations and Institutions; *Standards for public libraries*, 2nd ed, 1977, Verlag Dokumentation, Munchen.

International Labour Organisation; World Employment Report 2001: Life at work in the information economy, Geneva, ILO, 2001, p. 371

International Labour Organisation; World Labour Report 2000, Geneva, ILO, 2000, p. 18

JANAK RAJ.; National Policy on Education-1986 and libraries, *ILA Bulletin*, 24, 1; 1988; 4-13.

JANKIRAM (P).; Formal library and adult education: A master plan to eradicate illiteracy in rural India, *Herald of Library Science*, 27, 1-2; 1988; 35-43.

KAK (KK); Planning and non-literate Indian, *In Adult Education in India: Selected papers*, 2000, *Ed* by CJ Daswani and SY Shah, UNESCO, New Delhi, pp. 90-109.

KAK (KK); The non-literate as an instrument of progress, *Indian Journal of Adult Education*, 54, 1; Jan-Mar, 1993; 5-20.

KALIA (DR); A review of State Public Library System in India, *CLIS Observer*, 15, 1-2; 1998; 46-51.

KALIA (DR) and JAIN (MK); Library legislation and development: Need for uniform pattern, *Yojana*, 17, 6; 1973; 265-268.

KALIA (DR) and others; Guidelines for public library system and services, *Granthana*, 2, 1; 1991; 31-84.

KALIA (DR); The role of Delhi Public Library in adult education: A recapitulation, *CLIS Observer*, 8, 3-4; 1991; 33-42.

KAUL (HK); DELNET: The network of Delhi libraries, *IASLIC Bulletin*, 33, 4; 1988; 127.

KAUL (HK); Networking in public libraries in South Asia, *DELNET Newsletter*, 3, 1; July, 1996; 5-7.

KAUL (HK); Resource sharing in Indian libraries: The emerging laws, the growing agenda and DELNET experience, *In Library and Information Networking (NACLIN) 1998*, Delhi Library Network, New Delhi, pp.1-20.

KAULA (PN); Library movement in India: Papers for discussion at the First Delhi Library Conference held on 30-31 March, 1957, Delhi Library Association, Delhi.

KAULA (PN); A new approach to the development of libraries and information services in North-Eastern region, *Herald of Library Science*, 25, 1-2; 1986; 63-68.

KAULA (PN); A Study of library organizations in India, *Herald of Library Science*, 3, 2-3; 1964; 130-48.

KAULA (PN); Adult education and public libraries, *Herald of Library Science*, 38, 1-2; Jan -April, 1999; 62-69.

KAULA (PN); Library associations in India, *Unesco Bulletin for Libraries*, 24, 6; 1970; 319-25.

KAULA (PN); Professional organizations in India, *IASLIC Special Publication*, 6, 2; 1966; 122-44.

KAULA (PN); Role of public libraries in promoting literacy, *Herald of Library Science*, 22, 3-4; 1983; 226-27.

KEMPSON (Elaine); Information for self-reliance and self-determination: The role of community information services; *IFLA Journal*, 12, 3; 1986; 182-91.

KHAN (HA); Public library development: Policies, problems and performances; *Timeless-Fellowship*, 10; 1975-76; 20-33.

KRISHAN KUMAR; Literacy is more than mere brand recognition, *The Pioneer*, New Delhi, 18 November, 1993.

KRISHAN KUMAR, Role of public libraries in India in promotion of literacy; *Conference on Role of Public Libraries in Literacy Programme*; 15-19 Aug, 1989, IFLA, France.

KRISHAN KUMAR; Role of public libraries in promotion of literacy; *Library Herald*, 30, 2-4; July, 1991-Jan 1992; 155-61.

KRISHNAMURTHY (CS); Future of library associations; *Library Herald*, 6, 4; 1964; 226-31.

KUMAR (PSG); Role of libraries in adult education, *In* Twenty Eight All India Library Conference, Lucknow, 1982. pp.74-89.

KUMBAR (Mallinath) and BIRADAR (BS); Use of mass media and public library by the rural community: A study; *Annals of Library Science and Documentation*, 44, 3; 1997; 86-92.

LAUBACH (FC); *Forty years with the silent billion: Adventuring in literacy*; Flaning H. Revell Company, 1970, p. 115.

LAYMAN (Helen Huguenor); Literacy and the nation's libraries, 1977, American Library Association, Chicago.

LIMAYE (CB); Public libraries and adult education; *In* Twenty Eighth All India Library Conference, Lucknow, 1982, pp.96-103.

MAITRA (S); The public library and adult education in India; *International Library Review,* 6, 1974; 55-60

MALHOTRA (ML); Literacy programmes in India; *Bulletin of the UNESCO Principal Regional Office for Asia and Pacific,* No. 30; Dec, 1989; 127.

MANGLA (PB); Library legislation in India; *In* ROUT (RK), *Ed. Library Legislation in India,* 1986, Reliance, New Delhi, p. 19-50.

MANGLA (PB); Library legislation, *In* GEORGE (KM), *Ed. Indian libraries: Trends and perspectives,* 1985, Orient Longman, Calcutta, pp.179-205.

MARSHALL (DN); *History of libraries: Ancient and medieval,* 1983, Oxford and IBH, New Delhi.

MISHRA (Bhawanath); Role of public libraries in socio-economic development: promotion of literacy and adult education; *In Public library development perspectives and staffing pattern in libraries and information centres,* Thirty First All India Library Conference, Baroda, 1985, pp.215-19.

MITRA (Tarun Kumar); Social prospects of public library in a developing society; *In* Twenty Eighth All India Library Conference, Lucknow, 1982, pp.1-15.

MITTAL (RL); Perspective development plan for public libraries in India during the 7th plan period; *International Library Movement,* 7; 1985; 46-60.

MITTAL (RL); National policy on library legislation; *In* AGGRAWAL (SN), KHAN (RR) and SATYANARAYANA (NR), *Eds, Perspectives in library and information science,* 1982, V 2, Print House, pp.99-108.

MOHAN (VV); Community information sources: A framework for handling and services; *ILA Bulletin,* 24, 2; 1988; 68-75.

MOHANTY (BB) and SACHDEVA (JL); *Ed., Approaches to total literacy;* 1992, Indian Adult Education Association, New Delhi.

MUKHERJI (Barun Kumar); Multifacted approach towards development of public libraries in India, *In Two decades of the Foundation;* 1993, Calcutta, Raja Rammohun Roy Library Foundation, Calcutta, pp.78-82.

NARAYANA RAO (Kodati) and RAMACHANDRAN RAO (T); Rise and growth of the public library movement in India; *Herald of Library Science,* 16, 2-3; 1977; 131-64.

National Institute of Educational Planning and Administration; Education for All by 2000: Indian Perspective, New Delhi 1990.

National Literacy Mission awarded top UNESCO prize; *The Asian Age,* 22 July, 1999, p. 3.

National Policy on Library and Information System: A draft policy statement; *ILA Bulletin,* 21, 1-2; 1985; 43-48.

NAVALANI (K); Model public libraries acts: A comment, *ILA Bulletin,* 25, 3; 1989; 141-45.

NAYEEM (MA); Public library in a developing society; *In* Twenty Eighth All India Library Conference, Lucknow, 1982, pp.36-42.

NEELAMEGHAN (A); Information technology and rural development, *Information Studies*, 4, 1; 1998; 55-61.

NEELAMEGHAN (A); Literacy, numeracy..........informacy, *Information Studies*, 1, 4; 1995; 239-49.

NEHRU (JL); *The Discovery of India*, Meridian Books, London, 1960.

Organisation for Economic Cooperation and Development; Literacy and information age, OECD, Paris, 2000.

PARKER (JS); UNESCO and library development planning, 1985, Library Association, London.

PATEL (ILA); India: Adult education – the legislative and policy environment; *International Review of Education*, 42, 1-3; 1996; 75-96.

PILLAI (PG); Ernakulam: The first total literacy district in India, *Indian Journal of Adult Education*, 52, 3; 1991; 58-64.

Project Information Village; *NISSAT Newsletter*, 12, 1; 1993; 24.

RADHAKRISHNAN (MP); Kerala: The first fully literate State, *Yojana*, 35, 11; 1991; 7.

RAINA (BL); *Adult education in India*, The Indian Publications, 1994, Ambala Cantt. 80p.

RAJU (AAN); Constraints on the public library services in Andhra Pradesh; *CLIS Observer*, 7, 3-4; 1990; 69-72.

RAJU (KA); Information technology and public libraries in 21st century, *Herald of Library Science*, 38, 1-2; Jan -April, 1999; 52-62

RAJU (S); Female literacy in India; *Economic and Political Weekly*, 44; 1988; 57-64.

RAMAIAH (LS); The state of public libraries in India: The need for alternative finances to the library cess; *In* Two decades of the Foundation (1972-92): Souvenir; 1993, RRRLF, Calcutta, p.58-66.

RAMAKRISHNAIAH (Samson); Public libraries in India - A development perspective role of public libraries in socio-economic development in the promotion of literacy and adult education; *In Public library perspectives and staffing pattern in libraries and information centres*, Thirty First All India Library Conference, Baroda, 1985, pp. 85-91.

RAMAN NAIR (R); Principles for framing public library acts, *Lucknow Librarian*, 24,2; 1992. p.118-125.

RAMANAYA (IV); Role of public libraries in adult literacy work, *Herald of Library Science*, 16; 1977; 204-8.

RANA (JS); Public library network in Haryana; *ILA Bulletin*, 24, 4; 1989; 178-85.

RANGANATHAN (SR) and NEELAMEGHAN (A); Public library system, 1972, Sarada Ranganathan Endowment for Library Science; Bangalore.

RANGANATHAN (SR); *Education and library systems of the nation*; 1971, Mysore Library Association, Bangalore.

RANGANATHAN (SR); *Library development plan: The 5-year programme for India with draft library bills for the Union and constituent Sates*; 1950, Delhi University Press, Delhi.

RANGANATHAN (SR); *Library legislation: Handbook to Madras library Act*, 1953, Library Association, Madras.

RANGANATHAN (SR); Model public libraries bill, *Library Science*, 1, 4; 1964; 384-414.

RANGANATHAN (SR); National grid of public library system based on legislation; *In* KAULA (PN), *Ed. National grid of public library system of India based on library Acts.* 1972, *The Editor,* Varanasi.

Ranganathan's philosophy; assessment; impact and relevance; 1985, Vikas, New Delhi, p. 659-69.

RAO (VKRV) and DESAI (PB); *Greater Delhi: a study in urbanisation – 1940-57;* Asia Publishing House, New Delhi, p. 468.

RATH (Pravakar); *Public libraries finance;* 1996, Pratibha Prakashan, Delhi.

REDDY (V Sreenivas); Public libraries role in socio-economic development of the rural Indian masses; *In Public library development perspectives and staffing pattern in libraries and information centres;* Thirty First All India Library Conference; Baroda, 1985, pp.115-20.

Report of the Sub-group on public library system of the working group on "Libraries and Informatics" appointed by the Planning Commission for formulation of the Eighth Five Year Plan (1990-95); *CLIS Observer;* 13, 1-2; 1996; 27-94.

RICHARDSON (Joanna); The public library and the neo-literate in India: A literature survey, *Herald of Library Science*, 22, 3-4; 1983; 163-71.

ROUT (RK); (Ed.) *Library Legislation in India: Problems and Prospects;* 1986, Reliance Publishing House, New Delhi.

SACHDEVA (JL); Adult education: Challenges for the 21st century; *University News*, 36, 30; 1998; 4-6.

SACHDEVA (JL); Literacy campaigns - problems and prospects; *Indian Journal of Adult Education*, Oct-Dec, 1996; 51-58.

SARDA (K); *Rural library services in India;* 1986, Ess Ess Publications, New Delhi, p. 202.

SASTRY (RS); Public libraries: Modernisation and development, *ILA Bulletin,* 1-2; 1994; 2

SEN (NB); *Ed., Development of libraries in New Delhi;* 1965, New Book Society, New Delhi.

SEWA SINGH; Objectives and activities of national library associations in India: An evaluation; *In Ninth IASLIC Seminar*, Nagpur, Oct 23-26, 1980.

SHAH (SY); Contributions of Frank Laubach to the development of adult education in India (1935-70); *Perspectives in Education,* 16, 4; 1990; 221-35.

SHARADA RANGANATHAN ENDOWMENT; Public library development plan for fourth plan period; *Library Science*, Bangalore, 1, 4; 1964.

SHARMA (Pandey SK); *Public libraries in India;* 1985, Ess Ess Publication, New Delhi.

SHARMA (S); Bridging the difference between information sources and literacy around the world: India's global view; *ILA Bulletin*, 26, 2; 1990; 73-78.

SHARMA (Savitri); User's survey of Delhi Public Library: Karol Bagh Branch; *Library Herald*, 16, 1-2; 1974; 23-40.

SHUKLA (S); Literacy and development; *Indian Journal of Adult Education,* 54, 3; 1991; 5-11.

SINGH (S); *History of adult education during British period*; Delhi, Indian Adult Education Association, 1957.

SINHA (Arun Kumar); National adult education programme and public library; *Herald of Library Science*, 17, 4; 1978; 293-96.

SUBBA RAO (CV); Role of libraries in developing countries for rural upliftment; *ILA Bulletin*, 16, 1-2; 1980; 23-36.

Synopsis of DP Chattopadhyay Committee on National Policy on Library and Information System (NAPLIS); *CLIS Observer*; 15, 1-2; 1988; 11-45.

THOMAS (VK); Public library financing - analysis of RRRLF schemes assistance; *Herald of Library Science*; 38, 1-2; Jan-April, 1999; 27-39.

TILAK (Jandhyala BG); Education should be funded liberally by the government: Several poor countries ahead in literacy rate; *The Tribune*, Chandigarh, 22 May, 1998.

TREHAN (GL); A developing society and its library needs; *In* Twenty Eighth All India Library Conference, Lucknow, 1982, pp.17-29.

TRIPATHI (Virendra); Adult education and public libraries; *In* Twenty Eighth All India Library Conference, Lucknow, 1982, pp.52-63.

TYAGI (PN); *Education for all: A graphic presentation*; 1993, National Institute of Educational Planning and Administration, New Delhi.

UNESCO; Education for All, 1997, Paris

UNESCO; *New guidebook for development and production of literacy materials*; 1992, Paris.

UNESCO; *Public libraries for Asia: The Delhi seminar*; 1956, Paris.

UNESCO; *Public library in adult and fundamental education*, 1951, UNESCO, Paris.

UNESCO; *Public library legislation: A comparative study*; F.M. Gardner; 1977.

UNESCO; Standards for library service: An international survey; F.N. Withers; 1974.

UPPAL (SC); New National Education Policy and Libraries; *International Library Movement*, 8, 4; 1986; 183-87.

USMANI (SA); Role of library association in library movement with special reference to India; *Lucknow Librarian*, 59, 1-4; 1968; 34-44.

VED PRAKASH; Library legislation for Delhi; *In Public library development perspectives and staffing pattern in libraries and information centres*; Thirty First All India Library Conference, Baroda, 1985, pp.168-74.

VEERANJANEYULU (K) and SRINIVASRAO (T); Role of public library in development of culture and civilization - an overview; *Herald of Library Science*, 38, 1-2; Jan -April, 1999; 39-42.

VENKATAPPAIAH (V); *Indian library legislation*; 2V. 1990, Daya Publishing House, Delhi.

VENKATAPPAIAH (V); *Literacy campaign and libraries*; 1996, Ess Ess Publications, New Delhi, 188p.

VENKATAPPAIAH (V); Public library Acts in the states: A study; *ILA Bulletin*; 26,4; 1991; pp.187-197.

VENKATAPPAIAH (V); State policy for public library and information system and services; *Herald of Library Science*; 38, 1-2; Jan -April, 1999; 20-26.

VENKATAPPAIAH (V); States and UTs need comprehensive library legislation;

In VASHISHTH (CP) and GAKHAR (AP), *Eds.*; *In* Thirty Ninth All India Library Conference: Souvenir, 1994, ILA, Delhi, p.102-18.

VERMA (SL); Role of public libraries in promotion of literacy and adult education; *In Public library development perspectives and staffing pattern in libraries and information centres.* Thirty First All India Library Conference,. Baroda, 1985, pp.100-6.

VIDYAPATI; Nehru and literacy; *University News*, March 5, 1990; 1-3.

VIJAYADITYA (N); Information technology: A tool for rural community development; *DESIDOC Bulletin of Information Technology*; 20, 1-2; Jan-Mar, 2000; 53-9.

VISHWA MOHAN (V); Local information centres as harbingers of socio-economic development: A plan for the extension of public library services; *In* Thirty First All India Library Conference, Baroda, 1985, pp.107-114.

VISHWA MOHAN (V); Community information services: A framework for handling and service; *ILA Bulletin*, 24, 2; 1988; 68-75.

VYAS (SD); *Public library system*; 1998; Panchsheel Prakashan, Jaipur, p.188.

WALI (ML); Library association and their role in the development of library science and libraries; *ILA Bulletin*, 12, 3-4; 1976; 181-92.

WALIA (Meena) and AGRAWAL (SP); Role of public libraries in promotion of literacy and adult education; *In Public library development perspectives and staffing* pattern in libraries and information centres; Thirty First All India Library Conference, Baroda, 1985, pp.184-94.

WOOLIS (Blanche); Literacy and school libraries; *Journal of Library and Information Science;* 15, 2; 1990; 162-69.

WORLD BANK; *Human Development Report 2002: Deepening democracy in a fragmented world*; Oxford University Press, Oxford, 2002, p. 277

WORLD BANK; World Development Indicators 2002; CD-ROM, Washington DC.

WORLD BANK; *World Development Report 1999-2000: Entering the 21st century;* Oxford University Press, Washington DC, 2000, p. 301.

WORLD BANK; *World Development Report 2003: Sustainable development in a dynamic world: transforming institutions, growth and quality of life;* Oxford University Press, Washington DC, 2003, p. 250.

WORLD BANK; *World Development Report 2000-2001: At attacking poverty*, Oxford University Press, Washington DC, 2001, p. 335.

WORLD BANK; *World Development Report 1999*, Oxford University Press, World Bank, 1999, New York.

YOUNG (HEARTSTILL) and others; *Ed.*, ALA Glossary of Library and Information Science, 1983, American Library Association, Chicago.

DOCUMENTS FOR FURTHER READING

In conceptualising and writing this book, a large number of articles from books, journals, magazines and newspapers; views from individuals, statistical data from research reports, progress reports, annual reports of the Government Departments, Ministries, NGOs; vision documents, proceedings of the conferences and seminars; reports of the Boards, Committees and Task Forces, etc. have been consulted. Information extracted from these sources has been used in explaining a number of concepts. The following is the list of documents, which can help in understanding many issues to those interested in going into more details:

(A) Annual Reports of:

1. Delhi Public Library
2. Department of Culture
3. Department of Elementary Education
4. Department of Rural Development
5. Department of Women and Child Development
6. Directorate of Adult Education
7. Ministry of Finance
8. Ministry of Health and Family Welfare
9. Ministry of Human Resource Development
10. Ministry of Labour
11. Ministry of Social Justice and Empowerment
12. Ministry of Urban Affairs
13. Ministry of Youth Affairs and Sports
14. National Adult Education Association
15. National Informatics Centre
16. National Literacy Mission
17. Planning Commission
18. Raja Rammohum Roy Library Foundation
19. UNDP
20. UNESCO
21. World Bank

(B) Census of India 1981, 1991 and 2001.

(C) Tenth Five Year Plan 2002-2007.

(D) National Population Policy 2000.

Index